John Wells Foster

The Mississippi Valley

John Wells Foster

The Mississippi Valley

ISBN/EAN: 9783744693486

Printed in Europe, USA, Canada, Australia, Japan

Cover: Foto ©Andreas Hilbeck / pixelio.de

More available books at **www.hansebooks.com**

THE

MISSISSIPPI VALLEY:

ITS

PHYSICAL GEOGRAPHY,

INCLUDING SKETCHES OF THE

TOPOGRAPHY, BOTANY, CLIMATE, GEOLOGY, AND MINERAL RESOURCES; AND OF THE PROGRESS OF DEVELOPMENT IN POPULATION AND MATERIAL WEALTH.

BY

J. W. FOSTER, LL.D.,

PRESIDENT OF THE AMERICAN ASSOCIATION FOR THE ADVANCEMENT OF SCIENCE; JOINT-AUTHOR OF "FOSTER AND WHITNEY'S REPORT ON THE GEOLOGY OF THE LAKE SUPERIOR REGION;" LECTURER ON PHYSICAL GEOGRAPHY AND COGNATE SCIENCES IN THE UNIVERSITY OF CHICAGO, ETC., ETC.

ILLUSTRATED BY MAPS AND SECTIONS.

"Rerum cognoscere causas."

CHICAGO:
S. C. GRIGGS AND COMPANY.
LONDON:
TRÜBNER & CO
1869.

PREFACE.

HAVING devoted many years to explorations in different parts of the Mississippi Valley, and to the study of its soil, climate, and resources— mineral and agricultural,— and having been a witness, in part, of the gigantic strides which have been made during the lifetime of a generation, in those arts which contribute so essentially to the comforts and conveniences of man; — I propose to describe, in a comprehensive form, the Physical Geography of this wonderful region, and particularly of that portion which lies west of the great dividing line — the Mississippi River. Already this valley contains a majority of the people of the United States; and the developments which are now going on to bring it into close commercial relations with the mining regions of the Ultra-montane and Pacific States, and with the markets of the Orient, will add vastly to its resources, and to its commanding position as a part of the Great Republic.

With regard to the capacities of the region lying between the eastern rim of the Great Basin and the Missouri River, and known as the Plains, the vaguest ideas prevail. Some theorists, little versed in the laws of climatology, and over-sanguine as to the expansibility of our country, have anticipated the time when population would flow, in an unbroken wave, to the base of the Rocky Mountains; while others, more cautious, drawing their conclusiors from sources not less erroneous, have been disposed to regard this region as an irreclaimable desert. It is neither. While God has doomed certain portions of the surface to everlasting sterility, the greater portion will forever afford vast ranges for pasturage; and much of it, under a suitable system of irrigation, can be reclaimed and made to rival the ancient fruitfulness of the valleys of the Tigris and Euphrates.

The phenomena of forest-growth, of grassy plains, and arid wastes, it is believed, result from laws as constant and harmonious in their operation as those which regulate the planetary movements.

It was with a view of illustrating the gradations between the forest, prairie, and desert; the varying conditions of temperature and moisture, and their effects in determining the range of those plants cultivated for food; and, at the same time, to trace the character of the fundamental rocks over the whole of this region, pointing out the mode of occurrence of those ores and minerals useful in the arts; and, finally, to trace the colonization of this region from its feeble beginnings to its present magnificent proportions; that this work was undertaken. With the multiplication of observations — meteorological and geological, — it may be found necessary to modify some of the views herein expressed; and the most that I can hope is, that they may prove to be in the right direction.

No writer at this day upon physical geography can justly ignore the great name of HUMBOLDT. He explored nearly the whole realm of nature, and investigated her laws with a patient industry, and in a philosophical spirit, which have seldom been approached. He first reduced meteorology to the regular and consistent form of a science, when he mapped the lines of equal temperature, thus showing the distribution of heat over the seasons, and, in connection with the hygrometric state of the atmosphere, and the precipitation of rain, traced their effects upon the geographical range of plants. From confusion and uncertainty, he evoked order and harmony; out of materials apparently incongruous and misshapen, he erected a temple to science, proportionate alike in its outlines and in its several parts. He is emphatically the father of the science known as Physical Geography.

The scientific expeditions fitted out by the Government to determine the most practicable routes for railways between the Mississippi Valley and the Pacific Coast, have given us an insight into a vast region which before was almost a *terra incognita*. The results are embodied in a series of volumes, not accessible to the general reader, even if he had the time to peruse them, known as "The Pacific Railroad Surveys." The earlier expeditions of LEWIS and CLARKE, PIKE, LONG, FREMONT, WILKES, STANSBURY, and others, gave us general outlines of the physical geography; and yet, with the combined results of these observers, and of those who have subsequently become connected with the various mining enterprises, much is yet to be determined in every branch of natural history.

To Messrs. MEEK and HAYDEN the public are indebted for valuable contributions to the geology of the eastern slope of the Rocky Mountains.

The results of the Geological Survey of California, under the charge of Prof. J. D. WHITNEY, afford us a key to unlock the hidden mysteries of that complicated region; and it is to be regretted that so important a work has been suspended.

In the year 1819, a regular series of meteorological observations was instituted at the various Military Posts of the United States, under the authority of the Secretary of War, which has been continued to the present time. In 1857, these observations, together with those which had been made at other points by competent observers, were tabulated and brought out by Mr. LORIN BLODGET, in a work entitled "The Climatology of the United States." This work contains a vast amount of information, and is the foundation of most of our discussions in reference to the lines of temperature, the distribution of rain, and the prevalent direction of winds in the United States. But a work so thorough, must necessarily be encumbered with minute details, so that the generalizations are not presented in so compendious a form as to be appreciable by the cursory reader, nor are they, in all instances, carried to their legitimate results. The work is like an arsenal, to which the soldier resorts to equip himself with an armor suited to the actual conflict.

It is to be regretted that the Smithsonian Institution, which has been made the repository of these observations continued up to the present time, has not communicated to the world the tabulated results. These results, it is hardly necessary to say, are of great importance in enabling us to determine the varying fertility of the Continent.

Prof. ASA GRAY, in Silliman's Journal, 1857 and 1859, and Dr. J. G. COOPER, in the Patent

Office Report for 1860, have contributed valuable information on the geographical range of the forest-trees of North America; and it is to Sir JOHN RICHARDSON that we are almost entirely indebted for our knowledge of the climatology, in connection with the botany, of the circumpolar region of this Continent.

The work of HUMPHREYS and ABBOT, on "The Physics and Hydraulics of the Mississippi River," is of the very highest scientific interest. Principles the most elaborate, are patiently wrought out, and the results are clearly enunciated. From these demonstrations, it is evident that the views which formerly prevailed as to the extent of the delta, and the effects of fluviatile action upon the bed and enclosing banks of that river, were not understood.

This work,—which, with much distrust, I now submit to the public,—is not intended to be a purely scientific treatise. The severity of style and rigor of deduction which characterize such works, have been purposely avoided. I have attempted rather to present a series of graphic sketches of the great phenomena of the region under consideration, in a form which should interest and instruct the general reader, and, at the same time, to explain those natural laws to whose operation these phenomena are due. In preparing it for the press, I have been oppressed by a double fear,— lest, while

I might render it too abstruse for the comprehension of the general reader, at the same time, the specialties were not sufficiently exact to satisfy the requirements of those, who brought to the investigation of these subjects a purely scientific spirit. These details render science repellent to those who have not acquired a special knowledge of the elements on which it is based. It is believed, however, that generalizations may be set forth in a manner to interest and instruct the ordinary reader.

In discussing the operation of natural laws as manifested in climate, in the distribution of moisture, and even in the origin and spread of civilization, I have felt at liberty to draw my illustrations from every quarter of the world, and from almost every department of science. These illustrations will show that man, even, however much he may boast of his dominion over matter, is the creature of climate; and that, only under certain favorable conditions, does he attain to the full development of his physical and intellectual powers. Such conditions, it is believed, obtain in the Upper Valley of the Mississippi.

CHICAGO, *February* 1, 1869.

CONTENTS.

CHAPTER I.

THE MISSISSIPPI RIVER.

The magnitude of the Mississippi — Area — Subordinate basins — Internal navigation — Character of Lower Mississippi — Characteristic vegetation — Overflows — Bluffs — Levees — Outlets — Approaches — Phenomena of waters — Geology — Area of alluvium and delta — Earthquake-action. - - - - - Page 1

CHAPTER II.

MOUNTAINS AND PLAINS.

Character of the water-sheds — The Appalachain Range — The Rocky Mountains — The Sierra Nevada — The Cascade Range — The Coast Ranges — Ridges of the Great Basin — Character of the sources of the Mississippi — Of the Ohio Valley — The Llano Estacado — Rocky Mountain Valleys — Colorado Desert — Valley of the St. Lawrence — Pacific Railroad routes — Résumé. - 26

CHAPTER III.

THE ORIGIN OF PRAIRIES.

Distribution of forest, prairie, and desert — Prairies not due to peat-growth — Not due to the texture of the soil — Not due to the annual burnings — Zones of vegetation — The Great Basin — Climatic conditions — Mean annual precipitation — Source of moisture — Periodical rains of California — Conclusions. - - 71

CHAPTER IV.

THE ORIGIN OF PRAIRIES — *continued.*

South America — Primeval forests of Brazil — The Llanos of Caraccas — The Pampas of La Plata and the *Gran Chaco* — Patagonia —

Its deserts and mountains — Peru and the desert of Atacama — Wind and rain charts — Europe — Plains of the Black Sea — Steppes of the Caucasus — Plateau of Central Asia — Desert of Arabia — Africa — Sahara — Guinea — Basin of the Mediterranean — Australia — Résumé — Explanation of Map.   -   - 112

CHAPTER V.

FOREST-CULTURE AND IRRIGATION.

How plants grow — Effects of forests on health — On animal life — Effects of disrobing a country of forests — Rapid destruction of forests in the United States — Forests, their lessons — They modify climate — They retain moisture — Tree-planting — Irrigation — Practiced at an early day on both hemispheres — Successfully introduced on the Rocky Mountain slopes — Feasibility of its application in California, the Colorado Desert, and the Western Plains. -   -   -   -   -   -   -   -   -   - 141

CHAPTER VI.

CLIMATE.

Definition of climate — Atmospheric currents — Rains and winds — Cloud-bursts — Isothermal lines — Gulf-stream — Evaporative power of winds — Isotherms of the United States — Climate of the Pacific Slope and Great Basin — Phenomena of the seasons — Table of temperatures — Of rain-precipitation.   -   - 172

CHAPTER VII.

CULTIVATED PLANTS.

Conditions of climate and soil restricting the range of plants — Of the soil in reference to the growth of particular plants — Maize, — Wheat, — Oats, — Rye, and Barley — Natives of the plains of Central Asia — Rice — Sugar-cane — Sorghum — Potato — Cotton — Tobacco — Grasses for pasturage — Exhaustion of the soil — Facilities for cultivation — Tables of population and production.
209

CHAPTER VIII.

GEOLOGY—IGNEOUS AND METAMORPHIC ROCKS.

Geological structure of the Mississippi Valley — Tabular view of the different formations — Igneous rocks of different age — Systems of elevation of mountain chains — The Lake Superior system — The Primeval Continent — The Appalachian system — The Rocky-

Mountain system—The Pacific Coast Ranges—Igneous products—River systems—The Azoic system, associated with iron-ores—Iron-region of Lake Superior—Of Missouri—The Mythological age of metals—The present, the Iron age—Annual product of the world. - - - - - - - 242

CHAPTER IX.

GEOLOGY—*continued*,—SEDIMENTARY ROCKS.

Silurian system — First evidences of organic life—Area of Silurian—Lower Silurian—Potsdam sandstone—Pictured Rocks—Copper-region of Lake Superior—Lower Magnesian limestone—Lead-bearing veins of Missouri—St. Peter's sandstone—Cincinnati Blue limestone—Galena limestone—Upper Silurian system—Niagara limestone—Onondaga salt-group—Devonian system—Carboniferous system—Fluor spar, with veins of galena—Galena deposits—Silver ores of Mexico—Coal-Measures, their area—Thickness—Character of the coals—Permian system—Triassic and Jurassic series—Gold deposits of California—Copper deposits—Cretaceous deposits—Coal deposits. - - 272

CHAPTER X.

GEOLOGY —*continued*,— SEDIMENTARY ROCKS.

Tertiary system — Marine of the Atlantic Slope — Fresh-water of the Missouri Basin — Marine of the Pacific Coast — Economic value of the Tertiary coals — Igneous products of the Great Basin — Comstock lode, its yield in silver — Drift-epoch — Drift-action in the Mississippi Valley — Erosive action on the Pacific Slope and in the Colorado Plateau—Terraces of Modified Drift—Loess—Sand-dunes—The Great Lakes—Drift-phenomena—Denudation—Area, depth, and elevation—Résumé. - - - 318

CHAPTER XI.

INFLUENCE OF CLIMATE ON MAN.

Geographical range of man, as compared with that of plants—Conditions of human life under different zones—Arctic life—Tropical life—Life in Northern temperate zone—Human energy displayed within certain isothermal lines—In Europe—In North America—Climate of the Southern States, and the condition of society—Climate of the Northern States, and the condition of society—Effects of these differences seen in the Rebellion—Physical development. - - - - - 355

CHAPTER XII.
ORIGIN OF CIVILIZATION.

Valley of the Mississippi, its prospective population — Greece the cradle of civilization — Rome the inheritor of that civilization — Origin of Teutons and Celts — Characteristics of each race — Colonization of North America — National unity — Causes which promote it — English character — Their homogeneity as compared with that of the people of the United States — The civilizing effects of the Christian religion. - - - - - 377

CHAPTER XIII.
PROGRESS OF DEVELOPMENT.

Ordinance of 1787 for the government of the Northwestern Territory — Its effect upon the character of the colonization — First settlement of the region — Relative growth in population — Area of Western States — Agricultural products, their rapid increase — The assessed value of real and personal property — Indians — Their habits — Government policy towards them — The Moundbuilders — Their civilization — Antiquity of their works — Conclusion. - - - - - - - - - - - 401

ILLUSTRATIONS.

Map — Showing the distribution of Forest, Prairie, and Desert, - 140

Map — Showing the Isothermal Lines of the United States, - 200

Geological Sketch of the United States, - - - - 272

Index, - - - - - - - - - - - 433

THE MISSISSIPPI VALLEY:

ITS

PHYSICAL GEOGRAPHY.

CHAPTER I.

THE MISSISSIPPI RIVER.

THE MAGNITUDE OF THE MISSISSIPPI — AREA — SUBORDINATE BASINS — INTERNAL NAVIGATION — CHARACTER OF LOWER MISSISSIPPI — CHARACTERISTIC VEGETATION — OVERFLOWS — BLUFFS — LEVEES — OUTLETS — APPROACHES — PHENOMENA OF WATERS — GEOLOGY — AREA OF ALLUVIUM AND DELTA — EARTHQUAKE ACTION.

"THE beginnings of a river are insignificant, and its infancy is frivolous; it plays among the flowers of a meadow, it waters a garden, or turns a little mill. Gathering strength in its growth, it becomes wild and impetuous. Impatient of the restraints it meets with, in the hollows among the mountains, it is restless and fretful; quick in its turning, and unsteady in its course. Now it is a roaring cataract, tearing up and overturning whatever opposes its progress, and it shoots headlong down from a rock; then it becomes a sullen and gloomy pool, buried in the bottom of a glen. Recovering breath by repose, it again dashes along, till, tired of uproar and mischief, it quits all that it has swept along, and leaves an opening of the valley strewed with the rejected waste. Now, quitting its retirement, it comes abroad into the world, journeying with more prudence and discretion, through cultivated fields, yielding to circumstances, and winding round what it would trouble it to overwhelm and remove. It passes through populous cities, and all the busy haunts of men, tendering its services on every side, and becomes the support and ornament of the country. Increased by numerous alliances, and advanced in its course, it becomes grave and stately in its motions, loves peace and quiet, and, in majestic silence, rolls on its mighty waters, till it is laid to rest in the vast abyss." — *Pliny*, "*Hist. Nat.*," *Lib.* V.

Magnitude of the Mississippi — The Mississippi * River, when we consider its great length, the number and character of its tributaries — often exceeding the first-class rivers of Europe, — the area of country which it drains, the vast system of internal navigation which it affords, and the populous towns which have been founded on its banks, may be regarded as one of the most striking topographical features of the earth. The rivers descending from the Atlantic and Pacific slopes are, for the most part, short and rapid, and are not navigable beyond the reach of tide-water; but this

* The name is derived from the Algonquin, or Chippewyan, language — *Missi*, great, and *Sepi*, river. To the same root, or corruptions of it, may be traced several conspicuous bodies of water in the Northwest. The Indian name of Churchill River is *Missi-nepi*, probably identical in meaning with Mississippi. *Gummi* signifies water, or a collection of water, not running; thus, the aboriginal name of Lake Superior was *Kitchi*, great — allied to *Michi* or *Missi* — and *Gummi*, water; *Michi-gan* (Michigan) is a corruption of the same thing. In conversing with a Chippewyan Indian, he will describe any large body of running water, as *Missi*, or *Michi*. *Sepi*, or *Sebi*, and any large body of still water as *Mitchi*, or *Missi*, *Gummi* (great water); so that what he would regard as a generic term, we use as a *specific* term, which has become thoroughly incorporated with some of the most marked topographical features of the Northwest.

river-system penetrates to the heart of a continent, and, with its numerous tributaries, affords an inland navigation of unsurpassed magnificence.

Area—Subordinate Basins.—The Mississippi Valley comprises an area of 2,455,000 square miles, extending through 30 degrees of longitude and 23 degrees of latitude;—an area greater than that of all Europe, exclusive of Russia, Norway, and Sweden.

It is composed of several subordinate basins, whose area, elevation, drainage, etc., are as follows:*

RIVER.	DISTANCE FROM MOUTH. Miles.	HEIGHT ABOVE SEA. Feet.	WIDTH AT MOUTH. Feet.	DOWN-FALL OF RAIN. Inches.	MEAN DISCH'GE PER SEC. Cub.Feet.	AREA OF BASIN. Sq. Miles.
Upper Mississippi.	1,330	1,680	5,000	35.2	105,000	169,000
Missouri..........	2,908	6,800?	3,000	20.9	120,000	518,000
Ohio	1,265	1,649	3,000	41.5	158,000	214,000
Arkansas	1,514	10,000	1,500	29.3	63,000	189,000
Red River	1,200	2,450	800	39.0	57,000	97,000
Yazoo.............	500	210	850	46.3	43,000	13,850
St. Francis........	380	1,150	700	41.1	31,000	10,500
Lower Mississippi.	1,286	416	2,470	30.4	675,000	1,244,000

Internal Navigation.—The Mississippi and its tributaries afford an internal navigation for steam-

* Humphreys and Abbot, "Physics and Hydraulics of Miss. River."

boats, of more than 9,000 miles in extent.* They have proved the great highways by which, within a brief period, man has been able to penetrate to the interior of the continent, and to subdue it to his uses.

* The Mississippi is navigable —

From its mouth to St. Paul,	1,944 miles.
And from St. Anthony to Sauk Rapids,	80 "
Making a total navigation of	2,020 "

Several of its upper tributaries are navigable —

The Minnesota to Patterson's Rapids,	295 "
The St. Croix to St. Croix,	60 "
The Illinois to La Salle,	220 "
The Missouri is navigable, at high water, from its mouth to Fort Benton,	2,644 "
but ordinarily to 60 miles above the mouth of the Yellowstone (1,894 miles)	1,954 "

(The volume of water discharged by the Yellowstone is represented to be about the same as that of the Missouri; and after the junction, the river attains a width of 2,000 feet.)

The Ohio is navigable to Pittsburgh,	975 "
The Monongahela to Geneva,	91 "
The Tennessee to Muscle Shoals,	600 "
The Cumberland to Burkesville,	370 "

Some of its other tributaries, which have been slack-watered, give a navigation of . . . . 550 "

The Arkansas is navigable, in flood, to Ft. Gibson,	642 "
but during its lowest stage, it is difficult for boats of the lightest draught to reach Fort Smith,	522 "
The Red river is navigable, in ordinary stage, to Shrevesport,	330 "
but only in flood, to Preston,	820 "
The St. Francis is navigable to Wittsburg,	80 "
The White River is navigable to Batesville,	175 "
The Yazoo to Greenwood,	240 "
The Kaw has been ascended to Fort Riley,	100 "

but the navigation is ordinarily precarious.

The Platte is an important tributary of the Missouri, which, like the Canadian and the Arkansas, reaches to the base of the Rocky Mountains, and spreads out over a wide space, so that it is totally unfit for navigation.

Character of the Lower Mississippi. — "At the mouth of the Missouri, the Mississippi first assumes its characteristic appearance of a turbid and boiling torrent, immense in volume and force. From that point, its waters pursue their devious way for more than 1300 miles, destroying banks and islands at one locality, reconstructing them at another, absorbing tributary after tributary, without visible increase in size, — until, at length, it is in turn absorbed in the great volume of the Gulf." *

The shores of the Gulf, so far as relates to the Louisianian coast, are bordered, for fifty miles inland, by swamps, bayous, and lakes. The swamps generally consist of an oozy mass of mud, from twenty to forty feet in depth, resting on blue clay. Upon the hummocks, a variety of vegetable forms take root, unknown in the regions to the northward.

Typical Forms of Vegetation. — Conspicuous among these is the cypress, which is first seen near the mouth of the Ohio, and is always found on land subject to overflow. From a protuberance at the surface, a shaft rises straight to the height of sixty or eighty feet, without a limb, when it throws out numerous branches, umbrella-shaped, which sustain a foliage of short, fine, tufted leaves, of a green so deep as to appear almost brown. They grow so close together, that their branches inter-

* Humphreys and Abbot.

lock; and hence a cypress forest resembles a mass of verdure sustained in the air by tall perpendicular columns. From their branches, depend long festoons of moss, which sway to and fro in the wind, like so many shrouds,—communicating to the scene the most dismal aspect. Arranged around the parent stem, are numerous cone-shaped protuberances, known as "cypress knees," which enable the roots of the tree to communicate with the air; a provision of nature which is essential to its vitality.

The cypress loves the gloomiest and most inaccessible portions of the southern forest, and where, for one-half of the year, the surface is submerged. Repulsive, then, as is its habitat, it is the most valuable of all the southern lumber trees. Soft, free from knots, rifting straight, and easily wrought, it is fit for shingles, boards, and finishing material.

The palmetto, not the species of the Carolina coast, is another characteristic form of these swamps, and one which, by its peculiarities, at once arrests the eye of the northern traveler. It is perennial; and, from a large, tough root, throws up a stem six feet high, sustaining fan-shaped palm-leaves, exactly ribbed, and of a rich green verdure. These are used for fans, for braiding into hats, and for thatching the huts of the negroes.

These swamps, clothed with trees of abundant

and interlaced branches, springing from a mass of ooze tremulous to the foot, remind one of the estuaries and lakes, with their luxuriant vegetation, which stretched over large areas of the earth's surface during the Carboniferous epoch—a vegetation which furnished no sustenance to the higher forms of animal life, and which flourished in an atmosphere probably fatal to air-breathing animals. These swamps are the chosen retreats of the alligator, the lizard, and moccasin snake, and swarm with mosquitoes and other venomous insects. To man, they are impassable, except when flooded. To traverse them, he should be like Milton's fiend, qualified for all elements and all services; who,

> "With head, hands, wings, or feet, pursues his way;
> And swims, or sinks, or wades, or creeps, or flies."

In connection with the southern vegetation, two other types may be mentioned; the live-oak and the magnolia. The live-oak is a noble tree — tall, with long spreading branches, and presenting almost as great a mass of foliage as the northern elm. Its range does not extend beyond latitude thirty-one north.

The magnolia belongs to the tribe of laurels. The beauty of this tree has been greatly overrated. It is, according to Flint, only a fifth-rate tree, which grows in the rich alluvium of the Louisiana bottoms, where the soil is congenial to its full development. It is tall, graceful in form, with a smooth, light-colored bark, like that of the beech. The wood is soft and useless. The leaves are glossy on the upper surface, like those of the orange, with a yellowish down upon the under surface. The flower is large, and of a pure white, like those of the northern pond-lily, but twice the size. The odor is strong and not offensive. "Instead of displaying," says Flint, "a cone of flowers, we have seldom seen a tree in flower which did not require some attention and closeness of inspection to discover where the flowers are situated among the leaves." *

There are six or seven species among the laurels of the magnolia tribe.

Overflow of the Mississippi.—When in flood, the river extends to a width of thirty miles, and the surplus waters find their way to the ocean through deep forests and almost interminable swamps. The ordinary channel is marked by an outline of woods. As the flood recedes, it leaves behind, in the bottom lands, a sediment as fine and as fertilizing as the Nile mud. The course of the river is in a series of curves, from ten to twelve miles in diameter, sweeping round with great uniformity, until it

* "Mississippi Valley."

returns to a point very near the one from which it was deflected. The current continually encroaches on the alluvial banks, until finally, during high flood, a crevasse occurs, when nearly the whole volume of water rushes through the newly-formed channel, known as a "cut-off." Hence, along its whole course are seen numerous crescent-shaped lakes which owe their origin to this cause. Sandbars accumulate at the mouths of the ancient channels, on which first rushes take root, and subsequently cotton-wood, thus forming lakes which, except in flood, become isolated from the river.

The river being no where rock-bound in its lower course, and its banks consisting of the most comminuted materials, has great excavating power.*

Bluffs. — The alluvial bottoms are ordinarily impassable, and the bluffs only afford sites for habitations. In a few instances, they approach the river, as at the Iron Banks, near Columbus, and the Chalk

---

* The citation of a single case, which occurred at New Madrid, will suffice. Joseph Lewis (quoting, as authority, an old resident,) as marshal, in 1798, was ordered, by the local Spanish government, to move the church one mile north, to prevent its being undermined. The distance was measured by a surveyor, and the order was executed.

In 1811, the region having passed into the possession of another government, no pains were taken to protect the church against farther encroachments, when it fell into the river. My informant had seen the original plat of the town, which extended back from the river front four miles. There now remains a strip of the original plat, not more than sixty feet in width.

Banks, near Hickman, Kentucky; at Fulton, Randolph, Old River (but here the river has receded), and Memphis, Tennessee; at Walnut Hills or Vicksburg, Grand and Petit Gulf, Natchez, and Fort Adams, Mississippi; and at St. Francisville and Baton Rouge, Louisiana. All of the bluffs occur on the east side of the river, except the St. Francis Hills, and Point Chicot.

The bluffs, as first suggested by Lyell, belong to the age of the Rhenish Loess, and ordinarily consist of beds of yellowish loam, sand, and clay, with beds of lignite of an earlier age beneath.

Levees. — To protect the plantations from overflow, a system of levees was commenced many years ago; and, to aid the extension, Congress passed an act directing the proceeds of the sale of swamp-lands to be devoted to this purpose. Under the operation of this act, levees have been carried up the east bank, nearly as far as Memphis, and up the west bank to a point opposite the mouth of the Ohio. The peculiarity of the immediate banks of the river being higher than the alluvial plain, is characteristic of the whole course of the Lower Mississippi.

During the Rebellion, the levees, at many points, were destroyed as an act of war, and at others, were allowed to go to decay; and the result is, that large tracts of land, formerly as fertile as the valley of the Nile, have been surrendered up to the dominion of the river. To repair these levees at public expense, and to give employment to a class of people overwhelmed by misfortune, even if it be the result of their own rash acts, is a measure called for alike by a common humanity and an enlightened public policy.

Contrary to the received opinion, it is found that, where the current is confined, it has power to push forward its sediment, instead of allowing it to deposit on the bottom; so that the necessity will not arise of raising the levees higher, with the lapse of time.

Outlets.— The immediate channel of the river, after having received the contributions of its main affluents, is insufficient to discharge all of the waters which, from the drainage of the valley, find their way to the ocean. The first point of escape is at Cape Girardeau, Missouri, through the St. Francis, White, and several other rivers, before reaching the mouth of Red River. Here the volume of water is greater than at any other point; for, a few miles below, there are several lateral channels communicating with the Gulf. These outlets are known as Atchafalaya, which is supposed to be the ancient channel of Red River;

Bayou Manchac, cómmunicating with Lakes Maurepas, Ponchartrain, and Borgne; and Bayou Plaquemine and Bayou Lafourche.

Approaches to New Orleans.—Bars exist at the mouths of all the passes, so that it is difficult for large vessels to enter the river.

The Southeast Pass is apparently not over 2,000 feet in width, and the ordinary depth of water is 18 feet. The banks are low and lined with reeds. The few houses visible are perched on piles, and occupied by pilots, whose services are at all times required. There is no tide in the Mississippi, owing to its elevation above the Gulf, and its level is affected by winds, more than by other causes.

The Northeast Pass, which formerly was the principal one, now carries from 8 to 9 feet of water; and this is the depth of the Southwest Pass.

Another approach is through Barataria Bay, which admits of vessels drawing 10 or 12 feet of water. The Texas steamers go through the Grand Pass, into Vermilion Bay, and thence into Grand Lake. The New Orleans and Opelousas Railway extends to Berwick's Bay, which is the terminus of the southern steamship lines. The Teche is navigable as far as Franklin, which is quite a shipping point for sugars. The country to the west is high rolling prairie. There is another approach, through Lake Borgne and Pass Rigolet, into Ponchartrain, where the depth of water is from 8 to 15 feet.

Phenomena of the Waters.—The Upper Mississippi is as clear as the " arrowy Rhone;" and even at St. Louis, sixteen miles below the mouth of the Missouri, whose flood is densely charged with sediment, the thread between the differently-colored waters is distinctly preserved, so reluctant are they to commingle. Every one voyaging on the Lower Mississippi, must have been struck with the character of the current, as though some substance of the consistency of tar were boiling and bubbling in a great caldron.

Another feature of this river which has been remarked upon, is, that its width is not increased by the absorption of any tributary, however large: thus, at Rock Island, nearly 1,800 miles from its mouth, it is 5,000 feet wide, while at New Orleans, and where it enters the Gulf, swollen by the volumes of the Missouri, Ohio, Arkansas, and Red Rivers, it is dwarfed to 2,470 feet.* Standing on the levée at New Orleans, and looking across to Algiers on the opposite shore, one can hardly believe that within this narrow span is comprised the drainage of nearly half a continent.

* Humphreys and Abbot.

Geology of the River-Bed. — Its bed, all the way from Cairo to the Gulf, is not formed of its own alluvium, but is excavated in a tough blue clay of Cretaceous origin. By consulting the Geological Map, it will be seen that, outside of the immediate valley, the Cretaceous rocks extend on either side, from the mouth of the Ohio to within seventy miles of the Gulf, where they are overlapped by the Tertiaries. There is little doubt of the former continuity of these beds, or, in other words, that the Cretaceous sea extended from the base of the Rocky Mountains to the Atlantic Coast. It is evident, therefore, that the course of the Lower Mississippi has been determined subsequent to the Cretaceous age, since its bed has been excavated in this formation. It would further appear that, during the Tertiary epoch, there must have been an estuary extending as far north as the mouth of the Ohio, as indicated by the wedge-shaped body of these rocks observed there. Since the erosion of its channel to a far greater width than that now occupied by its waters, the immediate valley has been filled in with other formations; viz., the Loess and Recent Alluvium. An ideal section across the valley would exhibit the following arrangement of the several formations:

1. Upper Cretaceous.
2. Tertiary (Eocine).
3. Loess, or Bluff.
4. Modern Alluvium.

Pursuing our researches as to the origin of the river, it is inferred that it is subsequent to the Tertiary epoch, since outlying patches of this formation cap the summits of some of the hills of Illinois far beyond its ancient limits, and all of the associated fossils are of marine origin; thus showing that no large body of fresh water was discharged at this point into the Tertiary ocean.

In the deposition of the Loess, however, we have evidence that, at that period, the river had assumed its present channel, but with a vastly enlarged volume of water. The fossils are all of fresh-water origin, and of existing species, intermingled with quadrupeds, for the most part pachyderms now extinct but allied to existing genera,* which indicate the immediate presence of land under conditions of soil and vegetation such as now prevail;

* The fresh-water shells collected by Lyell, from the Loess, consisted of *Helix, Helicina, Pupa, Clystoma, Achatina,* and *Succinea,* all identical with shells now living; also, shells of the genera *Limnea, Planoibis, Paludina, Physa,* and *Cyclas.* Leidy has identified the following quadrupeds: *Felis atrox* (lion), *Ursus americanus, U. amplidens, Megalonyx jeffersoni, M. dissimilis, Mylodon harlani, Ereptodon priscus, Tapirus americanus, T. haysii, Equus americanus, Bootherium cavifrons, Elephas americanus,* and *Mastodon giganteus,* all extinct; and *Cervus virginianus,* belonging to a living species.

and yet, to account for the present position of the Loess, as pointed out by Lyell, we must presuppose a vertical movement or upheaval, of two hundred and fifty feet.

Area of Alluvium.—A wide belt of Recent Alluvium borders the Mississippi from the mouth of the Ohio to the Gulf, which is well delineated on one of Humphreys and Abbot's maps. This belt, in its greatest expansion, at Napoleon, is nearly 75 miles wide; while in its greatest contraction, at Natchez and Helena, it is about 25 miles. The area of the tract, above the delta is 19,450 square miles. According to the authority above cited, the alluvial deposit at Cairo is 25 feet thick; about 35 feet in the Yazoo swamps; and this thickness is maintained as far down as Baton Rouge. The borings of the Artesian well at New Orleans, indicate there a thickness of 40 feet; but at Bayou Plaquemine, the alluvial soil does not extend much below the level of the Gulf.

Area of the Delta.—The area of the delta, assuming that it begins where the river sends off its first branch to the sea—viz., at the head of Bayou Atchafalaya—is estimated by them at 12,300 square miles. This would be at the mouth of Red River, in latitude 31°, while the mouth of the Great

River is now in latitude 29°; thus extending through two degrees of space.

The rate at which the river advances into the Gulf is estimated by the same authority, at 262 feet per annum; and as its prolongation from its supposed original mouth is 220 miles, the age of the delta is computed at 4,400 years,—a period much at variance with the estimates of previous writers. That the Mississippi must have been a delta-forming river at an earlier period, is evidenced by the Loess which occurs along its banks, and which, at Natchez, attains a thickness of sixty feet.

The sediment held in suspension by the river, as determined by numerous experiments, is, by weight, nearly as 1 to 1.500; and by bulk, nearly as 1 to 2.900. The mean annual discharge of water is assumed at 19,500,000,000,000 cubic feet; hence, it follows that 812,500,000,000 pounds of sedimentary matter—equal to one square mile of deposit, 241 feet in depth—are yearly transported, in a state of suspension, into the Gulf.*

Depth and Slope.—The maximum depth of the Mississippi, as indicated by Humphreys and Abbot's tables, is, at Natchez, 118 feet; and the mean depth from below the mouth of the Arkansas to Red River, is 96 feet. The least low-water

* Humphreys and Abbot, "Physics of the Mississippi."

depths on the bars are: at St. Louis, 2 feet; Memphis, 5 feet; and Natchez, 6 feet. The range between low and high-water is: at Rock Island, 16 feet; at the mouth of the Missouri, 35 feet; at St. Louis, 37 feet; at Cairo, 51 feet; at Carrolton, 14 feet; and at the head of the Passes, 2.3 feet.

The fall of the Lower Mississippi is about $\frac{32}{100}$ of a foot per mile; of the Ohio, $\frac{43}{100}$ of a foot; of the Missouri, below Fort Union, $\frac{95}{100}$ of a foot; and of the Upper Mississippi, below St. Paul, $\frac{48}{100}$ of a foot.

EARTHQUAKE-ACTION IN THE MISSISSIPPI VALLEY.

The series of earthquake-shocks which occurred in the Mississippi Valley, commencing near the close of 1811, and continuing to 1813, were of sufficient violence to modify its surface to a considerable extent, creating yawning fissures, and converting dry land into lakes, some of which are fifty miles in circumference. The telluric activity of which these events were a part, extended over half a hemisphere, and was manifested in a series of stupendous phenomena, such as the elevation of the island of Sabrina, one of the group of the Azores, to the height of 320 feet above the sea; the destruction of Caraccas, with 10,000 of its inhabitants; the eruption of the volcano of St. Vincent; and the fearful subterranean noises which were heard on the Llanos of Calabazo, and at the mouth of the Rio Apure, and even far out at sea.

New Madrid, in the State of Missouri, and in the valley of the Mississippi, appears to have been one of the foci of this earthquake disturbance; and the shocks were repeated almost every hour for months in succession. Fortunately, the town as well as the surrounding region, was sparsely inhabited, and the houses (log cabins) were of a character little liable to be toppled over; but, so far as we can gather from the published accounts, and the personal recollections of those who were eye-witnesses of the scenes, we are satisfied that, if the same severity of shocks were to occur at this day, at St. Louis or Cincinnati, the destruction of life would be appalling, and those cities would become an undistinguishable mass of ruins.

Several years ago, in voyaging from Memphis to Cairo, I made the acquaintance of Mr. A. N. Dillard, who resided in the region of these disturbances, and who was a witness of the events which I shall record.

It was on the night of the 16th of December, 1811, that the first shock occurred. The weather had been warm and pleasant, and the air was filled with that peculiar haze characteristic of the Indian summer, except that it was more damp. About midnight, while the French, who constituted the bulk of the population at New Madrid, were engaged in dancing and frolicking, the first shock came on, and was of sufficient violence to shake down many of the houses and fences. The greatest consternation prevailed. The entire population rushed into the open air; and there, in the midnight darkness, and upon the rocking earth, Protestant and Catholic, side by side,

> "knelt down,
> And offered to the Mightiest"

solemn supplication; — for, in that fearful hour, human aid was unavailing.

"The shocks," my informant continued, "extended over a period of twenty or thirty months. Sometimes, they would come on gradually, and finally culminate; again, they would come without premonition, and in terrific force, and gradually subside.

"In every instance the motion was propagated from the west or southwest. Fissures would be formed, six hundred and even seven hundred feet in length, and twenty or thirty feet in breadth, through which water and sand would spout out to the height of forty feet. There issued no burning flames, but flashes such as result from the explosion of gas, or from the passage of the electrical fluid from one cloud to another. I have seen oak trees, which would be split in the centre and forty feet up the trunk, one part standing on one side of a fissure, and the other part on the other; and trees are now standing which have been cleft in this manner.

"My grandfather had received a boat-load of castings from Pittsburgh, which were stored in his cellar. During one of the shocks, the ground opened immediately under the house, and they were swallowed up, and no trace of them was afterwards obtained.

"I regard the region as still subject to these agitations. A few years ago, I saw the effects sufficiently violent to shake the bark off the trees, and to sway their tops to and fro.

"The region of the St. Francis is peculiar. I have trapped there for thirty years. There is a great deal of sunken land, caused by the earthquakes of 1811. There are large trees of walnut, white oak, and mulberry, such as grow on high land, which are now seen submerged ten and twenty feet beneath the water. In some of the lakes, I have seen cypresses so far beneath the surface, that, with a canoe, I have paddled among the branches. Previous to the earthquakes, keel-boats used to come up the St. Francis River, and pass into the Mississippi, at a point three miles below New Madrid. The bayou is now high ground."

From one of the fissures formed during these convulsions, was ejected the cranium of an extinct musk-ox (*Bootherium bombifrons*), now in the possession of the Lyceum of Natural History of New York.

Reel-foot Lake, on the opposite shore, in Obion county, Tennessee, nearly twenty miles long and seven broad, owes its origin to the sinking of the ground during this period. The trunks of dead cypresses are seen standing in the water; and the fisherman, as he plies his occupation in his canoe, floats above their branching tops.

Timothy Flint visited this region seven years after the occurrence of these terrible events, at a time when the recollections of the inhabitants were yet vivid. As the work in which he recorded his information has become rare, I may be pardoned for transcribing his graphic account almost entire:

"From all the accounts," he says, "corrected one by another, and compared with the very imperfect narratives which were published, I infer that the shock of these earthquakes, in the immediate center of their force, must have equaled, in the terrible heavings of the earth, any thing of the kind that has been recorded. I do not believe that the public have ever yet had any adequate idea of the violence of the concussions. We are accustomed to measure this by the buildings overturned and the mortality that results. Here, the country was thinly settled. The houses, fortunately, were frail, and of logs,—the most difficult to overturn that could be constructed. Yet, as it was, whole tracts were plunged in the bed of the river. The grave-yard at New Madrid, with all its sleeping tenants, was

precipitated into the bend of the stream. Most of the houses were thrown down. Large lakes, twenty miles in extent, were made in an hour; other lakes were drained. The whole country, to the mouth of the Ohio in one direction, and to the St. Francis in the other, including a front of three hundred miles, was convulsed to such a degree as to create lakes and islands, the number of which is not known, and to cover a tract of many miles in extent, near the Little Prairie, with water, three or four feet deep; and when the water disappeared, a stratum of sand, of the same thickness, was left in the place. Trees split in the midst, and lashed one with another, are still visible over great tracts of country, inclining in every direction, and at every angle to the earth and the horizon. They described the undulations of the earth as resembling waves, increasing in elevation as they advanced, and when they had attained a certain fearful height, the earth would burst, and vast volumes of water, and sand, and pit-coal were discharged as high as the tops of the trees. I have seen a hundred of these chasms which remained fearfully deep, although in a very tender alluvial soil, and after a lapse of seven years. Whole districts were covered with white sand, so as to become uninhabitable. The water at first covered the whole country, particularly at the Little Prairie; and it must, indeed, have been a scene of horror, in these deep forests, and in the gloom of the darkest night, and by wading in the water to the middle, for the inhabitants to fly from these concussions, which were occurring every few hours, with a noise equally terrible to beasts and birds, as to man. The birds themselves lost all power and disposition to fly, and retreated to the bosoms of men, their fellow-sufferers in the general convulsion. A few persons sank in these chasms, and were providentially extricated. One person died of affright; and one perished miserably on an island which retained its original level in the midst of a wide lake created by the earthquake. * *
* * * * A number perished, who sank with their boats in the river. A bursting of the earth just below the village of New Madrid, arrested the mighty stream in its course, and caused a reflux of its waves, by which, in a little time, a

great number of boats were swept by the ascending current into the mouth of the bayou, carried out, and left upon the dry earth, where the accumulating waters of the river had again changed the current. There were a great number of severe shocks, but two series of concussions were particularly terrible, far more so than the rest; and they remark that the shocks were clearly distinguishable into two classes: those in which the motion was horizontal, and those in which it was perpendicular. The latter were attended with the explosions and the terrible mixture of noises that preceded and accompanied the earthquakes in a louder degree, but were by no means so desolating and destructive as the other. When they were felt, the houses crumbled, and trees waved together, and the ground sank, and all the distructive phenomena were conspicuous. In the interval of the earthquakes, there was one evening — and that a brilliant and cloudless one — in which the western sky was a continued glare of vivid flashes of lightning and of repeated peals of subterranean thunder, seeming to proceed, as the flashes did, from below the horizon. They remark that the night, so conspicuous for subterranean thunder, was the same period in which the fatal earthquakes of Caraccas occurred; and they seem to suppose those flashes and that event parts of the same scene." *

Flint confirms the observations of others, that the chasms in the earth were in a direction from southwest to northeast, and were of an extent to swallow up not only men but houses; and that they frequently occurred in intervals of half a mile. The people felled the tallest trees at right angles to these chasms, and placed themselves upon their trunks, by which precaution many escaped destruc-

---

* "Recollections of the Last Ten Years in the Mississippi Valley." (1826.) P. 224

tion; for more than once the earth opened beneath, and would have engulfed them in the abyss.

So great was the destruction of property, and so irretrievably ruined were many of the farms by this series of events, that Congress, at a subsequent day, passed a law granting to each proprietor who had sustained serious loss, a section of land in what was known as the Boone-Lick country, on condition of his relinquishing his desolated farm to the Government.

Earthquake shocks yet occur in this region, and blasts of air and gas yet find their way to the surface through many of the half-filled fissures, but there has been no repetition of the terrible phenomena witnessed in 1811–12.

CHAPTER II.

MOUNTAINS AND PLAINS.

CHARACTER OF THE WATER-SHEDS — THE APPALACHIAN RANGE — THE ROCKY MOUNTAINS — THE SIERRA NEVADA — THE CASCADE RANGE — THE COAST RANGES — RIDGES OF THE GREAT BASIN — CHARACTER OF THE SOURCES OF THE MISSOURI — OF THE OHIO VALLEY — OF THE MISSISSIPPI VALLEY — THE LLANO ESTACADO — ROCKY-MOUNTAIN VALLEYS — COLORADO DESERT — VALLEY OF THE ST. LAWRENCE — PACIFIC RAILROAD ROUTES — RESUME.

Character of the Water-Sheds.—The Valley of the Mississippi may be regarded as a table-land between two diverging coast ranges — the Rocky and Appalachian Mountains,—with a slope on three sides towards the line of greatest depression occupied by the current of the river. The Ohio, at Pittsburgh, is 704 feet above the ocean; the watershed between Lake Michigan and the Illinois River is only 8 feet; the sources of the Mississippi, about 1,600; the sources of the Missouri, about 6,800 feet; the South Pass (source of the Sweetwater), 7,489 feet; Fort Bridger, 7,254 feet; and the divide between the Canadian and Pecos Rivers, about 5,543 feet. The elevations on the Western rim of the Basin, are attained by an inclined plane so slight that, in traversing it, the eye scarcely notices any deviation from a nearly uniform level. The ascent even to the South Pass, higher than that of Simplon or St. Gothard over the Alps, is so gradual that Frémont had to watch very closely to detect the culminating point.

The Appalachian Range.—This range, which divides the Atlantic slope from the Mississippi Valley, extends from Northern Alabama to the mouth of the St. Lawrence—a distance of more than 1,200 miles,—with a mean height of about 2,000 feet, and in a direction northeast and southwest. The culminating points, as determined by Guyot, are: Clingman's Peak, in the Black Mountains of North Carolina, being 6,702 feet; and Mt. Washington, in the White Mountains of New Hampshire, being 6,285 feet.

The Appalachian range does not exhibit a central axis, but, as first shown by the Rogerses, consists of a series of convex and concave flexures, giving rise to alternate ridge and valley, and affording few scenes of bold and rugged outline.

"The characteristic features," say they, "of the Appalachian ridges, are: their great length, narrowness, and steepness, the evenness of their summits, and their remarkable parallelism.

Many of them are almost perfectly straight for a distance of more than fifty miles; and this feature, combined with their steep slopes and sharp level summits, gives them the appearance, seen in perspective, of so many colossal entrenchments. Some groups of them are curved; but the outlines of all are marked by soft transitions and an astonishing degree of regularity. It is, rather, the number and great length of the ridges, and the magnitude of the belt which they constitute, than their individual height or grandeur, that places this chain among the great mountain systems of the world. * * * The rocks consist of the older metamorphic strata, including gneiss, and micaceous, chlorite, talcose, and argillaceous schists, together with masses referable to the earliest Appalachian formations."*

Flanking these ranges on the west, and coterminous with them in direction, is the Great Appalachian Valley, known by various local names. Its average width is about fifteen miles, and throughout it forms a nearly level plain.

Beyond this, to the northwest, and embracing an assemblage of rocks below the Coal-measures, is a series of long parallel ridges, which reach to the Cumberland and Alleghany Mountains, having a breadth of from thirty to sixty miles.

The northwestern portion of the Appalachian system is composed of what are known as the Alleghany and Cumberland Mountains, which are not protracted northeasterly beyond Southern New York. They embrace the Carboniferous series of rocks, and are about thirty-five miles in breadth.

While the general direction of the system is north-

* "Transactions of the American Association of Geologists."

east and southwest, there is a remarkable predominance of southeast dips throughout its entire length from Canada to Alabama, particularly along the southeastern or most disturbed side of the belt; but as we proceed towards the northwest, or remote from the region of greatest disturbance, the opposite or northwest dips, which previously were of rare occurrence, and always very steep, become progressively more numerous, and, as a general rule, more gentle, until they finally flatten down to an almost horizontality of the strata.

The Rogerses suppose that the movement which produced the permanent flexures "was compounded of a wave-like oscillation, and a tangential or horizontal pressure, both propagated northwestward across the disturbed belt, as indicated by the oblique character of nearly all the anticlinal and synclinal curves, both those which are closely folded and those which are obtuse;" and, resorting to forces now in operation for an explanation of these phenomena, they find analogies in the wave-like undulation of the surface, which occurs and is propagated over large areas during the throes and convulsions of the earthquake, as manifested in our time.*

* "Physical Structure of the Appalachian Chain," ("Trans. Amer. Association Geologists and Naturalists,") by Profs. Wm. B. and Henry D. Rogers.

It is desirable that there be recognized a division of the Appalachian

The Rocky Mountains. — The numerous ridges bounding the Great Valley on the west, pursue a general direction north of west and south of east, and are a part of a long axial line which extends almost uninterruptedly from Cape Horn to Behring's Straits, where, conforming to the great circle of the earth, it is protracted south, as first pointed out by Erman, through Western Asia, and terminates in Sumatra,—the whole length extending through 240° of latitude, or 18,560 miles.* In the United States, the Rocky Mountains extend from latitude 31° 30' to 49°, and from longitude 102° to 122½°, and embrace an area of more than 100,000 square miles. Their greatest width—between San Francisco and Fort Laramie—is 1,000 miles. In this area are included portions of Dakota, Montana, Idaho, Wyoming, Colorado, Utah, New Mexico, Arizona, California, Nevada, Oregon, and Washington. This vast assemblage of mountains is

Chain — a division founded on a difference in geological structure, and consequently on physical aspect. Let that portion which is characterized by the presence of crystalline and metamorphic rocks, and embracing the Unaka or Smoky Mountains of North Carolina, the Blue Ridge of Virginia and Pennsylvania, the Green Mountains of Vermont, and the White Mountains of New Hampshire, receive the generic name of *Appalachian Chain;* while that portion characterized by the coal-bearing rocks, and known as the Cumberland Mountains of Tennessee, and their extension into Virginia and Pennsylvania, retain the generic name of *Alleghanies.*

* Lieutenant (now General) Warren, " Pacific Railroad Survey," Vol. XI.

made up of several distinct chains, and will doubtless be found to consist of several distinct systems of upheaval. Sometimes they form central groups from which radiate subordinate branches, and again they present an endless maze of rugged flanks, with bare peaks sharply defined against the sky, and rising high above the line of vegetation into the region of perpetual snow.

It is between the parallels 40° and 41°, that they attain their greatest altitude and put on their sternest aspect; and as they range northward they sink down and become less serrated in contour. The most conspicuous peaks are: Frémont's, in the Wind-river Chain, (13,570); Long's Peak, in the North Park, (14,216); Gray's Peak, (14,245); and Spanish Peak is supposed to be equally high. These determinations, which differ somewhat from former ones, were recently made by Parry and Engelmann. To the south, the Raton Mountains project far into the plain. On the 35th° parallel there are two conspicuous landmarks, known as Mount Taylor or San Mateo, estimated at 11,000 feet, and San Francisco Mountain, estimated at 12,000 feet. All of these peaks are volcanic, and their elevation is among the most recent of geological events.

To the east, the plains along the parallel of the South Pass, are 6,000 feet above the sea-level. The western rim of the Great Basin is elevated 8,200 feet, while the Basin itself is 6,234 feet. To the north, about the sources of the Columbia, the mountains attain an altitude of from 7,000 to 8,000 feet above the sea, and are not snow-clad the year round.*

Many observers, like Warren and Abbot, looking at the topographical rather than the geological features of the region, have failed to recognize any thing like parallelism in the several chains. The Rocky Mountains, like the Alps, will doubtless be found to be intersected by numerous lines conforming to the great circle of the earth; but to develop those lines will be the work of long and patient investigation. The great frame-work of the region, we have reason to believe, was laid in a direction of N.N.W. and S.S.E.; but that frame-work has been repeatedly shattered, and the strata displaced, by more modern volcanic eruptions, the evidences of which exist almost every where throughout the whole region.

Topographers have laid down the trend of mountains and valleys, and of lakes and rivers, without comprehending the full import of apparently con-

---

* The following are some of the subordinate groups composing the Rocky Mountains: Bitter-Root, Cœur d'Alene, Kootanie, Salmon-River, Rocky Mountains (proper), Wind-River, The Parks, Raton, Santa Fé, Sandia, Manzana, Organ, Gaudalupe, Hucco, San Juan, Chusca, and Sierra Madre.

forming lines; but geologists, following in their wake, and carefully studying the strata which have been disturbed by these lines, resulting from igneous invasions, have been enabled to eliminate some of the grandest deductions in physical science. Let any student of structural geography plat upon a map the outlines of the great Appalachian and Illinois coal-fields; let him then examine the river-systems in connection with the mountain-systems of North America, and he will see that these topographical features are not the result of accidental upheaval, but of forces acting over vast areas, and in determinate directions,—evincing that, even amid apparently chaotic materials, there was still a presiding spirit of law and order.

It must be ever borne in mind that, between the Mississippi Valley and the Pacific Slope, there is a great swelling of the land, in an axial form, or a series of axes, to the height of from 5,000 to 7,000 feet; and from this elevated plateau, as in the Andes, the Caucasus in Central Asia, and other mountainous districts, rise still loftier ranges, various in direction and in age. Humboldt has pointed out this notable fact which has been ignored by less skillful physicists:

"The arrangement of these partial groups," he remarks, "erupted from fissures not parallel to each other, is in its bearings for the most part independent of the ideal axis which may be drawn through the entire swell of the undulating flattened ridge. These remarkable features in the formation of the soil give rise to a deception which is strengthened by the pictorial effect of this beautiful country. The colossal mountains, covered with perpetual snow, seem, as it were, to rise out of a plain. The spectator confounds the ridge of the soft-swelling land, the elevated plain, with the plain of the low lands; and it is only from the change of climate, the lowering of the temperature, under the same degree of latitude, that he is reminded of the height to which he has ascended." (This swelling of the soil belongs to a different epoch from the rampart-like chains with which it is crowned.) "The immense swelling of the surface of land," he continues, "which goes on increasing in breadth towards the north and northwest, is continuous from tropical Mexico to Oregon; and on this swelling or elevated plain, which is itself the great geognostic phenomenon, separate groups of mountains, running often in varying directions, rise over fissures which have been formed more recently and at different periods. These *superimposed* groups of mountains — which, however, in the Rocky Mountains, are for an extent of 8° of latitude connected together almost like a rampart, and rendered visible to a great distance by conical mountains, chiefly trachyte, from 10,000 to 12,000 feet high, — produce an impression on the mind of the traveler which is only the more profound from the circumstance that the elevated plateau which stretches far and wide around him, assumes in his eyes the appearance of a plain of the level country. Though in reference to the Cordilleras of South America, a considerable part of which is known to me by personal inspection, we speak of double and triple ranges, we must not forget that even here, the directions of the separate ranges of mountain-groups, whether in long ridges or in separate domes, are by no means parallel, either to one another, or in direction to the entire swell of the land." *

The Sierra Nevada or Snowy Range forms the western rim of the Great Basin, and is more

---

* "Cosmos," Vol. V., Art. "Volcanoes."

rugged and rises to loftier elevations than any other mountain-chain in the United States. The Sierra itself is a granitic crest, pursuing a course of about N. 30° W., flanked by metamorphic shales and sandstones. The culminating points are between the parallels 36° and 37° of latitude. Mount Silliman, as determined by the Geological Survey of California, is in height 11,623 feet; Mount Brewer, 13,886; Mount Tyndall, 14,386; and Mount Whitney, 15,000 feet,—probably the highest point of land in the United States.

The volcanic cones which have been lifted up since the Sierra Nevada assumed its direction, have an elevation little inferior. The Shasta Butte, as determined by Whitney, rises 14,440 feet, and Lassen's Peak is 10,577 feet.

The strata of Triassic age, metamorphosed and tilted, pursue a direction along the foot-hills of the Sierra Nevada of great uniformity, and the Cretaceous and Miocine tertiary are observed to rest undisturbed upon their upturned edges until traced to the vicinity of Shasta, where it is found that the continuity of the former is interrupted, and the latter are lifted up at high angles, thus showing that the volcanic action which elevated this butte was subsequent in age to that which formed the Snowy Mountains, and operated in a different line of direction.

The Cascade Range.—This range pursues a course nearly north and south, and is characterized by a series of lofty volcanic cones, among which are Mount St. Helen's, estimated by Dana at 16,000 feet; Mount Hood, 11,225 feet, as recently determined by Williamson; Mounts Jefferson and Adams, unmeasured; Mount Rainier, (according to Johnson) 12,330 feet; and Mounts Olympus and Baker, unmeasured. It is probable that the estimated height of St. Helen's is exaggerated; so that it is still doubtful whether any peak in the United States overtops Mount Blanc (15,810 feet).

Most of these peaks have trachytic cones, which were ignited up to a recent period; and the peperino and scoriæ which have been ejected from these vents cover large areas of country, and effectually conceal the fundamental rocks.

The Coast Ranges.—According to Antisell,* these ranges exhibit a remarkable parallelism, and show unmistakable evidence of ancient volcanic action. Their general direction is N. 70° W.; but Whitney gives N. 54° W. as the strike of the Mount Diablo Range. They have, in their course north of San Francisco, some lofty peaks, but the chains are short and ill-defined. San Francisco itself reposes on Cretaceous strata. South of the city,

* "Pacific Railroad Report" Vol. VI.

the ranges preserve much uniformity through 4° of latitude, until, in the vicinity of Fort Tejon, they become blended with those of the Sierra Nevada, and are prolonged into the sea at San Louis Bay.

Monte Diablo, which stands as a sentinel over the approach to the Golden Gate, is, according to Whitney, 3,856 feet high; Mount Hamilton, 4,440 feet; and Mount Carlos, 4,977 feet.

The elevation of the Coast Ranges above the sea-level was an event subsequent in time to that of the Sierra Nevada, since it brought up and metamorphosed into jaspery materials the sandstones and shales of the Cretaceous and Miocine-tertiary series which now form the wall of the Pacific Coast. This uplift may be regarded as one of the most recent of the dynamical events which has determined the outlines of the continent.

The Great Basin.—This remarkable plateau is elevated about 4,500 feet above the sea-level, and is traversed by successive ridges running north and south, which preserve a considerable degree of parallelism. These ridges are generally short and ill-defined, and some of them are a deviation from the general course which characterizes the Rocky Mountains. Thus, the Humboldt Range bears N. 20° E., and the Uintah Range runs east and west.

Within this basin is contained the Washoe

Mountains, which include the famous Comstock silver-lode. These mountains, according to Baron Richthofen, are separated from the steep slope of the Sierra Nevada by a continuous meridional depression marked by the deep basins of Truckee Valley, Washoe Valley, and Carson Valley. Though irregular, a general direction may be traced in the summit range from north to south, where it slopes down to a smooth table-land, traversed from west to east by the Carson River flowing in a narrow crevice, beyond which the Washoe Range is protracted in the more elevated Pine-Nut Mountains. The culminating point of the range is Mount Davidson, whose elevation, as determined by Whitney, is 7,827 feet. Virginia City is 6,205, Washoe Lake is 5,006 feet, and Dayton 4,490 feet.

"The aspect of the Washoe Mountains," remarks the Baron, "is exceedingly barren; so is the view from Virginia over the hilly country to the east. Yet there is a remarkable grandeur and sublimity in it. The air is extraordinarily pure and transparent, so as to allow every gulch and declivity in the slope of mountains a hundred miles off to be distinguished. The eye wanders over an unbroken desert, where barren hills alternate with sandy basins. There is no beauty in this scenery, but it has a strange charm; the constant enjoyment of the distant view is a redeeming feature of life in Virginia." *

In the report of the expedition under Governor Blasdel to Pahranagat, in Southeastern Nevada,

---

* "Report on the Comstock Lode," by Ferdinand Baron Richthofen.

the chief features of the country are noted: the parallelism of the mountain ranges, which are nearly northwest and southeast; wide valleys, often covered with artemisia, and often bare of all vegetation; the presence of volcanic overflows along the foot-hills; the entire absence of timber, the only wood being mezquite bushes near the springs; great scarcity of water; the occurrence of wide gravel washes at the mouths of the cañons; and a general air of sterility and desolation pervading the whole region.

CHARACTER OF THE MAIN VALLEYS.

The Missouri River is the longest affluent of the Mississippi — though the volume of water discharged is not so great as that of the Ohio, — and by reason of its length ought to be regarded as the main stream. It has its sources in longitude 112° and latitude 47°, where they nearly interlock with those of the Columbia, — the only river which rises in the Rocky Mountains and breaks through the Coast Ranges, in the vast extent from British Columbia to Mexico. Standing on the summit at any point, Captain Mullan remarks, you can see the waters that flow into the two oceans; and no where on the continent do we find such a perfect net-work of water-courses. Amid an innumerable number of sheltered valleys found embosomed in the mountains, stock can graze on the hill-sides in winter, without forage being provided for them; and here the Indians, during that season, find abiding places.

"When we reach," he continues, "the Great Falls, there for thirteen miles, the river, in a series of cascades, falls, chutes, and rapids, has a total fall of three hundred and eighty feet. The land to the north, and for four or five miles back from the river, is much broken by coulees and ravines; but to the south, and distant three miles, the country is a flat plain." *

After leaving this region, according to Humphreys, the streams flow through almost treeless plains. Near the foot-hills, the soil is good, and receives a greater supply of moisture than the region further east. Extending to longitude 97°, and thence southward, there is a belt of country which, without putting on the features of a desert, has yet an aspect of sterility not to be mistaken. The meteorological conditions (deficiency of moisture), and the nature of the soil (alternations of sand and clay), render it unfit for agricultural purposes. The soil produces luxuriant grapes in the spring, but in the dry season the sun withers the vegetation, and parches, bakes, and cracks, the clayey surface; a process which gives it not only a sterile

* Mullan, "Address before Geographical Society," N. Y.
† Humphreys, "Pacific Railroad Survey," Vol. I.

aspect, but renders it uncultivable.† This region is known as the *Mauvaises Terres*, or Bad Lands.

The Yellowstone is the principal affluent of the Missouri, whose volume, as estimated by General Warren, is as large as that which is considered the main stream; and Jefferson, Madison, and Gallatin Forks, are by no means inconsiderable rivers.

The country drained by these tributaries, according to Mullan, before quoted, is among the most beautiful to be found west of the Mississippi,— gently undulating prairie, dotted here and there with clumps of timber. All the streams are fringed with forest growth, the soil is rich, the climate mild and invigorating, and here exist all of the elements for happy homes.

That portion of Oregon and Washington Territory west of the Coast Range, and bounding the Pacific, with the exception of the meadow or prairie bottoms, is a dense forest, timbered with fir, pine, and oak. The lumber trade is large; and is maintained with China, Japan, Australia, and the Sandwich Islands. The finest spar and mast timber is here found, and is sent to the ship-yards of France and England.*

The Columbia is navigable for four hundred and fifty miles from its mouth to South Fork, subject, however, to two interruptions by falls, around

---

* "Address before the Geographical Society," N. Y.

which railroads have been constructed; and there is a project to extend its navigation to Fort Boise, three hundred miles further, and reach the heart of Idaho.

Thus the vision of the poet has passed away. Those deep solitudes,

> "Where rolls the Oregon, and hears no sound
> Save its own dashings,"

have become the abodes of an active population, and the river itself is made the great highway to the interior of a continent.

The Ohio Basin is so well known that a brief description will suffice. It is diversified by hills of no great elevation, and by valleys of no great width. The rocks are of sedimentary origin, and but slightly metamorphosed; so that almost every where, from their yielding nature, the hills present rounded outlines, and are cultivable to their summits. The valleys are fertile, and abundantly watered by running streams. The surface, with the exception of a few wet prairies, was originally clothed with magnificent forests of several species of the oak, together with black walnut, hickory, sugar maple, and the liliodendron; while the undergrowth was composed of azaleas, rhododendrons, and many creeping plants;—altogether presenting a diversity of vegetable forms rarely to be seen over an equal area on other portions of the earth's surface.

The Sources of the Upper Mississippi are among the great forests of conifers, white birches, and aspens — subarctic types — which continue north, but dwarfed in stature, until the limits of arborescent vegetation are reached; and its mouth is in the region of the orange, the magnolia, and even the palm,— thus approaching the verge of tropical forms. A navigable river, flowing through a region so diversified in climate and productions, can not but become the source of a vast inland commerce.

Its central portion is through a magnificent region of alternate forest and prairie. The vegetation of the latter is largely represented by the *Compositæ*. This belt, so far from being restricted to the Mississippi Valley, extends southwesterly through the Osage and Cherokee countries, and is prolonged into Western Texas, constituting the best agricultural region of the United States, where the conditions of soil and climate are well adapted to the cultivation of those plants useful to man.

Captain (now General) Pope thus describes the region:

"By far the richest and most beautiful district of country I have ever seen, in Texas or elsewhere, is that watered by the

Trinity and its tributaries. Occupying, east and west, a belt of one hundred miles in width, with about equal quantities of prairie and timber, intersected by numerous clear, fresh streams and countless springs, with a gently undulating surface of prairie and oak openings, it presents the most charming views, as of a country in a high state of cultivation; and you are startled at the summit of each swell of a prairie, into a prospect of groves, parks, and forests, with intervening plains of luxuriant grass, over which the eye in vain wanders in search of the white village or the stately house, which seem alone wanting to the scene." *

Leaving this beautiful country and proceeding westward, the traveler enters one of the most desolate portions of the United States, known as the Llano Estacado, or the *Staked Plain*,—a treeless plateau, elevated 4,000 feet above the sea, a hundred miles or more in breadth, and stretching from the Canadian to beyond the northern confines of Mexico, unbroken by a single peak, and underlaid by nearly horizontal strata of red clay and gypsum. It is without wood or water. For thirty miles east of the Pecos, the surface is hard, and covered with grama grass; and from thence to a point about thirty miles west of the Colorado of Texas, the hard surface alternates with patches of dark-red sand, covered with coarse bunch-grass. The Llano Estacado presents no inducements to cultivation.†

* "Pacific Railroad Surveys," Vol. III.

† Pope, "Pacific Railroad Surveys," Vol. II.

Rocky-Mountain Valleys.—Between Great-Salt Lake and the base of the Sierra Nevada—a space, according to Humphreys, of 500 miles—the country consists of alternations of mountains and plains, the latter gradually rising from the lake to the base of the Humboldt; that is, from 4,200 feet to 6,000 feet above the sea. The mountains are sharp, rocky, and generally inaccessible, and rise from 1,500 to 3,000 feet above the valleys. The greater part of these valleys are sparsely sprinkled with several varieties of artemisia, presenting the aspect of a dreary waste; but on the flanks of some of the mountains, which are more liberally supplied with moisture from the melting snows, grama grass flourishes. Immediately west of Great-Salt Lake, there is a desert plain of clay and sand, impregnated with salt, seventy miles in width, and extending through five degrees of longitude.

The southern rim of the Great Basin is not hemmed in by any great mountain range, but is formed by a gradual swell of the plain, traversed by detached ranges, whose passes are only 400 or 500 feet above the general level, thus preventing the drainage into the Pacific. This water-shed separates the Great Basin from the Colorado Valley, the most desolate portion of the United States.

The Colorado Desert.—This desert, according to Blake,* extends from the base of San Bernardino Pass to the Gulf of California, the distance, between latitudes 32° and 34° N., being about 140 miles. Its greatest width is 75 miles, and the entire area is about 9,000 square miles. Portions of the surface, instead of being composed of drifting sands, are of compact blue clay, with a floor-like appearance, hardly indented with the mule's hoof in passing over it. A similar desert borders the Colorado River on the east side, which extends for a long distance up the Gila, and reaches the base of the mountains in the region of Sonora.

The desert spreads out as a wide and apparently limitless plain; not a green spot, not a shrub, not a solitary tree is to be seen, and the mountains which hem it in, are so bald that there is not soil enough to cover the rocks.

Blake notices the variety and intensity of colors in the light which invests every distant object, as characteristic of that region, the result of the extreme purity and dryness of the atmosphere, which is so transparent that small objects may be seen at extraordinary distances, robed in a peculiar azure hue.

Upon these desolate plains are witnessed all of the phenomena of a tropical twilight. The shadows

* "Pacific Railroad Survey," Vol. V.

of the distant mountains, sharply defined, are projected on the surface of the ground, and these again are reflected upon the apparently glassy vault above. While yet the distant summits are gilded with the rays of the setting sun, the plain itself is enveloped in darkness, and the stars sparkle like diamonds in a setting of jet,—thus realizing the vision of the Ancient Mariner:

> "The sun's rim dips; the stars rush out;
> At one stride comes the dark."

Valley of the St. Lawrence.—So little elevated is the *divortia aquarum* between the river-systems of the St. Lawrence, Hudson's Bay, the Mississippi, and the Hudson Rivers, that it opposes slight impediments to navigation. The Mississippi and St. Lawrence have their sources in a labyrinth of lakes,—so numerous, indeed, as, according to Richardson, to cover at least one-half of the surface. The commerce of the Hudson's Bay Company, extending over a vast region, embracing the sources of the Columbia, Mackenzie, Lake Superior, Hudson's Bay, and the Saskatchawan, is carried on through a great net-work of natural channels. The voyageur, starting at a common point on that slightly elevated plateau, in a light canoe, may pass, by easy portages, to the Arctic Ocean, to Astoria, to Hudson's Bay, to Chicago, to Quebec, and to New

York. Between the Minnesota branch of the Mississippi and the Red River of the North, loaded bateaux are transferred each year. During flood, the Muskingum of the Ohio, interlocks with the Cuyahoga of Lake Erie; the Des Plaines of the Illinois, with the Chicago River of Lake Michigan; and the Wisconsin River of the Mississippi, with the Fox River of Green Bay.

By reason of a notable physical fact, the sinking down of the Alleghany Ridges, in their northeasterly prolongation, a continuous water communication has been established between Lake Erie and the Hudson-River Valley, which will, at no distant day, be enlarged into a ship-canal; while the Ohio River and Lake Erie, and the Mississippi and Lake Michigan, have been connected by similar artificial communications, and have been made the great highways of an unsurpassed internal commerce.

On the destinies of New York City, this peculiar topographical feature has exercised a dominating influence, enabling her to hold easy and expeditious communication with the Great Interior, and to become alike the depository and the distributing point of the vast mass of vegetable and animal food which annually moves from West to East, through this channel, to the markets of the world. It has been the main-spring of her opulence and commercial greatness; the Aladdin's lamp, by the rubbing of which, the baser materials have been transmuted into gold; the secret, by the possession of which, she has been enabled to outstrip all of the rival sea-board cities in population and material prosperity, and to become the connecting link in the traffic of two hemispheres. The highlands of the Hudson are the gateways of a commerce such as Venice in her palmiest days never dreamed of, and such as Holland, rescued from the sea and fortified by dykes, can not surpass. In access to the ocean, New York has not, perhaps, advantages superior to Norfolk, Baltimore, Philadelphia, or even Boston; but in access to the great FOOD-PRODUCING STATES, she has unrivaled facilities, which she can for all time retain, if she lends her credit to the opening of enlarged routes of communication, thereby producing cheap and easy modes of transit.

To many unacquainted with the conditions of soil and climate, it might appear that New Orleans, situated at the outlet of this great river-system, would become a powerful competitor in the career of commercial greatness; but a few facts will serve to dispel this illusion. Several years ago, I expressed the following sentiments, which, in the light of subsequent events, I am not disposed to retract or modify:

"In the early settlement of the West, the Mississippi was the only outlet for the products of the country; but the opening of the New York and Canadian canals, and the construction between the East and West of not less than five trunk railways, have rendered the free navigation of the Mississippi a matter of secondary importance.

"The heated waters of a tropical sea, destructive to most of our articles of export; a malarious climate, shunned by every Northerner for at least one-half of the year; and a detour in the voyage of over three thousand miles in a direct line to the markets of the world; — these considerations have been sufficiently powerful to divert the great flow of animal and vegetable food from the South to the East. Up to 1860, the West found a local market for an inconsiderable portion of her breadstuffs and provisions in the South; but, after supplying that local demand, the amount which was exported from New Orleans was insignificant, hardly exceeding two millions of dollars per annum."

This system of internal navigation, if platted on the map of Europe, would stretch from the North Sea to the confines of Tartary, and from the Mediterranean to the Baltic. We have, within this area, a people united and prosperous, and acknowledging allegiance to one all-protecting Government, while there, the area is divided into principalities and empires for ages disunited, and differing in laws, language, and race. No one fact can impress the American more profoundly than this, of the prospective grandeur of his country.

The external commerce of the nation is but a tithe of that which is carried on through this internal system of communication.

PACIFIC RAILROADS.

Two railroads, the Union Pacific and the Union Pacific Eastern Division, are in progress of construction between the Missouri River and the Pacific Slope; and one other, the Northern Pacific, is projected to connect the waters of Lake Superior with those of Puget Sound.

Union Pacific Railroad.—This railway starts at Omaha, on the Missouri River, at an altitude of 968 feet above the ocean, and follows the valley of the Platte to the forks, where, leaving the North Fork, it follows the South Platte to Julesburg, and thence to the mouth of Lodge-Pole Creek. This station is 484.75 miles distant, and the altitude attained is 3,528 feet. This portion of the route is through a region highly favorable to the construction of a road; requiring few bridges, and little excavation.

Here the engineering difficulties begin. From Lodge-Pole Creek to Evans's Pass, in the Black Hills, 545.62 miles, the altitude rises to 8,248 feet. This is the culminating point on this line between the two oceans, and is 75 feet higher than the Pass of Great St. Bernard in the Alps. The highest points of the Black Hills, in this vicinity, are from 9,000 to 9,500 feet.

The table-lands between the Black Hills and Medicine-Bow Mountains, have an elevation between 6,000 and 7,000 feet, and are nearly barren of vegetation, except the characteristic artemisia.

The next highest summit is that between Bear River of Salt Lake and Muddy Creek, a tributary of Green River flowing into the Colorado. This point, on the eastern rim of the Great Basin, is 893 miles distant from Omaha, and has an altitude of 7,567 feet. Salt-Lake City, distant 1,026.76 miles, has an elevation of 4,285 feet. The road, as finally located, leaves Salt-Lake City to the left, crossing Bear-River Bay, and curves round the head of the lake, on whose borders is founded, by that peculiar people known as Mormons, the largest "settlement" in any of the territories; and however much we may deplore the social economy of this people, all must admit that they have exhibited a degree of thrift and patient industry which is highly to be commended.

Materials for construction of a railroad abound along this portion of the route. Pines suitable for timber clothe the ridges, and lignite is found in the earth, at intervals, as far east as Boulder Creek, sufficiently pure to furnish fuel for locomotives. Between Salt Lake and Reed's Pass, in the Humboldt Mountains (altitude 5,550 feet), the country is said to abound in grasses, and also in timber and water.

From Reed's Pass, 1,259.47 miles, the route follows one of the branches of the Humboldt River. The mountains on the south have an elevation of 8,000 feet, and the loftiest peaks are perpetually covered with snow. The valley is well-watered by numerous streams which have their sources in the melting snows, and is adapted to agricultural purposes.

At Copper Cañon, the river is from 150 to 200 feet wide, and passes 18,000 cubic feet of water in a minute. "This section," remarks the engineer, Mr. Bates, "is the most remarkable and interesting feature of the line. A range of mountains, having a direction nearly north and south, in remote ages, formed a barrier to the flow of the water between this point and Humboldt Wells, and the valley has probably been the bed of a lake. All along the slopes of the hills, the water-line can be seen several hundred feet above the river-bed. . . . They rise several thousand feet in height, with mountain on the top of mountain, rolling off, in the dim distance, in almost every conceivable shape."

The lower valley of Humboldt River is susceptible of cultivation, and several ranches have been established along its course.

The route between Humboldt Lake and Truckee

Desert, traverses a region where the soil is so light that it blows and drifts like snow, requiring ballast to protect the road-bed. The Truckee-River Valley, where intersected, is narrow and tortuous, but finally emerges into the Big Meadows, which are surrounded by mountains of great height. These meadows are inhabited by a mixed population of 500 souls, occupied in agriculture, trade, and mining. The proposed termination of the road is on the Truckee River, near Crystal Peak, at the boundary of California;—5,195 feet above tide, and 1,550.50 miles distant from Omaha.

The Central Pacific Railroad of California.—This road extends from Sacramento to Truckee Valley, and in its construction, impediments which a few years ago would have been deemed insurmountable by the civil engineer, have been successfully overcome.

Leaving Sacramento in June, the passenger, in the course of a few hours, experiences as great a change of temperature as though he were to pass from New York to Greenland. The valley, at this season, is clothed with a semi-tropical vegetation, and the balmy air is laden with the fragrance of flowers.

From the treeless plain to the eastward, the Sierra Nevada looms up like a great cloud-bank, the snow-fields on the summits flashing in the morning sun with opalescent hues. Soon he becomes involved in the foot-hills, and the view of the distant mountains is shut out. The cars wind around a projecting promontory, and far down is seen, like a silver thread, the foaming torrent of a branch of the American River. Ere long a glimpse of the snow-capped mountains is gained, and the air is tempered by their proximity. The flanks of the subordinate hills are clothed with dense forests of pine and other evergreens.

As the engine continues to climb, the country becomes still more inhospitable, and, seventy-five miles from Sacramento, and 4,500 feet above the sea, the snow-fields descend to the level of the track; and at intervals, through deep cuts, are constructed steep-roofed sheds with heavy timbers, to ward off the avalanches.

Still ascending, the pines are replaced by the cedar and tamarack, until finally the limit of vegetation is attained, and the hills rise up bare and desolate. The track is through tunnels in the solid rock, and along immense fields of snow, and icicles hang pendent from every projecting crag.

About one hundred miles from Sacramento, the summit is attained—7,042 feet, being 1,206 feet less than Evans's Pass; and, two miles beyond, the train enters the Great Tunnel, 1,659 feet in length.

The aspect here has all the rigors of an Arctic winter. Deep snow-banks, glacier-like torrents, and stalactites of ice, are on every side.

And now commences the descent. Steam is shut off, the breaks are applied, and the train moves forward by its own momentum. Far below, the eye catches a glimpse of Donner Lake, cradled in the hills, and surrounded by a fringe of pines. Around this lake, the road makes a circuit of seven miles, to gain an advance of only one-fourth of a mile, and in this distance accomplishes a descent of 783 feet. Truckee Station, in the valley of the Great Basin, is 119 miles from Sacramento, and 5,860 feet above the sea.*

The entire distance from Omaha to Sacramento is 1,669 miles,—to San Francisco, 1,793 miles.

Humboldt Valley is represented as rich in the precious metals, but the products are unavailable, by reason of inaccessibility and cost of transportation. Virginia City, the seat of extensive and prosperous mining, is sixteen miles south of the road, but owing to the topography of the country, forty miles of construction are required to make the connection.

The mining interests of Nevada will receive a prodigious impulse on the completion of this great

---

* The details of the passage of the first passenger train, are abridged from the Correspondent of the "New York Tribune."

work,—in the accession of population; in the diminished cost of transport of mining machinery and supplies of every kind; and in the facilities of communicating with both slopes of the continent.

Union Pacific Railroad, Eastern Division.— This road runs nearly due west from Kansas City, Missouri, up the valley of the Kaw, of which the Smoky Hill River is the continuation, to Pond Creek, near Fort Wallace, 412 miles distant. The route is through a region highly feasible for the construction of such a work, the country rising by an almost uniform slope to the height of about 2,200 feet.

The valley of the Kaw, for more than 100 miles, is well wooded, while the uplands rise in gently-swelling hills. The precipitation of rain is sufficient, during the spring and summer, to mature all the cerealia usually cultivated at the West. The western portion of the State is unfitted for agriculture, without a resort to irrigation, but affords an unlimited range of pasturage, which was, up to a recent time, the favorite resort of the buffalo.

To make Pond Creek the terminus of the road, or to continue it to Denver, seems a short-sighted policy, as it simply gives an additional outlet to the mining regions of Colorado and Nevada, of which there is no pressing necessity. The Company now propose, by Government aid, to deflect the road southwesterly to Fort Lyon; thence, after ascending the valley of the Purgatoire, to cross the eastern spur of the Raton Mountain; and thence, passing Fort Union, to continue onward to the Rio Grande, at Albuquerque, 872 miles. The highest summit encountered is at the head of Cañon Blanco — latitude 35°, and about thirty miles south of Santa Fé, — 7,136 feet above the sea. From Albuquerque, the survey has been protracted nearly along the 35th parallel, over the axial line of California, and thence northwesterly into the San Joaquin valley; and, crossing a gap in the Diablo range, reaches San Francisco. Such a route would develop a region rich in mineral resources, and over portions of which the dominion of the Government is but imperfectly asserted and maintained.

Dr. Le Conte, who accompanied the expedition as far as New Mexico, has briefly reported on the geology of the country.

The region from Fort Wallace to the Arkansas (seventy miles) is deficient in water; the annual rain-fall at Fort Lyon being 11.25 inches. The Arkansas furnishes an abundant supply of good water, and the valley contains much land capable, under irrigation, of yielding abundant harvests. Occasional groves of cotton-wood are seen in the valley; but the Purgatoire is fringed with a growth of cotton-wood, box, elder, and willow. The hills, within thirty miles of the Arkansas, are thickly covered with cedars; and on the higher ridges, adjacent to the cañon, pines of good quality appear.

Important beds of coal (Cretaceous) were observed along the foot-hills of the mountains, eight and ten feet in thickness. Enough is known to justify the conclusion that there are several places in the neighborhood of the line surveyed, which will furnish sufficient supplies of fuel adapted to railroad and domestic purposes.

Rich deposits of placer gold exist near Maxwell's, and gold quartz, argentiferous galena, copper, limonite, specular, and magnetic oxide of iron, are found in quantities of economic value.*

The country between the Rio Grande and the Colorado of the West, presents far different physical aspects. Instead of gentle slopes, composed of thick beds of water-worn materials, we find abrupt cliffs, barren rocks excavated into deep cañons, and sheltered valleys, where the herds are secure against the severest storms which rage on the mountains. To add to the desolation of the scene, extinct volcanic cones and long lines of erupted rock are by no means rare.

* Dr. John L. Le Conte's "Preliminary Report to General Palmer, in charge of Survey," 1868.

"The Navajo Country," according to Dr. Parry, "comprises a similar character of broken highlands, with fertile valleys, grassy slopes, and deeply-sheltered cañons.

"In passing to the valley of the Colorado, we descend by a succession of irregular mountain ranges and basin valleys, becoming more arid as they reach the lower elevation, and finally passing into the valley of the Colorado, characterized by its bare mountain ranges, desert uplands, and broad alluvial bottoms, supporting their peculiar semi-tropical vegetation." *

The features of the Colorado Desert, as well as of the western slope of the Sierra Nevada, require no further description. Dr. Parry traces the peculiar coal-deposits two hundred miles west of the Rio Grande. Over all of the region, between the Rocky Mountains and the Sierra Nevada, placer gold is known to exist. Silver is very generally associated with lead and copper, and it also occurs in the form of chloride and black oxide, with more or less gold. Copper is mined on Williams's Fork of the Colorado, and shipped to Swansea. Absence of water and fuel, the difficulty of transporting machinery, and the insecurity of life, have thus far prevented the development of this region. The extension of this railroad has already become a matter of commercial importance, and will soon become one of national necessity.

* Dr. C. C. Parry, "Preliminary Report," 1868.

Northern Pacific Railroad. — It is contemplated by a company of capitalists, aided by a government subsidy, to construct a railroad from the Fond du Lac of Lake Superior, to the Great Bend of the Missouri, thence through the valley of the Yellowstone River, and across the Rocky Mountains, through Cadott's Pass, to the valley of the Columbia ; and. thence, to Seattle, in Washington Territory, with a branch to Portland, on the Columbia River.

This road will traverse an entirely new region, which is supposed to contain resources, both mineral and agricultural, not to be developed by the roads now in progress of construction.

The estimated distance is 1,775 miles. From Fond du Lac to the main divide of the waters of the Missouri and Columbia, — according to Mr. Edwin F. Johnson, Chief Engineer of the road, — a distance of over 1,000 miles, there is no mountain range to be overcome. The elevation of the ground between the Mississippi and Lake Superior, in the direction of Crow Wing, is 1,158 feet above the ocean, or 558 feet above Lake Superior. The highest elevation encountered, is at Cadott's Pass, 5,330 feet, and the second, Snoqualmie Pass, 3,000 feet. The main range of mountains which forms the axis of the Continent where the proposed line crosses, is broken down, so as to permit the sources of the Missouri and the Columbia nearly to interlock.*

The general sterility of the valley of the Upper Missouri has been dwelt upon, but to the north of this, there lies a region drained by the Red, Mouse, Assiniboin, and Saskatchawan Rivers, which are navigable for long distances, — a region which, owing to the rapid trend of the isothermal lines to the northward, after passing longitude 98°, has a climate far more genial and a soil far less sterile than that of New England. So far as known, it is better adapted to the growth of wheat, rye, and oats, than the prairies of Illinois and Wisconsin. Herds

* My young friend, William H. Dall, who, for five years past, has been engaged in investigating the natural history of the region of Alaska, has furnished me with the following topographical notes, as to the northern extension of the Rocky Mountain ranges:

"1. ROCKY MOUNTAINS. — From the reports of the explorers of the Telegraphic Expedition, and the employés of the Hudson's Bay Company, and my own explorations, the following are our conclusions: First, the prolongation of this chain, northwesterly to the Arctic Ocean, as laid down on most physico-geographical maps, is erroneous.

"The Rocky Mountains lose their distinctive character, *as a range*, about latitude 60° N. The country here to the west and northwest, becomes mountainous, rolling, and broken. This conglomeration of mountains extends to the north and northwest, perhaps as far as the parallel 64°. About longitude 147° west, the Coast Mountains (being the prolongation of the Cascade Range, and probably the same in age) also lose themselves in this rolling country. Through these hills — 1,200 to 2,500 feet — the Youkon River cuts its way in a northwest direction. These mountains gradually close up their ranks as we go west, and about longitude 140° or 145°, they are united in a clearly defined range, which has a trend parallel with that of the coast, and which I have named the Alaskan Mountains. (See Proc. Boston Society of Nat. Hist., Nov. 4, 1868). This range contains of buffalo range over plains of rich pasturage, and winter even on the sources of the Athabasca,— a pretty conclusive evidence of the mildness of the climate.

This region, as large as the original Thirteen States in area, would be directly dependent on this route for its commercial intercourse; and, though under the dominion of a foreign power, its people would naturally gravitate to us as the centre of their political system.

The Pacific coast has a climate as congenial as that of Western Europe. Its fiord-like character,

many high volcanic peaks, and forms the back-bone of the peninsula of Alaska, and the Aleutian Islands.

"2. ROMANZOFF MOUNTAINS. — These mountains extend along the coast, from near the mouth of the Mackenzie River, gradually rising, till they culminate near the mouth of the Colville River. Several fine peaks are visible from Ft. Youkon, at the junction of the Porcupine and the Youkon Rivers. Near the Mackenzie River they are comparatively low and insignificant.

"3. Between the eastern end of this range, and the high, rolling country mentioned above, there is a broad extent of surface comparatively free from mountains. It is a rolling country, and these hills attain their highest point (2,000 feet?) at the water-shed between the sources of the Porcupine and the Peel Rivers. This permits the westward migration of eastern species of birds — summer visitors, — and the Alaskan Range to a great extent, if not entirely, arrests the northward progress of the typical west coast land-birds.

"There is no defined northerly current through the Ounimak Pass, but to the westward the Japan Current, or a branch of it, extends north through Behring's Straits, into the Arctic Ocean.

"The other mountains, in the valley of the Youkon, are low, none exceeding 3,000 feet, and probably only one or two attain over 1,500 or 2,000 feet. There are no large rivers emptying into Kotzebue Sound, or the Arctic Ocean. The Kouskoquim River is the only large one south of the Youkon.

"Isanotsky Pass is a cul-de-sac, and impassable for vessels."

and the deep articulations through the Straits of Fuca into Puget's Sound, afford harbors unsurpassed in ease of approach, anchorage, and shelter.

Lignite of a superior quality is found at Bellingham Bay and in the Willamette Valley. The interior affords magnificent forests, which already yield large supplies of lumber. From the Douglas pine, or the sugar pine, may be hewn spars fit

> "to be the mast
> Of some great ammiral."

The mountains of Idaho and Montana already yield $20,000,000 annually of the precious metals.

It will thus be seen that two lines of Pacific railway are under construction, and a third is projected. Already is the commercial interest of the valley of the Mississippi beginning to feel the effects of this new impulse communicated to its trade, as the ocean is affected by a large stream discharging its waters into its abyss. That the completion of these lines is to have an important bearing on our own commerce and that of the world, is not to be gainsayed; and yet these benefits may, by many, be overestimated. Viewed as a work of art, spanning such rivers as the Mississippi and Missouri, and scaling the crests of ridges like those of the Rocky Mountains and Sierra Nevada, it may be pronounced the most magnificent example of ancient or modern engineering. Viewed as a commercial problem, while it may not divert the commerce of the world, so far as relates to bulky articles which have received little enhanced value from the skill or industry of man, from its accustomed channels; but, so far as relates to human intercourse by travel, to the transmission of intelligence through the mails, to the development of mines of the precious metals, to the conveyance of the spices, silks, and teas of the Orient to their appropriate markets, its benefits will be great. But, viewed as a political measure, building up lines of States across the Continent, linking together parts of the Republic now widely separated by ties of the closest intimacy, and consolidating the strength and glory of a nation, it presents an aspect far more important than any mere commercial enterprise, and amply justifies the expenditure of all the money which has been appropriated to this object.

The construction of these roads will be regarded, in all coming times, as among those great works dictated by a wise patriotism and a far-seeing sagacity, which have for their object the substantial welfare of every portion of the Great Republic. Undertaken, too, at a time of great national depression, and when the burdens of taxation bore heavily on all classes, they are illustrious examples of what a free people can accomplish to develop those resources which shall contribute to the national strength and unity.

RESUME.

I have thus attempted to sketch the physical features of the United States; and, in doing so, have purposely avoided, except incidentally, all reference to those portions which are well known to the general reader.

This country has within itself elements of wealth such as are possessed by no other nation. On other continents, the progress of nations and the unity of the people have been interrupted both by physical restraints, such as impassable mountains and vast deserts, and by artificial restraints, such as civil disabilities and inequality of condition. "The feeble barrier of the Cheviot Hills," says Mrs. Somerville, "between England and Scotland, and the moderate elevation of the Highlands, have prevented the amalgamation of the Anglo-Saxons and Celts, even in a period of high civilization. The Franks and Belgians are distinct, though separated by hills of still less elevation." * Thus, slight physical barriers have controlled the migration of races, and checked the spread of civilization.

* "Physical Geography."

> "Lands intersected by a narrow frith
> Abhor each other. Mountains interposed
> Make enemies of nations, who had else,
> Like kindred drops, been mingled into one."

Our own country, with the internal improvements already completed, presents no such obstacles to inter-communication. With a vast body of agricultural lands in the interior, capable of producing a diversity of products, with great manufacturing capacities at one extreme, and great mineral resources at the other, the whole intersected by navigable rivers and far-stretching railroads, by which expeditious communication is had with the most distant parts, and maintaining an oceanic commerce both with Europe and Asia, soon to be more intimate than that of the most favored nations,—all these conditions are conducive to national strength and unity.

Nor are the peculiar tendencies of our political system to be overlooked. Founded, as it now is, upon the basis of equal rights to all men, every citizen is animated with the sentiment that he constitutes a part of the State. This sentiment will impress him with the value and efficiency of the ballot, and the importance of its use in checking abuses and promoting reforms. To those who, born in a foreign land, have been accustomed to see the right of empire exercised by a rule of succession as inexorable as the decrees of fate, and the most obsequious devotions paid by the wisest statesmen and the most renowned warriors to one who has inherited this right by the mere accident of birth, irrespective of public capacity or private worth,—to those, we repeat, who arrive on our shores and become invested with citizenship, there is no inducement to maintain the distinctions of nationality or the prejudices of race, whether he be Celt, Teuton, or Sclavonian. By the removal of all restraints upon intermarriage, by bringing together the children in the public schools and teaching them from the same text-books, and by enlisting men in the pursuit of the same industries, a spirit is evoked whose tendency is to soften the asperities of local association, and to fuse incongruous materials into harmonious proportions,—in fact, to Americanize all nationalities.

The recognition, in its broadest sense, of individual and political freedom, will produce unity and fraternity; it will "humanize men, and give them a common country." *

Our country has yet vast tracts of rich land whose surface has never been furrowed by the plough, and whose sod has never been upturned to the light of the sun. It is as fresh in rural beauty

---

* "Humanitatem homini daret, breviterque una cunctarum gentium, in toto orbe patria fierat." (Pliny, "Natural History.")

as when first it came from the hand of nature. Apart from the tumuli and embankments of that mysterious race, the Mound-Builders, or occasional patches of greensward, to indicate the spot where the Indian once pitched his lodge, there is little to remind us of the former occupancy of the continent. How different this from the aspects of the Old World! There are the remains of human structures whose origin stretches back to the dawn of the historic epoch; — pyramids, obelisks, and sphinxes, to remind us of an Egyptian civilization; winged bulls, colossal in size, hanging gardens, and spacious palaces, monuments of the former greatness of the Assyrian empire; statues of matchless proportions, temples of faultless architecture, and colisseums vast in extent, to remind us of the refinements of a Grecian or Roman civilization; and Gothic cathedrals, castles, and towers, to recall the rude civilization of the Middle Ages. But these are monuments of an effete civilization, indicative of long ages of crime and oppression, when man remorselessly appropriated the unrequited toil of his fellow-man. There is nothing to symbolize the moral or intellectual elevation of the masses; and, while we may admire these ruins of former greatness, the true philanthropist does not regret that such civilizations have been swept from the earth. They proclaim a relation which, throughout all history, has been adverse to human progress,—that of tyrant and people, of patrician and plebs, of lord and vassal, of master and slave.

But the contemplation of the physical aspects of our country awakens far different thoughts. Its vast primeval forests of rich and varied verdure; its almost boundless plains of waving green, spread out far as human vision can range; its noble rivers, thousands of miles in length, often expanding into inland seas, which serve as the great highways of an extended and prosperous commerce; its lofty mountains, whose crests penetrate high into the region of perpetual snow, and whose flanks are stored with the precious metals;—all remind the statesman and the philanthropist that here are the elements of material wealth and of human power, such as the world never saw; that here is a field for the display of the most vigorous manifestations of physical or intellectual force; and that here, under a beneficent form of government, man may rise to his true dignity,—a position in the order of creation "a little lower than that of the angels."

CHAPTER III.

THE ORIGIN OF PRAIRIES.

DISTRIBUTION OF FOREST, PRAIRIE, AND DESERT — PRAIRIES NOT DUE TO PEAT-GROWTH — NOT DUE TO THE TEXTURE OF THE SOIL — NOT DUE TO THE ANNUAL BURNINGS — ZONES OF VEGETATION — THE GREAT BASIN — CLIMATIC CONDITIONS — MEAN ANNUAL PRECIPITATION — SOURCE OF MOISTURE — PERIODICAL RAINS OF CALIFORNIA — CONCLUSIONS.

Distribution of Forest, Prairie, and Desert.— Whenever we examine a continental mass, we ordinarily find a wooded belt along the shores, succeeded, as we advance inland, by grassy plains, and graduating in the interior into inhospitable deserts. Whenever we study the annual precipitation of moisture, in connection with the lines of temperature, we find that, wherever the moisture is equable and abundant, we have the densely-clothed forest; wherever it is unequally distributed, we have the grassy plain; and wherever it is mostly withheld, we have the inhospitable desert.

The varying supply of moisture, then, is sufficient to account for the diversity of vegetation, modified to some extent by the physical features of the country, altitude above the sea, and the extremes of heat and cold.

Most of us were born in a wooded region, and in the vicinity of the moisture-distilling sea. In our childhood, we were accustomed to look out upon a landscape diversified by mountain and valley. Every hill had its crown of forest, and every stream its waterfall. To subdue the soil by cutting down these aborescent forms, was an herculean task. Thus, then, from early associations, we were led to infer that this was the primal condition of the earth's surface.

Transported to a region with a combination of features far different, with a soil composed of the most comminuted materials, where in a day's journey we should fail to see the underlying rock or even an erratic block, with a surface stretching out in vast savannas, either level or thrown into gently-rounded outlines, like the waves of the ocean arrested and petrified,— the whole waving with a luxuriant growth of vegetable green,— while in the distance, the eye would discern a clump of trees, like an island in mid-ocean, or a long line of trees, like a low coast, fringing a stream which wound its sluggish way through this mass of verdure, and where the whole plain seemed to be spread out like a hemisphere bounded by the sky;—transferred to such a scene, our ideas of the earth's surface would be very different from those of our youthful remembrance.

If we were to penetrate still further into the interior, and behold plains equally extended, the surface covered with efflorescences of salt which glittered like snow-flakes in the morning sun, or with a rank growth of artemisia which perfumed the air as with camphor, or with cacti which we had seen cultivated as hot-house plants, shooting up in tree-like forms; our ideas of the earth's surface would be still further modified. And yet, such are the diversities which nature presents in every continental mass.

The Prairies not due to Peat-Growth.—It is a microscopic view to undertake to trace analogies between the formation of the prairies and that of the treeless morasses known as peat-swamps, as has been done by Lesquereux, a distinguished botanist, in the first volume of the "Illinois Geological Reports." It is a theory which presupposes a humid climate, a level country with imperfect drainage, and with a surface dotted over with lakes and sheltered from the winds, where the peat-producing plants could grow,—conditions none of which obtain where the prairies assume their grandest proportions. *

---

* Take, for example, Kansas: So great is the relief and depression of the soil, that, standing on one of the "rolls," I have commanded a view of forty miles in extent. The rise of the Kansas Slope is 2,200

We can hardly conceive of conditions by which the whole surface of a country would be converted into a peat-bog. Such bogs are generally found occupying erosions in the surface, and where they are sheltered from the winds. There is no tendency to the formation of peat along the shores of the Great Lakes, where the waters are agitated by storms, nor along the margins of rivers of briskly-running water. Peat-vegetation, then, only thrives in still waters, and where there is a tendency to stagnation; and the area over which it extends in a given region is inconsiderable, compared with the area occupied by other vegetable forms. *

feet in the distance of 400 miles. What struck me as remarkable, in traversing that region, was the entire absence of peat.

Dr. Logan ("Report on the Geology of Kansas," 1866,) remarks: "There is but little marshy or spongy soil in the whole State; the surplus water coursing down the natural conduits, leaves no opportunity for the saturation of the ground, which is observable in some of the other States, and particularly the prairie States east of the Mississippi River. * * * Kansas, as said before, by reason of its physical features, its soil, and its winds, is thoroughly drained. The streams usually have high banks and run in narrow channels, and the water is carried off with great rapidity. * * Hence, no ponds or sloughs are formed, and but rarely any spongy soil."

Thus, while the treeless region of Kansas is characterized by an absence of peat, the densely-wooded region of Massachusetts contains, by estimate, 120,000,000 of cords.

* Staring gives the following explanation of the formation of peat: The first condition on the surface of the fens, is stillness of water. Hence, it is not formed in running streams, nor in pools so large as to be subject to frequent agitation of the wind. Aquatic plants of various genera, such as *Nuphar, Nymphæa*, etc., fill the bottom with roots and cover the surface with leaves. Many of the plants die each year, and furnish a soil fit for a higher order of vegetation, viz., *Phragmites*,

The aromatic sage-plants, the cacti, and the bunch-grasses, are forms of vegetation which characterize the Western Plains, and are unknown in a region favorable to the growth of peat.

The Llanos of Venezuela have many features in common with the prairies, but they are subject, each year, to droughts so long-continued and intense that the soil cracks and bakes, and the carbonized particles of vegetation are whirled through the air in the form of fine dust. Such climatic conditions would preclude the growth of peat-vegetation.

It is evident, therefore, that we must resort to other and different causes to explain the phenomena of these grassy plains.

Acorus, Sparganium, etc. In course of twenty or thirty years, the muddy bottom is filled with roots of aquatic and marsh plants, which are lighter than water; and if the depth is great enough to detach the vegetable net-work, it rises to the surface, bearing with it, of course, the soil formed above it by decay of stems and leaves. New genera now appear upon the mass, such as *Carix, Menyanthes,* and others, which quickly cover it.

The turf has now acquired a thickness of from two to four feet, and floats about. In about half a century, the mass, having increased in thickness, reaches the bottom and becomes fixed. Arborescent plants, *Alnus, Salix,* etc., appear, and these contribute to hasten the attachment of the turf to the bottom, both by their weight and by sending their roots through into the ground. This is the method employed by nature for the gradual filling up of shallow lakes and pools, and converting them first into morass and then into dry land. (Staring, "De Bodem van Nederland," i., 36.)

Hundreds of acres of floating pastures, which have nothing to distinguish them from grass-lands, resting on solid bog, are found in North Holland. Cattle are pastured on these islands, and sometimes large trees are found growing on them. There is little evidence that the surface of the prairies has been thus formed.

Not due to the Texture of the Soil.—Other physicists would attribute the formation of prairies to the mechanical or chemical composition of the soil,—a theory which we think equally untenable, when we reflect that the surface of these treeless plains may vary in every degree between drifting sands and impervious clays, and that the efflorescences of soda and gypsum which are the evidences of an arid climate at one extremity of the Continent, would become fertilizing agents at the other.

The forest of Fontainbleau thrives on a plain composed of sand to the extent of ninety-eight per cent. of the whole contents; the region of the Colorado Valley, the most desolate portion of the United States, is often underlaid by a blue clay so indurated as hardly to be impressed by a mule's hoof in passing over it; the soil of the Llano Estacado is red clay and gypsum, which, under certain conditions of moisture, would be highly productive; and even the entire area of Sahara is far from being a mass of drifting sands.

Not due to Annual Burnings.—The theory very much in vogue before the laws of climatology were fully understood, which attributed the formation of prairies to the annual fires set by the Indians, is deserving only of a passing notice. If these regions were once wooded, we should expect to find the remains of an arborescent vegetation entombed in the sloughs, where they would be capable of indefinite preservation. If their treeless character is due to such causes, we should expect to find similar tracts east of the Alleghanies; particularly, as it is a historical fact that, when this country was first known to the European, the Indian lived in the wooded region, and not on the prairies.

In traversing the great forests adjacent to Lake Superior, where, owing to the resinous nature of the trees, the fires at times rage with unabated fury, consuming even the turf, until quenched by drenching rains, we have seen large areas thus burnt over; but we never saw a grassy plain which could be traced to such a cause.

In order to fully comprehend the origin of these vast savannas, and to trace that origin to the operation of known laws, it becomes necessary to consider the varying distribution of moisture in connection with the geographical distribution of plants.

ZONES OF VEGETATION.

North America may be divided into five zones of vegetation, resulting from its climatic conditions:

1. *The Region of Mosses and Saxifrages.*
2. *The Densely-wooded Region.*
3. *Alternate Wood and Prairie.*
4. *Vast Grassy Plains, where the Trees are restricted to the immediate Banks of the Streams.*
5. *Vast Arid Plains, often bare of Vegetation, and covered to some extent with Saline Efflorescences.*

Region of Mosses and Saxifrages. — From latitude 60° N., on Hudson's Bay, and thence extending northwesterly as far as the Arctic Ocean, lie the "Barren Grounds," so well described by Richardson. They are treeless, and the simpler kinds of vegetation abound, such as lichens, mosses, and fungi. Still north, beyond the flood, is the *Terra Damnata* of the Laplanders; there,

> "A frozen continent
> Lies dark and wild, beat with perpetual storms
> Of whirlwind and dire hail, which on firm land
> Thaws not, but gathers heap, and ruin seems
> Of ancient pile; all else deep snow and ice."

This peculiar vegetation is the result of diminished temperature, rather than of deficient moisture, where every hill is sculptured in ice, and every stream has a viscid flow to the oceanic abyss.

Densely-wooded Belt. — Below the "Barren Grounds," we enter upon a forest-belt which stretches continuously to the Gulf of Mexico.

ZONES OF VEGETATION.

The prairie has its greatest transverse expansion in the Missouri Basin, and narrows as it goes north. In the temperate zone, the western line of the forest-belt would bear southeast, passing west of the head of Lake Superior, and striking the west shore of Lake Michigan, whence it is protracted southwest into Eastern Texas. Clumps of spruce-fir form its outliers to the north, while its southern extension embraces the magnolia and palmetto.

With reference to the forest-range, as determined by lines of latitude, *and, therefore, by the vicissitudes of summer and winter temperature, rather than by the varying supplies of moisture*, it may be stated than many of the Canadian types, following the course of the Alleghanies, reach as far south as Virginia, and even Georgia, where they intermingle with forms purely sub-tropical. Thus, on the crests of the Alleghanies, in Pennsylvania, may be seen the hemlock of the north holding divided empire with the magnolia of the south,— sub-arctic and sub-tropical species intermingling,— and both withstanding alike the rigor of our winters and the heat of our summers; both hybernating during the winter, and both displaying during the summer, in the most vigorous manner, the functions of foliation and fructification. Thus it is, by reason of these excessive variations of summer and winter temperature, an American forest presents an assemblage of trees and a variety of foliage, of which Europe affords no parallel. The former has about one hundred and twenty different species, while the latter has only thirty-four.

In the forests adjacent to the Great Lakes, the Coniferous or Pine tribe is largely predominant. While this group occupies a region little prized for agriculture, by reason of the poverty of the soil and the rigor of the climate, it is fortunately contiguous to a region where both of these conditions are wanting, and where the presence of dense forests would be a serious obstacle to the development of the country.

Taking root in a soil which may contain but two per cent. of organic matter, and which, but for its vegetable covering, would become a mass of drifting sands, the white pine (*P. strobus*) becomes the monarch of our forests, symmetrical in form where grown in the open air, and the most valuable of all our trees when felled for lumber. I cite this example to illustrate the fact, that certain forms of vegetation are far more dependent for their growth upon a regular supply of moisture, than upon the quantity of organic matter in the soil.

While the sub-arctic types, in their southern prolongation, cling to the crests of the Alleghanies, there are other types, characteristic of a more temperate climate, such as the oak, the hickory, and tulip, which clothe the slopes; and still other types, such as the mulberry, black-walnut, papaw, buckeye, honey-locust, and persimmon, which seek the rich, mellow bottoms.

While the geographical range of certain arborescent forms is mainly limited, north and south, *by the conditions of temperature*, their eastern and western range, taking the Alleghanies as the axis, is limited *by the conditions of moisture;* and these limits are more circumscribed by the latter cause than by the former.

The eastern rim of the Mississippi Valley contains many characteristic trees which are but feebly represented where the prairies commence, and disappear altogether beyond the Missouri, where they assume their full development. On the other hand, vegetable forms are not represented on the eastern margin, which attain their full development as we approach the base of the Rocky Mountains. These changes are wholly independent of isothermal lines, but dependent on the variable supply of moisture.

Alternate Wood and Prairie.—In this zone, we would include the region between the eastern shore of Lake Michigan and the eastern slope of the Missouri Basin, in Iowa, latitude 42° N., longitude 95° W.; and thence the western boundary is protracted a little west of south, towards the mouth of the Rio Grande. This line is far from being well-defined, since the trees follow all of the great valleys of the Mississippi and Missouri, to within five or six hundred miles of the Rocky Mountains.

With regard to the botany of this region, Dr. J. G. Cooper, who has paid much attention to the geographical distribution of plants in the United States, remarks, that "no new forms of trees appear, while those found farther eastward rapidly diminish towards the west. Thirteen species have not been traced west of its eastern border; about ninety extend pretty far into the Texan and Illinois regions; but only five or six cross the eastern limit of the Camanche and Dacotah regions, which, however, receive nine more from the west and south." The cause of the disappearance of trees, he attributes to the deficient and irregular supply of moisture. "It is true," he adds, "that this does not materially affect agriculture in the more eastern regions; in fact, most crops will succeed better with less rain than is necessary for most trees to thrive." [*].

It is in this region that the grasses become predominant over the forest, usurping, for the most part, the high and dry rolls, and hedging the trees to the immediate valleys, or to such uplands as have a stiff, clayey, retentive soil. That the limits

* "Smithsonian Report," 1858.

of the forest were not more extended in former times, is evident from the fact that the sloughs yield no entombed trunks of trees which, we know, in other regions, are preserved for an indefinite period of time.

The differences in the retentive power of moisture in the soil, give to the eastern line of the prairie-region an irregular outline, which may be likened to a deeply-indented coast,—far-entering bays, projecting headlands, and an archipelago of islands.

What are known as "oak openings," indicate the transition from the densely-wooded region to the treeless plains. The trees stand as in an artificial park, shading a green-sward devoid of underbrush, so that the traveler may ride or drive in any direction. This characteristic feature I have noticed almost continuously from Green Bay to the western borders of Arkansas. The trees appear dwarfed and sickly; the extremities are often dead, while the main body is covered with foliage, and the trunks, when felled, are found to be more or less decayed. *

---

* As illustrative of the retentive power of a soil in modifying vegetation, I would state that, in the lead-bearing region of Wisconsin, the Galena limestone is a porous rock, intersected by numerous fissures; and hence, where it prevails, we almost invariably find a growth of scrub-oaks or prairie-grass. In the denudation of that region, during the Drift-period, there were left behind patches of the Cincinnati blue limestone, which is here a shale decomposing into clay, and is much more retentive of moisture than the subjacent formation.

These patches form forest-crowned mounds, and are so distinct

The change in the character of the grasses and herbaceous plants is more marked, even, than in the trees. These are largely *Compositæ*, with the genera *Helianthus, Actinomeris, Coreopsis, Echinacea*, etc. The compass-plant (*Silphium laciniatum*), which arranges the margin of its leaf north and south with so much uniformity that the traveler, in a cloudy day, may determine the direction of the magnetic meridian, forms one of the most noticeable plants of the prairie.

These plants are the pioneers of a more marked change in a vegetation which finds its full development still farther in the interior of the Continent, and may be regarded, I think, as the unerring index of a change in the conditions of humidity in the atmosphere.

Vast Grassy Plains, with Trees restricted to the immediate banks of the Streams.—This is the character of the country between the Missouri River and the base of the Rocky Mountains; but as the traveler advances from east to west, he begins to notice increasing signs of dryness in the atmosphere, and of a more marked continental cli-

in character from the general plain, that the geologist can map the boundaries of the two formations, without an examination of the respective strata,—the vegetation of the one being dwarfed, while that of the other is luxuriant. Such is the origin of the Sinsinowa, Blue, and Scales's Mounds, Gratiot's Grove, and several other forest-crowned eminences.

mate. The rain-fall becomes insufficient for the cultivation of crops, and the diurnal changes of temperature are too abrupt to permit the growing and maturing of the sub-tropical plants cultivated for food. The thermometer may rise to 70° or 80° at mid-day, and drop to below the freezing-point at night. Not a cloud, for days, dims the lustre of the sun; and at night, are shed no refreshing dews. The purity of the air is so great that wild meats are cured without the aid of salt, and the grasses dry up without a loss of their nutritive properties. Surrounded by a medium so dry, elastic, and bracing, the voyageur toils under a heat of 90° without exciting excessive perspiration, and at the same time his system is proof against the chilling air of the night. Those stifling and enervating heats, and those cold and disagreeable storms, characteristic of the humid regions to the east, are here unknown, and the atmosphere itself becomes highly electrical.

There are other indications of an arid climate. The soil becomes sandy and porous; the surface, in places, is covered with incrustations of soda and gypsum; and the streams are rendered unpalatable by reason of the solution of these salts in their waters. Such phenomena occur in most regions where evaporation is equal to precipitation. Where there is an excess of precipitation, the water leaches out these salts from the soil, and bears them to the ocean.

Salt lakes and saline efflorescences were observed by Stevens, as far east as longitude 101°, northwest of the sources of the Mississippi; by Frémont, in longitude 100°, south of the Platte; and by Marcy, in longitude 101°, on the Red River. They extend even farther east, as salt-flats have been observed near the Red River of the North; in Nebraska, within seventy miles of Omaha; in Kansas, seventy-five miles northwest of Fort Riley, and in the valleys of the Republican, Saline, and Solomon Rivers; on the Great Bend of the Arkansas, in beds from six to twenty inches deep; and between the Arkansas and Canadian, as far east as longitude 97°.

The vegetation indicates a similar change of climatic conditions. While the cotton-wood, the box-elder, and occasionally a dwarfed red-cedar, are almost the only representatives of the noble forests to the east, and these hug the moist alluvium of the streams, there are other forms which here attain their full development. These are the artemisia, the cactus, and the buffalo or bunch grass.

The artemisia (*A. tridentata*) first attracts attention on the Kansas River, as far east as longitude 95°, but it attains a ranker development nearer the base of the Mountains, where saline efflorescences are more common, and its full development in the Great Basin. The narrative of every explorer contains notices of the "interminable deserts" of wild sage. Frémont ("Expedition of 1842,") remarks:

> "With the change in the geological formation, on leaving Fort Laramie, the whole face of the country has entirely altered its appearance. Eastward of that meridian, the principal objects which strike the eye of the traveler are the absence of timber, and the immense expanse of prairie, covered with the verdure of rich grasses, and highly adapted to pasturage. * * * Westward of Laramie River, the region is sandy, and apparently sterile; and the place of the grass is usurped by the artemisia and other odoriferous plants, to whose growth the dry air and sandy soil of this region are favorable. * * * They grow every where, — on the hills and over the river-bottoms, in tough, twisted, wiry clumps; and wherever the beaten track was left, they rendered the progress of the carts rough and slow. As the country increased in elevation, they increased in size; and the whole air is strongly impregnated and saturated with the odor of camphor and spirits of turpentine which belongs to this plant."

Bigelow, on the journey between Fort Smith and Santa Fé, does not record the occurrence of this plant.

The cactus is another characteristic form of an arid climate. Although occasionally seen as the prickly pear on the sandy shores of Lake Michigan, and within the sparsely-wooded belt of southern Missouri, yet on the Plains it puts on a variety of forms, and attains, at times, tree-like dimensions.

Bigelow notes the occurrence of *Opuntia* as far east as Fort Smith. The Llano Estacado, however, is emphatically the region of the cacti, which ascend even the slopes of the mountains, as at Santa Fé. Frémont remarks that there "cacti become rare, and mosses begin to dispute the hills with them,"— a conclusive evidence of the increasing humidity of the air; for lichens and mosses are the first to attach themselves to trees and rocks, where they pave the way for the higher orders of plants. The crests of the Sierra Madrè, which are sufficiently high to condense the moisture which is withheld from the plains, become clothed with arborescent forms, such as the Douglas pine, the Mexican yellow-pine (*Piñon*) and the balsam-fir. Accustomed as we are to see the *Cactaceæ* cultivated as hot-house plants, we can form very imperfect ideas of their luxuriance and magnificence where they flourish in their native arid wilds,— some of them rising in candelabra-like forms, or like the pipes of an organ, to the height of thirty or forty feet. One species (*Cereus giganteus*), it is said, on the Gila, reaches sixty feet, and shoots up twenty-five or thirty feet without a branch, yielding an edible fruit much prized by the natives. The melon-cactus contains within its prickly envelope a watery pulp which the mule, parching with thirst, opens with his foot and extracts with his lips.

The cactus is characteristic of the arid region both of North and South America, but is rarely seen under like conditions in the eastern hemisphere.

The buffalo or "grama" grass, of which there are several species, is another marked type of the Plains. It grows in tufts, having a narrow, slender leaf, and where it exists in all its perfection, the surface of the soil resembles a sheep-lawn. It dies down under the heats of summer, and the climate is so dry that its nutritive properties are preserved; and thus, at all seasons of the year, it affords sustenance to the immense herds of buffalo which roam over the plains. Bigelow first noticed its appearance on a small branch of the Canadian, about longitude 96°, and it extends thence to the Sierra Nevada. On the Smoky-Hill route, I have observed it about thirty miles west of Fort Riley.

Vast Arid Plains, often bare of Vegetation, and covered, to some extent, with Saline Incrustations.—The Rocky Mountains form a well-marked division in the climatology of the United States, both in reference to the fertility of soil and the distribution of plants. Newberry has remarked that, while on the eastern slope, we have immense grassy plains, large accumulations of detrital materials, and a gently-rolling surface; on the western slope, we have large tracts of sandy wastes, of rocky surfaces bare of covering, and intersected by numerous and deep cañons, so intricate as to bewilder and impede the explorer. The Great Basin and the Colorado Desert occupy the region between the Rocky Mountains and the Sierra Nevada, from the head of the Gulf of California as far north as latitude 42°, and in many respects present physical aspects not elsewhere recognized in North America.

The Great Basin.— This remarkable plateau has a lake and river system of its own, and is cut off from communication with the sea. It embraces an area, triangular in shape, of 700 miles in length and 500 in width. It is elevated from 4,000 to 6,000 feet above the ocean, and is traversed by bare and rocky ridges, having a general parallelism with the intervening valleys, which are of a desert-like character, and are sprinkled over with the ever-present artemisia. Throughout, hot springs and salt lakes abound, the most notable of the latter class being the Great Salt Lake, whose outlines have been faithfully mapped by Stansbury. *

* The water, according to Stansbury, ("Expedition to the Great Salt Lake,") contains more than twenty per cent. of chloride of sodium, and is so buoyant that, in bathing, a man may float, stretched at full length on his back, having most of his person above water. In a sitting posture, the shoulders remain above the surface. The brine is so strong that the least particle getting into the eyes, causes the most acute pain. Whole tracts of land on the borders of this lake are cov-

The Dead Sea, with its river Jordan, here finds its counterpart. Its bleak and rugged shores are without a tree to relieve the eye, and its waters apart from animalculæ sustain no organic life.

The mountains which rim this Basin are sufficiently high to condense the vapors of the clouds and cause them to descend in showers, thus forming the sources of streams which, as they reach the margin of the valleys, are absorbed by the thirsty soil. Hence, the plains are absolute deserts, whilst the slopes are clothed with grama grass. Salt beds and alkali flats are abundant. "They are situated," says Ross Brown, "in valleys from which the waters, having no escape, are spread out over large surfaces, and soon evaporate, leaving the salt and other substances behind. * * Upon the great saliniferous fields of Nye county, Nevada, millions of tons could be shoveled up, lying dry and pure upon the surface, to a depth varying from six inches to three feet." *

The salt is extensively used in the metallurgy of the silver ores which occur so abundantly in Nevada.

The mountains almost every where, except where

ered with saline incrustations having all the purity of snow-flakes, and the amount in one field, ten miles long and seven miles broad, was estimated at 100,000,000 of bushels,—equal in bulk to the entire wheat crop of the United States.

* "Mineral Resources of the United States." 1867.

they reach the snow-line, are clothed with forests of pine, spruce, and fir, of sufficient size to afford the materials for lumber.

The Sierra Nevada.—Bounding the Great Basin on the west, as with a wall, is the Sierra Nevada. The vapors rolled up from the Pacific are here arrested and wrung of their moisture; and hence, each side of the axis is distinguished by well-marked differences in climate and vegetable forms. The sea-ward slope is densely wooded, and contains many peculiar forms, among which is a species of red-wood (*Sequoia gigantea*), the monarch of all arborescent forms. *

---

* Many of the trees of the Pacific Coast are peculiar. Among them may be mentioned:

Pinus lambertiana (Sugar Pine). It grows to the height of 200 feet. The grain is so straight that shingles and clap-boards may be rifted out of the trunk. Whitney speaks of it thus: " The sugar pine is the grandest tree. It occurs at all altitudes between 3,000 and 4,000 feet, but attains its greatest dimensions between 4,000 and 5,000 feet, where it is frequently 300 feet in height. Its trunk is perfectly straight, its head symmetrical, and from the slightly-drooping ends of its horizontal branches, the enormous cones hang down in bunches of two or three, like tassels. One tree, measured by us, was found to be 300 feet high, without a flaw or curve in its trunk, and only seven feet in diameter at its base. These forests are rather open. the trees being seldom densely aggregated; and, owing to the dryness of the air, their trunks are very free from mosses and lichens." (" Geology of California," p. 336.)

P. ponderosa (Pitch Pine). The wood is very coarse and durable, and well-fitted for the purposes of construction.

P. sabiniana (Sabine's Pine.) Grows to the height of 150 feet. Timber soft and durable.

P. insignis (Seal Pine). A noble tree, with bright grass-green leaves.

Abies douglasii (Douglas Fir). A tree characteristic of the northern

ZONES OF VEGETATION. 93

As we descend the slopes towards the sea, where the conditions of moisture are less constant, we encounter changes in the vegetable forms so abrupt as at once to attract observation.

The forests of California are mainly restricted to the sea-coast or the mountain slopes, while the longitudinal valleys are covered with herbaceous plants, with trees bordering the immediate banks of the streams,—presenting features not unlike the prairie region of the Mississippi Valley. From May to November is the dry season, in which rain rarely falls, and clouds and mists rarely veil the

Pacific coast, from latitude 40° to Alaska, and only found east of the Cascade Range. This is principally the timber used at the saw-mills on Puget's Sound, and is both strong and durable; in fact, says Ross Brown, it is the strongest timber on the Coast, both in perpendicular pressure and horizontal strain. According to experiments made in France, at the imperial dock at Toulon, masts from this tree are superior to the best Riga spars. In flexibility and tenacity of fibre, these trees are rarely surpassed; they may be bent and twisted several times in contrary directions without breaking, and they possess other rare qualities, such as superficial dimensions, strength, lightness, and absence of knots. ("Mineral Resources of the United States," 1868.)

There are other pines which occur on the Rocky Mountain Slope, deserving of notice:

P. edulis (Piñon of the Mexicans), grows from 40 to 50 feet high. The seed is about the size of a hazel-nut, and is used as food by the Indians.

P. flexilis (Rocky Mountain White Pine), has many of the qualities of the *P. strobus* of the East. Dr. James, who first discovered it, asserts that its nuts are edible. It is used as a lumber tree.

The Balsam Fir (*P. abies*), and Red Cedar (*Juniperus virginiana*), range from the Atlantic to the Mountains. The latter maintains its existence, with great tenacity, nearly to the base of the Mountains, and reappears upon their flanks.

All the species of firs, according to Whitney, are very beautiful.

sun; under whose intense rays the temperature often rises to 112°–115°, vegetation is consumed, the soil cracks and bakes, and the germination of seeds is effectually arrested. With the setting in of the autumnal rains, vegetation at once quickens into life, and the surface becomes clothed with a greensward, interspersed with a multitude of variously-tinted flowers.* These effects are clearly traceable

They attain a large size, are very symmetrical in their growth, and have a very dark-green and brilliant foliage, which is very fragrant. The branches are often regularly and pinnately divided, producing a "most brilliant effect. The color of the sky is perceptibly darker, as seen through this peculiar foliage, raised in a canopy so high above the observer."

Sequoia sempervirens (Red-wood). A noble tree, growing 200 feet in height, with a trunk ten feet in diameter; wood soft, durable, and easily wrought; one of the most valuable lumber trees on the Pacific Coast, and in the absence of its namesake would be regarded as the giant of the forest.

S. gigantea (Giant Red-wood). The most colossal of all forms of forest growth. One prostrate trunk, according to Blake. ("Pacific Railroad Survey,") must have been 450 feet in height, and 45 feet in diameter. The Mariposa grove, containing these trees, is scattered over an extent of six miles or more, and includes about six hundred trees. They stand in groups of twos and threes. The largest is 102 feet in circumference, and there are four others which exceed 100 feet. There are other groves, but the trees have no great geographical range, and it is to be feared that they are undergoing the process of extinction. From the number of annular rings counted on some of the prostrate trunks, the age indicated was not less than 1,300 years. The British botanists were the first to become aware of this gigantic tree, and gave it the name of Wellingtonia. American botanists proposed the name of Washingtonia, but they could not assert priority of discovery. It is found, however, to belong to the genus *Sequoia*, and, hence, must bear that name.

Mariposa grove is included in the grant made by Congress, of the Yosemite Valley, to the State of California, to be used as a public park; and it is to be hoped that these noble trees will be preserved.

* See Newberry's "Botanical Report," in "Pacific Railroad Reports."

to the unequal supply of moisture. The Coast Ranges absorb whatever is derived from the local winds of the Pacific, and the melting snows of the Sierra water the mountain-slopes, while the valleys are given up to unmitigated drought. These conditions fully explain the limits of tree and herbaceous growth.

The Yosemite Valley, though illustrating no meteorological fact, forms one of the most marked physical features, not only of California, but of the world. A narrow valley, walled in by precipices two and three thousand feet in height, with a great dome 4,600 feet in height, dominating over the whole; a cataract, falling with an unbroken plunge 1,600 feet, another 950 feet, and still another of 350 feet, whose waters at length commingle in a river known as the Merced, which winds its way through grassy meadows, occasionally expanding into pools, from whose glassy surface is faithfully reflected every tint, not mingled, but sharply-defined, of rock, tree, and sky;—the whole forms a combined scene of rugged grandeur and picturesque beauty, which is probably unequaled on the face of the earth.

Thus, then, the traveler, in crossing the Continent from east to west, passes through every gradation, from a luxuriant forest-growth to one completely bare of all vegetation; and, in his progress, is impressed with the constantly-increasing signs of aridity, until he comes within the influence of the moist breath of the Pacific Ocean.

SOURCES OF MOISTURE.

Let us now inquire into the sources of moisture which fertilizes the Continent, and its mode of distribution.

1. The rains which water the Atlantic Slope are *equally distributed*, the variations between the four seasons being very slight.

2. Those which water the Mississippi Valley are *unequally distributed*, those of spring and summer being greatly in excess; a fact which has been overlooked by most meteorologists, in reference to the geographical distribution of plants.

3. Those which water the Californian Coast are *periodic*, marking a well-defined wet and dry season.

In examining Blodget's Rain-Chart of the United States, showing the mean distribution for the year, we find that, leaving out the Pacific Slope and the extreme peninsula of Florida, the greatest precipitation is in the vicinity of Pensacola, where it annually reaches 63 inches. This area is extremely limited, and presents a rounded outline, from which the lines of diminished precipitation rapidly decrease in intensity, like the eddying circles from the point where a stone first strikes the water. The Alleghanies, so far from condensing the vapors and causing increased precipitation, seem to serve only as an entering wedge to separate the vapor-bearing currents, and cause a more copious precipitation on their slopes than on their crests. The Great Lakes, too, instead of generating moisture to be distributed over the adjacent regions, seem to repel it; so that it is dryer in their immediate basins than on the plateaux which surround them.

When we examine the precipitation of rain, as distributed over the four seasons, there is, owing to the two systems of *equal* and *unequal* distribution, a strange inosculation of lines.

Winter.—The mouths of the Mississippi and the region of Pensacola are in the area of greatest precipitation (18 inches). From this centre, the lines of equal precipitation on the west, maintaining a considerable parallelism, first bear northwest along the Texas coast; then, rapidly curving, bear northeast; then east; and, as they leave the Continent, northeast.

The conditions of moisture are as follows:

In the Densely-Wooded Region,	18 to 7 inches.
In the Prairie Region,	5 to 3 "
On the Treeless Plains,	2 "

Autumn.—The mouths of the Mississippi and the region of Pensacola are within the area of greatest precipitation (12 inches). The lines of equal precipitation pursue a north-northeast direction, and, in the distribution of moisture, exhibit the following results:

In the Densely-Wooded Region,	12 to 8 inches.
In the Prairie Region,	8 to 5 "
On the Treeless Plains,	4 "

Summer.—The lines of summer precipitation, owing to the operation of the law of unequal distribution, are very irregular. On the Plains, they bear nearly north and south; but, as protracted east, they make one curvature to the south, as they approach Lake Michigan, and another, still more abrupt, as they approach the Alleghanies, equal to five degrees of latitude,— after passing which, they curve abruptly to the northeast. The conditions of moisture are as follows:

In the Densely-Wooded Region,	15 to 12 inches.
In the Prairie Region,	12 to 8 "
On the Treeless Plains,	8 to 4 "

Spring. — The lines of equal precipitation exhibit a remarkable deflection to the northwest, caused, as we shall show, by the prevailing summer winds, and which, but for this deflection, would render the region at the base of the Rocky Mountains an uninhabitable desert. While the mouths of the Mississippi and the region of Pensacola still receive the greatest amount of precipitation (15 inches), Fort Laramie, on the Plains, is nearly as well watered as New York, on the sea board (10 inches); and Chicago receives no more rain than falls in Cheyenne, at the base of the Rocky Mountains (8 inches).

There is this noticeable fact, illustrated in the preceding remarks: that while, on the Atlantic Slope, the precipitation is pretty equally distributed over the four seasons, the tendency to unequal precipitation, comparing spring and summer with autumn and winter, begins to manifest itself on the Prairies, and as we enter the Plains it becomes still more marked, — the fall, and especially the winter, being the dry season.

Making a section across the Continent, from New York to San Francisco, we have the following results:

MEAN ANNUAL PRECIPITATION.

STATIONS.	SPRING.	SUMMER.	AUTUMN.	WINTER.	YEAR.
New York[1]	11.55	11.33	10.30	9.63	42.23
Ann Arbor[2]	7.30	11.20	7.00	3.10	28.60
Fort Leavenworth[3]	7.92	12.24	7.33	2.75	30.29
Fort Riley[4]	7.91	7.15	5.58	1.26	21.90
Fort Laramie[5]	8.69	5.70	3.96	1.63	19.98
Fort Yuma[6]	0.27	1.30	0.86	0.72	3.15
San Francisco[7]	7.56	1.09	2.96	11.34	21.95

1 Wooded. 2 Verge of Prairie. 3 4 5 Prairie. 6 Desert. 7 Periodical Rains.

Contrasting the two stations, New York and Fort Laramie, it will be seen that on the sea-board about 48 per cent. of the yearly precipitation occurs during the fall and winter, while on the Plains only 25 per cent. occurs during that period; and that, while on the sea-board the precipitation is nearly uniform during the four seasons, three-fourths of the precipitation on the Plains occurs during the spring and summer months.

At Fort Riley, the immediate valley of the Kaw is well-wooded, and the trees derive moisture, apart from the annual precipitation, from the stream itself; but when we ascend the bluffs which line its shores, the eye roams over a region of bold, rounded outlines, without a tree or a shrub to break the monotony of the scene.

A region where the annual precipitation is slightly in excess of twenty inches, I infer from observation, is unfavorable to the growth of trees, even were that moisture equally distributed; but where three-fourths of it is precipitated during the spring and summer, the grasses flourish and mature to the exclusion of arborescent forms. The effect of this peculiarity of the climate is to extend the cultivation of the cereals much farther west than could be done, if the moisture were equally distributed, and to afford rich pasturage to immense herds of buffalo, up to the verge of the Rocky Mountains, over a region which, if the rains were equally distributed, would present still more inhospitable features.

California. — Turning now to California, we find that far different conditions prevail, and new elements enter into the combination. There, a well-defined wet and dry season is observed,— 86 per cent. of the annual precipitation of rain taking place during the winter and spring, and nearly 50 per cent. during the winter. While, therefore, winter is the dry season on the Plains, it is the season of most profuse rains on the California coast,— a pretty conclusive proof that the vapor-bearing winds which water the Plains, do not come from the southwest.

More than one writer on the Climatology of the United States,* has maintained that the moisture which bathes the Continent is mainly derived from the Pacific Ocean, and distributed by the great southwest current of winds, without taking into consideration how far that current is modified by the configuration of the Continent.

If this theory of a southwest origin of the moisture be true, we should justly infer that the winds of the Pacific, however highly charged, and apart from a great mountain barrier, in passing over 17° of longitude, would become dry winds long before reaching the Atlantic Slope, and the conditions of the fertility of the Continent would be reversed. The Alleghanies would be as desolate as the Purple

---

* It may be stated that the National Observatory at Washington, under the control of the Navy Department, and maintained by liberal appropriations from Congress, was for years in charge of Lieutenant Maury; and among the fruits of his labors was a work on the "Physical Geography of the Sea," in which it was maintained that the moisture which waters this Continent is taken up from the Pacific Ocean and carried into the higher regions, and then precipitated by a descending current, first striking the land in the region of Salt Lake, *among the most desolate portions of the United States.*

Berghaus and Johnston ("Physical Atlas") have mapped the United States as being mainly in the belt of southwest winds; and Coffin, by tabulating numerous results ("Smithsonian Institute Contributions,") has shown the existence of a great westerly current, north of the parallel 35°, and about 23½° in breadth, which encircles the globe.

The winds which water the Great Valley, as will be seen, are the result of the peculiar configuration of the coast adjacent to the Gulf of Mexico and the Caribbean Sea, by which they are diverted from their uniform course; and that diversion explains the phenomena of our climatology.

Hills, and the Colorado Desert would be as fertile as the Valley of the Shenandoah.

Source of Moisture.—That portion of the Continent which embraces the United States, is situated in the zone of southwest winds, and these winds are found to prevail with wonderful regularity on the Atlantic, north of the calms of Cancer; but in the region of the Caribbean Sea and the Gulf of Mexico, there are abnormal conditions which present a marked deviation from the fixedness and uniformity observable in the winds of the mid-Atlantic and the north of Africa. Both southerly and northerly winds blow with violence across the parallel 30° (in the belt of the calms of Cancer) which, away from the American continent, acts as a great wall between the southwest and northeast winds. In the summer season, the northeast trades, hot and moist from the equatorial zone, as they enter the Caribbean Sea, are deflected by the lofty chain of the Andes which girds the coast, and pass into the Gulf of Mexico, where they become inland breezes on the Coast of Texas; and as they penetrate the interior, they are gradually deflected east, until they reach about latitude 39°, when they assume the direction of the great southwest aerial current. It is this deviation from the regular flow, which gives to the Mississippi Valley its moist, tropical summer climate.

Volney was the first to point out this deflection:

"Mariners relate that from Cape Vela, a projecting point of the Gulf of Maracaybo, the winds vary and swerve into a course parallel to the stream which flows into the Caribbean Sea. On entering the Bay of Honduras, it veers a little, and blows from the southeast. The bank of sand called Yucatan, is interposed between the two bays, but is so low and level that it is no obstacle to its progress. Bernard de Orto, who has published some useful information on the winds of Vera Cruz, tells us that southeast winds prevail in those parts."

He further adds that the trade-winds are deflected by the table-lands of Mexico, and become the south winds of the Mississippi Valley. Redfield admits that it is to this current that the Mississippi Valley owes its fertility; and Russell, whose work I have consulted with satisfaction, sustains the same view.*

Blodget remarks that southeast winds prevail almost exclusively, from April to October, or during the whole period of the warm months, when the western plains receive their excess of moisture. "These winds are also stronger at the most distant of these posts from the sea,— a proof that the impulse is not wholly at the coast, but that some ade-

---

* Russell, Robert, in his work on "North America, its Agriculture and Climate," elaborately discusses this question, and calls attention to the remarkable generalization of Volney, made at a time when no wind or rain charts were available. Russell has overlooked the earlier generalizations of Blodget, and the facts on which they are founded.

quate cause, at least for their continuance, exists in the interior." " There is no preponderance of these winds at Fort Scott or Fort Leavenworth."* At Natchez, the winds are southerly and easterly to the extent of one-third; at St. Louis, according to Engelman, the south and southeast winds are the prevailing ones from April to October, in the other months the west and northwest; at Cincinnati, according to Dr. Ray, west and southwest winds are the prevailing ones the year round. Thus, " these statistics are decisive," says Blodget, " that the southerly winds have ceased before reaching Cincinnati."

Humphreys and Abbot remark:

" Diagrams of the winds have been plotted from the 'Army Meteorological Observations,' for five years, at Key West, from June, 1850, to June, 1854, and also for the year from June, 1851, to June, 1852, at the same place. Similar diagrams have been made from the wind observations of the Delta Survey, at Fort St. Philip, and at Carrollton. The great resemblance between the winds at Key West and those near the mouth of the Mississippi, is apparent when these diagrams are compared. Both have, in part, the characteristics of the northeast trade-winds. Blowing chiefly between northeast and southeast, they veer towards the south as summer approaches, and continue to blow from that quarter and from the east during the summer and early part of the autumn; changing towards the north upon the approach of winter, they blow principally from that direction during the winter months." †

* " Climatology of the United States."

† " Physics and Hydraulics of the Mississippi River."

This course conforms, too, to the track usually pursued by the great hurricanes which, originating in the West Indies, first blow southeast, then curve abruptly, and sweep the Atlantic Coast in a northeast direction.

Periodical Rains of California.—The Pacific Slope affords another illustration of the law, every where observed, of diverse climates on opposite sides of a great mountain chain. It is evident that the high lands in Central America interrupt the flow of the northeast winds between the Gulf of Mexico and the Pacific Coast, giving origin to two distinct systems of aerial circulation. That of the Pacific Coast appears to partake of the periodical character of the Tropics, there being well-defined monsoons, whose movements are dependent on the sun. As in autumn he retires southward, the southwest winds, charged with the moisture of the Pacific, set in and water the land, until they strike the crests of the Sierra, where they part with the remainder of their moisture, and flow over the Great Basin as dry winds. As the sun returns north, an opposite set of winds become predominant. Day after day and month after month, the sun flames in an unclouded sky; and under the intensity of his rays, vegetation withers and shrivels up, and the ground bakes and cracks as if in an oven.

At few places on the earth's surface does the thermometer mark a higher range of temperature than at Fort Miller, amid the foot-hills of the Sierra.

Parry is of the opinion that the configuration of the southerly slope of the interior district between the Rio Grande and the Colorado Basin is such that, while it weakens the force of the cold northern currents, it permits the warm winds from the south to precipitate their moisture on the higher slopes in the form of summer rains and winter snows; and hence, we have in these elevated districts, a climate favoring the growth of trees, and a more equable precipitation of rain and dew throughout the year. These features are particularly noticeable along the elevated slopes of the San Francisco mountains, where magnificent pine forests are agreeably interspersed with grassy valleys and parks, and numerous springs, together with an invigorating atmosphere.*

The details embodied in this chapter may fail to enlist the attention of the general reader, but they contain the causes of the variable fertility of the Continent, and should be mastered by every one who would acquire a comprehensive knowledge of its Physical Geography.

* Report on "Kansas Pacific Railroad," along the thirty-fifth parallel. By C. C. Parry.

CONCLUSIONS.

Regarding, then, the Gulf of Mexico as the proximate source of the rains which water the Great Valley, we can explain the following phenomena, which are inexplicable on the supposition that the southwest winds are the great vapor-bearing current:

1. Why the greatest precipitation takes place along the shores of the Gulf of Mexico.

2. Why the Llano Estacado, the Colorado Desert, and the Great Basin, almost wholly within the zone of the southwest winds, are dry.

3. Why the Western Plains, during the spring and summer, are nearly as profusely watered as the Atlantic Slope.

4. Why the Valley of the Mississippi, during the prevalence of these winds, has an almost tropical climate.

5. And why the Atlantic Slope, instead of being the most arid, as it would be if the southwest winds furnished the moisture, is within the region of equally-distributed rains.

Thus it is believed that a study of the physical features of this country, in connection with the prevailing winds, and the consequent distribution of moisture, and also in connection with the lines of equal temperature, will show:

1. That these great changes in the geographical distribution of plants, under nearly equal lines of temperature, are not due to the mechanical texture or chemical composition of the soil, but to the variable supplies of moisture.

2. And that in the winds, as the agent in the distribution of that moisture, we have an adequate cause to explain all of the phenomena of forest, prairie, and desert.

NOTE.— Since the completion of this Chapter, which is but an expansion of the views expressed by me in a "Report to the Illinois Central Railroad Company," in 1858, my attention has been directed to a Report "On the Flowering Plants and Ferns of Ohio," by Dr. J. S. Newberry, (1860,) in which that distinguished physicist holds the following language:

1. "The great controlling influence which has operated to exclude trees from so large a portion of our territory west of the Mississippi, is unquestionably a deficiency of precipitated moisture. To this cause are due the prairies of Oregon, California, New Mexico, Utah, Nebraska, Kansas, Arkansas, and Texas. Throughout this great area, we find every variety of surface, and soil of every physical structure, or chemical composition, — unless in exceptional circumstances, where it receives an unusual supply of moisture, — if not utterly sterile, covered with a coating of grass.

2. "To the Great Plains, the typical prairies of the Far West, the theories proposed for the Origin of Prairies, viz.: that of Professor Whitney, that they are due to the fineness of soil; or that of Mr. Lesquereux, that they are beds of ancient lakes; that of Mr. Desor, that they are the lower and level reaches of sea-bottom; or, finally, that which attributes them to annual fires; are alike wholly inapplicable.

3. "The prairies bordering on, or east of, the Mississippi, may be, and doubtless are partly or locally, due to one or more of the conditions suggested in the above theories; but even here, the great controlling influence has been the supply of water. The structure of the soil of the prairies coinciding with the extremes of want and supply of rain characteristic of the climate, have made them now too dry and now too wet for the healthy growth of trees. A sandy, gravelly or

rocky soil or subsoil, more thoroughly saturated with moisture and more deeply penetrated with the roots of forest trees, affords them constant supply of the fluid which to them is vital. This, as it seems to the writer, is the reason why the knolls and ridges, composed of coarser materials, are covered with trees; while the lower levels, with firmer soil, are prairies. Where great variation of level exists, the high lands are frequently covered with trees, in virtue of the greater precipitation of moisture which they enjoy."

Dana ("Manual of Geology," 1863, p. 46), without going into details, announces the general result, thus: "That prairies, forest regions, and deserts, are located by the winds and temperature, in connection with the general configuration of the land." Cooper, before quoted, has shown the geographical distribution of plants; and Blodget, the annual precipitation of rain. But, to fully explain the Origin of Prairies, requires the combined observations of the Meteorologist, the Botanist, and the Geologist.

CHAPTER IV.

THE ORIGIN OF PRAIRIES (*Continued*).

SOUTH AMERICA — PRIMEVAL FORESTS OF BRAZIL — THE LLANOS OF CARACCAS — THE PAMPAS OF LA PLATA AND THE GRAN CHACO — PATAGONIA, ITS DESERTS AND MOUNTAINS — PERU, AND THE DESERT OF ATACAMA — WIND AND RAIN CHARTS — EUROPE — PLAINS OF THE BLACK SEA — STEPPES OF THE CAUCASUS — PLATEAU OF CENTRAL ASIA — DESERT OF ARABIA — AFRICA — SAHARA — GUINEA — BASIN OF THE MEDITERRANEAN — AUSTRALIA — RESUME — EXPLANATION OF MAP.

A THEORY, such as we have announced, in order to command assent, must not be used to explain local phenomena, but must be applicable to the explanation of the physical features of every continental mass. Without deviating too far from the scope of this work, and avoiding unneccessary details, we propose to make such an application.

SOUTH AMERICA.

In instituting a comparison between the two portions of the Western Hemisphere, we have not, so far as relates to South America, a series of meteorological observations to guide us; but we know the topographical features of the country, and the prevailing direction of the winds, as well as the boundaries of the forests, llanos or pampas, and the deserts of the interior.

The Andes border the western coast of the Continent, from one extremity to the other, rising up rugged and rock-ribbed into the region of perpetual snow, and leaving on the Pacific side a narrow and abrupt slope to the ocean, while on the Atlantic side the country stretches out in gently-undulating plains. The mountains are every where sufficiently high to arrest the floating clouds and deprive them of their moisture; and hence, on opposite sides, we find not only the most marked diversity of climate, but of vegetable forms. *

---

* The Andes assume their most colossal proportions in the vicinity of Lake Titicaca (Peru). It is from this point, according to Squier, ("Harper's Magazine," April, 1868,) that the traveler has a full view of the massive bulk of Illampu, the crown of the Continent, the highest mountain of America, rivaling if not equaling in height the monarchs of Himalaya. "Observers vary in their estimates and calculations of its altitude, from 25,000 to 27,000 feet; my own estimates place it at not far from 26,000. Extending southward from this, is an uninterrupted chain of *Nevados*, or Snowy Mountains, no where less than 20,000 feet in height. which terminates in the great mountain of Illamini, 24,500 feet in altitude."

"No where in the world, perhaps," he continues, "can a panorama so diversified and grand be obtained from a single point of view. The whole great table-land of Peru and Bolivia, at its widest part, with its own system of waters, its own rivers and lakes, its own plains and mountains, all framed in by the ranges of Cordillera and the Andes, is presented like a map before the adventurous visitor who climbs the *apacheta* of Tiahuanaco. Grand, severe, almost sullen, is the aspect

Like North America, this continent has its region of luxuriant forests, grassy plains, and inhospitable deserts.

Primeval Forests of Brazil.—Brazil is fed by perpetual currents of moisture, which are exhaled from the Atlantic and distributed over half a continent. A vast forest region fills the connected basins of the Orinoco and Amazon, extending to the base of the Andes,—a primeval forest, as graphically described by Humboldt, so impenetrable that it is impossible to clear with an axe a passage between trees eight and twelve feet in diameter for more than a few paces, and where the chief obstacle presented is the undergrowth of plants, filling up every interval in a zone where all vegetation has a tendency to assume a ligneous form,— a region traversed in all directions by systems of rivers, whose tributaries even sometimes exceed the Wolga or the Danube, and whose courses are the only highways into the interior. This connected forest has an extent of surface, and a grandeur of arborescent forms, unequaled on any other portion of the earth.

<small>which nature presents here. We stand in the centre of a scenery and a terrestrial system which seems to be, in spirit as well as in fact, lifted above the rest of the world. * * * Clouds surge up from the dank plains and forests of Brazil, only to be precipitated and dissolved by the snowy barriers which they can not pass."</small>

The Llanos of Caraccas.—Bounding this forest-belt on the north, the Llanos stretch from the lofty gigantic crests which gird the Caribbean Sea southward to near the channel of the Amazon, and from the base of the Andes east to the mountains of La Paramé, constituting a plain of irregular dimensions, 180 by 200 leagues in extent. It is thus walled in, with a single outlet through the valley of the Orinoco. The valleys of Caraccas are fertile beyond compare, and grow all of the tropical fruits so highly prized by man; presenting an abrupt contrast to these vast treeless plains. "Fresh from the richest luxuriance of organic life," says Humboldt, "the traveler treads at once the desolate margin of a treeless desert. Neither hill nor cliff rises to break the uniformity of the plain. * * * The steppe lies stretched before us, dead and rigid, like the stony crust of a desolated planet."

During the rainy season, these plains are clothed with a rich carpet of verdure; but in the dry season, every form of vegetable organism is withered and burned, as if by an all-consuming fire, and the very air is filled with particles of carbonized dust.

The contrast of seasons is graphically described by Humboldt:

"When, under the rays of a never-clouded sun, the carbonized turfy covering falls into dust, the indurated soil cracks asunder as if from the shock of an earthquake. * * The lowering sky sheds a dim, almost straw-colored light on the desolate plain. The horizon draws suddenly nearer; the steppe seems to contract, and with it the heart of the wanderer. The hot dusty particles which fill the air, increase its suffocating heat, and the east-wind, blowing over the long-heated soil, brings with it no refreshment, but rather a still more burning glow. The pools which the yellow-fading branches of the fan-palm had protected from evaporation, now gradually disappear. As in the icy north the animals become torpid with cold, so here, under the influence of the parching drought, the crocodile and the boa become motionless and fall asleep, deeply-buried in the dry mud. Every where the death-threatening drought prevails; and yet, by the play of the refracted rays of light, producing the phenomenon of mirage, the thirsty traveler is every where pursued by the illusive image of a cool, rippling, watery mirror. * * * At length, after the long drought, the welcome season of rain arrives; and then how suddenly is the scene changed! The deep blue of the hitherto perpetually cloudless sky becomes lighter; at night, the dark space in the constellation of the Southern Cross is hardly distinguishable; the soft phosphorescent light of the Magellanic clouds fades away; even the stars in Aquila and Ophiucus, in the zenith, shine with a trembling and less planetary light. A single cloud appears in the south, like a distant mountain rising perpendicularly from the horizon. Gradually the increasing vapors spread like mist over the sky, and now the distant thunder ushers in the life-restoring rain. Hardly has the earth received the refreshing moisture, before the previously barren steppe begins to exhale sweet odors, and to clothe itself with a variety of grasses. * * * Sometimes (so the Aborigines relate) on the margin of the swamps, the moistened clay is said to blister and rise slowly in a kind of mound; then, with a violent noise, like the outbreak of a small mud volcano, the heaped-up earth is cast high in the air. The beholder acquainted with the meaning of this spectacle, flies; for he knows there will issue forth a gigantic water-snake or scaly crocodile, awakened from a torpid state by the first fall of rain. * * * A portion of the steppe now presents the aspect of an inland sea; and now nature constrains the same animals who in the first half of the year panted with thirst on the dry and dusty soil, to adopt the amphibious life. * * Such a sight reminds the thoughtful observer involuntarily of the capability of conforming to the most varied circumstances, with which the all-providing Author of Nature has endowed certain animals and plants." *

Such a region could never tempt the natives to leave the beautiful cacao groves of Caraccas, but since it has been open to European occupancy, vast herds of cattle here find pasturage.

The Pampas of La Plata.— In the northern portion of the Argentine Republic, there is an immense tract of country known as the *Gran Chaco*, occupying a triangle between the rivers Paraguay and Solado, and reaching north to Bolivia,— an area of more than 100,000 miles square. It is of variable fertility. The northern part is forest-clothed, but the southern part is arid, sandy, and uninhabitable. West of the Vermejo, is the great desert of Salinas, covered for the most part with mineral efflorescences which sparkle like dew-drops in the sun.

The Pampas, from the Indian name *valley*, are immense plains which commence as high as latitude 33°, and extend over the whole country, graduating into the stern deserts of Patagonia, and their

---

* Humboldt, "Aspects of Nature." Title, "Steppes and Deserts."

area is not less than 300,000 square miles. In the main, they are fertile, being dotted with numerous lakes of a brackish character; but the wells afford palatable water.

Proceeding inland from Buenos Ayres, the character of the country undergoes marked changes. For the first two hundred miles, the surface is covered with clover and thistles, which grow in alternate crops, conforming to the seasons. The succeeding belt, four hundred and fifty miles broad, is clothed with grass alternately brown and green, as spring or autumn prevails; and to this succeeds the wooded region, consisting of scrubby trees and shrubs, which stretches to the base of the Cordilleras. The trees, mostly evergreens, do not form tangled thickets, but are grouped in a park-like arrangement. "The whole country," according to Head, "is in such beautiful order that, if citizens and millions of inhabitants could suddenly be planted at proper intervals and situations, the people would have nothing to do but drive their cattle to graze, and, without any previous preparation, to plough whatever quantity of ground their wants may require." *

In the region of grass and wood, the climate is exceedingly dry: there is no dew at night; in the hottest weather, the most violent exertions of man

---

* Sir Francis Head's "Journey over the Pampas."

produce very little perspiration; and the animals which die, lie upon the plain dried up in their skins.

Patagonia. — The southern extremity of the Continent, on the western coast, is girt with a range of mountains, reaching high into the air; while the eastern coast, so far as known, is arranged in stair-like terraces, which sustain a coarse, wiry grass, with belts of stunted trees along the water-courses. The plain, or interior region, is one of unmitigated sterility; but that which borders the Pacific, is surfeited with rain. Twelve feet have been known to fall within forty days; and navigators report that, off the coast, pools of fresh water have been found floating above the briny waters of the ocean, so pure that it may be scooped up for the use of the vessel's crew.

Peru. — Although this region occupies the same relation to the Pacific Coast as the western border of Patagonia, yet it presents an abrupt contrast in climate. Rains are unknown, and with the exception of occasional fogs, called *garua*, the inhabitants enjoy a perpetual serenity of sky. So constant is this condition of the atmosphere, that those ordinary forms of civility which, in the northern temperate zone, usually succeed an introduction, and are the prelude to more intimate relations, such as "A fine day!" or "A prospect of a shower!" are here obsolete terms. Ridiculous as this custom, abstractly considered, may seem, it after all paves the way to more confidential relations; it is the bridge which spans an otherwise almost impassable gulf. In the mountainous regions, rains occasionally fall, when the sands at once attest the quickening power of nature, and become clothed with peculiar forms of vegetation.

Between the parallels 21° 30' and 25° 30' S., lies the desert of Atacama. Towards the north, there are some fertile spots, but to the south it is not only uninhabited, but uninhabitable. The surface is covered with dark movable sands; the air is dry; no refreshing dews descend at night; no clouds discharge refreshing showers by day; but, from the abundant presence of salt, the surface glistens in the clear sunlight, as though studded with a floor of diamonds.

Such are some of the physical features of South America,—luxuriant forms of vegetable life, far-stretching plains robed in grasses, deserts of drifting sands, or covered with saline incrustations, and mountains shooting far up into the regions of perpetual snow.

We find a solution of these phenomena in the variable supply of moisture. The effect of the

Andes in condensing the vapors, come from what quarter they may, has been adverted to. Hence, while there is a wet and dry side throughout their entire range, the conditions are not constant, as seen in the contrast between Patagonia and Peru, for the reason that the winds which supply the moisture are not constant.

WIND AND RAIN CHARTS.

If we examine the Map (Plate I.), we shall find that the climatic centre of the earth—the Zone of Variable Winds and Calms, and at the same time the Zone of Constant Precipitation—lies about 6° north of the Equator. This belt is not stationary, but advances and recedes with the sun, over a space of about a thousand miles, carrying with it its attendant rains, winds, and calms, and giving origin in the tropics to a well-defined wet and dry season.

North of this belt, about 28° in width, is the Zone of the Northeast-Trades, and south of it that of the Southeast-Trades. On the north next succeeding, we have the Calm Belt of Cancer, and on the south the Calm Belt of Capricorn. North of Cancer is the Region of Southwest Winds, and south of Capricorn the Region of Northwest Winds. In the calm belts, the under-currents proceeding from the Poles meet the downward returning currents from the

Equator, in which the latter prevail; so that, in the Northern Hemisphere, we have two sets of aerial currents blowing in opposite directions, southwest and northeast; and in the Southern Hemisphere, northwest and southeast, with a belt of Variable Winds at or near the Equator.

Applying this system of winds and rains to the physical features of South America, as modifying the direction of the currents and the distribution of moisture, we find that the Llanos are situated in the Belt of Variable Winds, and are, therefore, subject to a wet and dry season. Walled in as they are on nearly every side by lofty mountains, which exclude the local moisture of the ocean, with heated columns of air rising from the glowing surface, to dissipate each forming cloud,— giving origin to droughts so protracted as to burn up every form of vegetation and cause the particles to fill the air with carbonized dust,—succeeded by inundations so copious as to convert vast tracts into inland seas;—these would be conditions highly unfavorable to the growth of trees, while they would not be unfavorable to the growth of grasses. It is, then, to the unequal distribution of moisture that we are to attribute the origin of the Llanos.

Brazil, on the other hand, lies between the Equatorial Belt and the Belt of Capricorn; while Peru occupies the same position to the west, but separated by the culminating peaks of the Andes, not less than 24,000 feet high. In the one region, as we have seen, there is an unequaled forest-growth, and in the other nothing can be grown except by artificial irrigation.

Whence proceeds this diversity? The Southeast Trades, laden with moisture perpetually distilled, strike the Atlantic Coast, and, as they sweep over the Continent, make a perpetual deposit; until, reaching the snow-capped Andes, they are wrung of their remaining moisture, and pass over to the Pacific as dry winds. Hence, then, as these winds blow constantly, the constant serenity of the Peruvian skies; and hence, too, the nearly unvarying flood which the Amazon, without a shoal or a rapid between its mouth and the base of the Andes, pours into the ocean.

Below the tropic of Capricorn, the prevailing winds become northwest, which have a long seaward sweep before striking the shore. The high and abrupt coast, aided by the low temperature, at once arrests and deprives them of moisture; and hence the western coast of Patagonia is among the most profusely-watered portions of the earth's surface, while the opposite slope is in an almost rainless region.

La Plata occupies an intermediate position between the luxuriant forest-growth of Brazil and the barren steppes of Patagonia; and as nature, like a skillful painter, always blends and harmonizes her lines, we should not look for abrupt transitions. The northern portion is in the Movable Belt of Capricorn, where the conflict takes place between the under-currents of the Southern Pole and the upper descending currents from the Equator, and is the best-watered; while the southern portion is in the Belt of Northwest Currents, which are dry off-shore breezes, and hence there is a deficiency of moisture. There is a local monsoon, too, along the coast, whose effects in distributing moisture do not extend far inland.

Combining, therefore, in one view, the varying distribution of moisture, as influenced by the prevailing winds, we find the dense forest, where it is constant and abundant, as in Brazil; the pampas and llanos, where it is deficient or unequally distributed, as in Venezuela and La Plata; and the inhospitable desert, where it is nearly withheld, as in Patagonia and Peru.

EUROPE.

The great Southwestern aerial Current, described in the previous Chapter, as it leaves the coast of the United States, is dry; but in its passage across the Atlantic, it imbibes the warmth and moisture of the Gulf Stream, which it exhales on the western coast of Europe. It is to the warmth and moisture thus communicated, that Ireland owes her rich pasturage, verdant in all vicissitudes of the seasons; that England has a precarious wheat-harvest, and that the Atlantic Coast of United States exhibits a depression equal to 11° of temperature. As these winds penetrate interiorly, they gradually part with their moisture, and the climate assumes a more continental character. To the forest-growth, succeed grassy steppes; then, plains covered with saline efflorescences; and finally, as in the United States and in South America, inhospitable deserts.

Starting eastward from the German Ocean, between the parallels 52° and 53°, the traveler may advance to the river Lena, without having passed a mountain-range higher than 2,000 feet; thus traversing 130° of longitude, or more than one-third part of the curvature of the earth.

Western Russia, in the Temperate Zone, is covered almost entirely with a dense forest,—so dense that it has been said a squirrel might travel on the tree-tops from St. Petersburg to Moscow, without touching the ground. Leaving this forest-region and penetrating still further into the interior, vast steppes succeed, which graduate into inhospitable wastes.

Plains of the Black Sea.—These plains have been celebrated from the earliest historical period, for their productiveness in human food; and the nations of the Mediterranean, before the Christian Era, as they now do, drew large supplies from this source.

Herodotus, the Father of History, has described this region as possessing the same features which we now behold. "Across the Borysthenes (the Don), the first country after you leave the coast is Hylea (Woodland). Above this, dwell the Scythian Husbandmen. * * Crossing the Panticapes and proceeding eastward of the Husbandmen, we come upon the wandering Scythians, who neither plough nor sow. Their country, and the whole of this region except Hylea, is quite bare of trees." *

General Turchin, of Chicago, whose early life was passed in this region, has furnished me with an elaborate paper upon its soil and climate, an abstract of which I shall embody here. Between these plains and the prairies of the Mississippi Valley, there is a marked similarity in soil and climate, confirmed by the observations of one familiar with both regions.

Starting at Lublin, Poland, about latitude 51°, the northern boundary of the wheat-region, and, at the same time, the southern boundary of the forest,

* Herodotus, Book IV.

the dividing line runs north of east to Penza, comprehending the whole eastern portion of Russia, and thence is produced along the southern boundary of Siberia. The whole area of the wheat-growing region is not less than 500,000 square miles; from which, deducting the area of timber, and the salt and sandy steppes, we have 375,000 square miles. These steppes may be thus classified:

1. *Those of a rolling character, well supplied with Timber, Springs, and Streams.*
2. *Those partly-rolling, with scarcely any Timber, but possessing a sufficient quantity of Streams.*
3. *The level Steppes, intermixed with those of a Salt and Sandy character, with no Timber and few Streams.*

1. The first class of steppes comprehends the region lying north of the Caucasus Range. These steppes, particularly those of the Ukraine, are extremely beautiful, and, where not cultivated, are clothed with grasses and wild flowers; while the streams, which are numerous, are bordered with trees. The soil is very rich—humus and clay,—well supplied with different salts, such as potash, magnesia, lime, nitre, etc., which, pulverized and intermixed, give it a brownish-yellow color; but, in the eastern portion of the region, it is dark-brown. Almost all of the nitre of Russia is manufactured in the Ukraine. The Coal-Measures in

many cases constitute the underlying rock, and yield an excellent quality of coal. These are best developed along the north line of the Caucasus. The soil of the Caucasus is extremely rich, and the timber attains an uncommon size, particularly the walnut and *tchinor*, the latter strongly resembling the cotton-wood of the Mississippi Valley.

2. The second-class steppes include the southern part of Bessarabia, the province of Kherson, and the peninsula of Crimea. The soil is a very rich black mould, produces every variety of grain, and very much resembles the black prairie-soil of Illinois. Its composition does not materially differ from that of the first class, except that it contains more humus. These steppes differ from the prairies in being dryer, in having sloughs only near the streams, in furnishing grass of a finer texture, and presenting a surface almost bare of trees. The traveler may journey for hundreds of miles without meeting with a belt or grove, or seeing aught but the green waves of the grassy steppes spread around him like a vast sea, and melting away imperceptibly into the distant horizon.

3. The third class of steppes comprises the country extending along the coast of the Black Sea, the Sea of Azov, the interior of the Crimea, the eastern portion of the country between the Black and Caspian Seas, and the vast region on the left bank of

the Wolga. These steppes are level, treeless, with few streams, but contain numerous salt and sandy patches. In the province of Sartov, there is a salt lake from which are annually extracted vast quantities of this material.

Thus far have I extracted from General Turchin's MS. In examining the Rain-Charts of this region, we find that the same law prevails as in the Mississippi Valley; that is, instead of the precipitation being distributed nearly equally over the four seasons, the spring and summer rains are greatly in excess.

In explanation of the phenomena of this region, it may be remarked that the Caucasus Range occupies the country between the Black and Caspian Seas (a distance of 700 miles), the highest peaks penetrating the snow line, and one peak (Elbrouz, 17,785 feet,) rising 2,000 feet higher than Mount Blanc (15,744 feet). A portion of the moisture borne by the Southwest Trades against these summits, is condensed; and here a precipitation takes place, amounting to 60 inches, which is far in excess of what falls on the steppes. On the first and second-class steppes, the rain-fall is from 35 to 20 inches; on the third class, 15 inches; in the salt-region of the Caspian, 10 inches.*

---

* Compare these figures with those of the United States: Greatest precipitation along the Gulf Coast (densely wooded), 63 inches; prairies of Iowa and Wisconsin, 35 inches; plains at base of the Rocky Mountains, 15 inches; and in the Great Basin, 10 inches.

PLATEAU OF CENTRAL ASIA.

The Caspian region is but an outlier of the Great Asiatic Plateau, the vastest, if not the most elevated, according to Humboldt, on the surface of the globe. Instead of drifting sands, the Asiatic steppes, like the Great Basin, are crossed by ranges of hills clothed with coniferous woods. There are, too, grassy plains; other parts are covered with succulent evergreen plants; and "other parts," quoting from Humboldt, "glisten from a distance with flakes of exuded salt, which cover the clayey soil, not unlike in appearance to fresh-fallen snow." Of this character is the great desert of Gobi, walled in on the north by the Altai Range, and on the south by the Kuen-lun. Nor are these steppes uninhabitable. Tartars and Mongolians, swarming forth from their desert retreats, have at different times exercised the most direct influence on the destinies of mankind.

Thus situated in the interior of a Continent, in the lee of the monsoons which sweep the Indian Ocean, and sheltered by the loftiest mountains of the world, it is to be inferred, in the absence even of precise meteorological statistics, that this Great Plateau would present varying aspects of sterility. The southern slope of the Himalaya is intersected by deep-entering bays, like the Arabian Sea and the Bay of Bengal, which give it a peninsular character. The southwest monsoons blow from April to October, and the northeast monsoons the other half of the year, and both expend their moisture upon the southern slope of the great mountain barrier. The rain-fall here reaches 200 inches a year; and thus it is we have another illustration of the physical fact of a rainless district on one side of a great mountain chain, and a district on the other most abundantly watered.

Arabian Desert.—The desert of Arabia may be considered as an extension of that system of arid wastes which finds its full development in the Sahara of Africa.

An historian versed in philosophy, while yet the laws of climatology were not understood, has thus graphically described that inhospitable region:

> "It is a boundless waste of sand, intersected by sharp and naked mountains; and the face of the desert, without shade or shelter, is scorched by the direct and intense rays of the tropical sun. Instead of refreshing breezes, the winds, particularly from the southwest, diffuse a noxious and even deadly vapor; the hillocks of sand which they alternately diffuse and scatter, are compared to the billows of the ocean, and whole caravans, whole armies, have been lost and buried in the whirlwind. The common benefits of water are an object of desire and contest; and such is the scarcity of wood, that some art is requisite to preserve and propagate the element of fire.
>
> "Arabia is destitute of navigable rivers, which fertilize the soil, and convey its products to adjacent regions. The torrents

that fall from the hills are imbibed by the thirsty earth; the rare and hardy plants, the tamarind or the acacia, that strike their roots into the clefts of the rocks, are nourished by the dews of the night; a scanty supply of rain is collected in cisterns and aqueducts; the wells and springs are the secret treasures of the desert; and the pilgrim of Mecca, after many a dry and sultry march, is disgusted with the taste of the waters which have rolled over a bed of sulphur or salt. Such is the general and genuine picture of the climate of Arabia. The experience of evil enhances the value of any local or partial enjoyments. A shady grove, a green pasture, a stream of fresh water, are sufficient to attach a colony of sedentary Arabs to the fortunate spot which can afford food and refreshment to themselves or their cattle, and which encourage their industry in the cultivation of the palm-tree or the vine.

"The high lands that border the Indian Ocean are distinguished by their superior plenty of wood and water; the air is more temperate, the fruits are more delicious, the animals and the human race more numerous; the fertility of the soil invites and rewards the toil of the husbandman; and the peculiar gifts of frankincense and coffee have attracted, in different ages, the merchants of the world. If it be compared with the rest of the peninsula, this sequestered region may truly deserve the appellation of HAPPY; and the splendid coloring of fancy and fiction has been suggested by contrast, and countenanced by distance. It was for this earthly paradise, that nature had reserved her choicest favors and her most curious workmanship." *

AFRICA.

A grander and a more desolate aspect characterizes the plains of Africa. "They are," says Humboldt, "parts of a sea of sand which, stretching

---

* Gibbon, "Decline and Fall," Ch. L.

eastward, separate fruitful regions from each other, or encloses them like islands. Neither dews, nor rains, bathe these desolate plains, or develop on their glowing surface the germs of vegetable life; for heated columns of air, every where ascending, dissolve the vapors, and disperse each swiftly-vanishing cloud." *

And yet these plains do not present one wide waste of desolation. They have their oases, which are habitable by man;—

> "The tufted isles
> That verdant rise amid the Libyan wild."

They have their fountains, shaded by the palm, where the weary traveler may slake his thirst.

Approaching the Great Sahara from the Mediterranean or the Red Sea, we view it where it puts on its sternest features. The extreme northwestern portion of the Continent, lying in the Zone of Southwest Winds, has a strip of cultivable land; while the Nile, by its annual inundations, maintains a green thread of vegetation through a region of desolate sands.

There is no region of the earth where the conditions of climate are more constant than those which embrace the sources of the Nile. When the Dog-Star rises, the inhabitants of the Lower Valley look

---

* "Aspects of Nature," Title, "Steppes and Deserts."

for a swelling of the river. If the Nilometer which measures the height of the flood, indicates but eight cubits, the crops will be scanty; but if it reaches fourteen cubits, they will be abundant.

"Where the Nile," says Draper, "breaks through the mountain gate at Essouan, it is observed that its waters begin to rise about the end of the month of May, and in eight or nine weeks the inundation is at its height. The flood in the river is due to the great rains which have fallen in the mountainous countries among which the Nile takes its rise, and which have been precipitated by the trade-winds that blow, except where disturbed by the monsoons, over the vast expanse of the tropical Indian Ocean. Thus dried, the East-Wind pursues its solemn course over the solitudes of Central Africa, a cloudless and a rainless wind, its track marked by desolation and deserts. At first the river becomes red, and then green, because the flood of its great Abyssinian branch, the Blue Nile, arrives first; but soon after, the White Nile makes its appearance, and from the overflowing banks, not only water, but a rich and fertilizing mud, is discharged." *

Those portions of the Great Desert accessible from the Mediterranean and the Nile, are wholly within the Belt of Northeast Winds, which, in their passage over other lands, have been wrung of all their moisture; and hence, as observed by Marsh,† the present general drift of the sands appears to be to the southwest and west.

The coast of Guinea, the strike side, is in the Zone of Periodical Rains, and is most profusely

---

* "Intellectual Development of Europe."

† "Man and Nature."

watered. In 1838, during three months, at Sierra Leone, the prodigious quantity of 314 inches of rain fell; and in two days, nearly 20 inches, an amount equal to two-thirds of the annual precipitation in the British Isles. The rainy season lasts from May to November, and is ushered in and carried off by tornadoes. To the inhabitants, it is a period of gloom and apprehension. The hills are wrapped in impenetrable fogs, and the rains fall in such torrents that all out-door exercises are suspended. It is the period, too, of fevers and malarious diseases.

Vast and impenetrable forests stretch into the interior, which afford teak and cam-wood. A range of mountains, whether mythical or real I know not, is laid down by most geographers as reaching from the coast eastward into the interior, which should serve as a wall to arrest the vapor-bearing currents and prevent their flow into the region of the Great Desert.

In the absence of positive information, then, we would presuppose that a section extended from the Coast of Guinea to the Mediterranean Sea would exhibit somewhat the following features: A luxuriant growth of arborescent vegetation on the Atlantic Coast, developed under tropical heats and oceanic moisture; alternations of grove and grass; and last, wild wastes of drifting sands. A theory which supposes that these arid wastes originated in and are maintained by the circulation of an atmosphere previously robbed of all moisture, is just as plausible and tenable as one which presupposes that these sands are but a portion of an elevated ocean-bed, from whose glowing surface arise heated currents of air, which dissolve every vapor-bearing cloud. It is simply a question whether we have not confounded cause with effect.

The strip of cultivable land bordering the Mediterranean, including Morocco and Algeria, is in the Region of the Southwest Currents, and affords many fruitful valleys. It is shut off from the desert by the stupendous chain of the High Atlas, whose range is east and west. In the basin of the Mediterranean, evaporation is far in excess of precipitation, and hence there is a constantly-flowing current from the Atlantic, through the Straits of Gibraltar, to supply the vacuum thus created.

AUSTRALIA.

Australia has been characterized as "a land of anomalies,"—where the fishes, in some instances at least, approach in structure those of the Old Red Sandstone epoch; where the birds, recently extinct, were furnished with wings simply to enable them to run; where we find mammalia that do not suckle their young; where reptiles are warm-blooded; where animals bring forth a few days after conception—the fœti being without limbs or external organs; and where other animals whose fore-legs are nearly useless for locomotion, accomplish this operation by employing their hind-legs and tail; and finally, where there is a paradoxical animal, with the bill and feet of a duck, the body of a mole, and the general structure of a reptile. The vegetation is equally strange, where the margin of the leaves, and not the surface, as in other lands, is upturned to the sun.

The physical features of the country are no less strange,—a Continent without rivers, and where fertility is confined to the summits of considerable hills. Surrounded by the ocean, yet its interior is an arid waste. While subject in some degree to a wet and dry season, there are cycles of ten or twelve years of unmitigated drought, during which no rain falls; close upon which, is a year of floods. The floods of the coast are simultaneous with drought in the interior, and *vice versa.*

Australia lies partly within the influence of the Southeast Trades, and partly within that of the Northwest Currents; while the northern portion is swept by the Periodical Monsoons. The highest mountains are on the Pacific side, and hence prevent the passage of the Northwest Currents into the interior. According to Dana, the Australian

Alps, which face the southwest shores, have peaks 5,000 to 6,500 feet in height, which are continued northward in the Blue Mountains, whose general elevation is 3,000 to 4,000 feet, with some more elevated summits, and beyond these, in ridges under other names, — the whole range being between 2,000 and 6,000 feet in elevation. The elevated grounds to the east perform the same office, and thus we have a Continent with high borders around a depressed interior. Of all continents, Australia is the most arid and inhospitable.

RESUME.

If we examine a geological map of the world, we shall find that these vast plains and deserts were sea-bottoms during the Cretaceous, and in many instances, during the Tertiary epoch, and the mountains by which they are girt were the ancient shore-lines. But this does not justify us in the inference that their desert-like character is due to this cause, for the sedimentary rocks of every age, which, as a general rule, afford a far more hospitable soil than those of igneous origin, have undergone the same process. There is little doubt that, if the most inhospitable portions of Sahara had been exposed to the direct action of the winds of the region of monsoons, which give origin to the inundations of the Nile, they would have been robed with an appropriate vegetation, whose decay, in the course of ages, would have created an amount of humus which, incorporating itself with the soil, might have made this desolation a garden.

Embracing the whole subject in a comprehensive glance, we believe that it will be found:

That the phenomenon of varying vegetation, throughout every continent and throughout every zone, is, primarily, dependent on the varying supply of moisture; modified, secondarily, by altitude of surface above the sea, diversity of soil, its evaporative power, and the climatic conditions of temperature.

The winds and the rains, heat and cold, light and and darkness, are the great powers, whether manifested in the tempest or in the gently-distilling dew; whether in Arctic colds or tropical heats; whether in midnight darkness or in the full glare of the midday sun; whether in the structure of the rugged oak, or in the delicate tissues of the unfolding flower;—these, we repeat, are the great powers which every where act in accordant harmony, to produce the infinite diversity of vegetable life; they are the agents by which Nature perpetually renews the youth, the beauty, and the fertility, of our planet.

And yet, all these apparently complicated phenomena are but emanations from a single source, the SUN,—the "lantern of the World" (*lucerna mundi*), as described by Copernicus; the all-vivifying, pulsating "*heart of the Universe*," as described by an ancient philosopher;* or, as described by a modern philosopher,† the primary source of light and radiating heat, and the generator of numerous terrestrial, electro-magnetic processes, and, indeed, of the greater part of the organic vital activity on our planet.

"By its rays," quoting the greatest of living astronomers, ‡ "are produced all winds, and those disturbances in the electric equilibrium of the atmosphere which give rise to terrestrial magnetism. By their vivifying action, vegetables are elaborated from inorganic matter, and become in their turn the support of animals and man, and the sources of those great deposits of dynamical efficiency which are laid up for human use in our coal-strata. By them, the waters of the sea are made to circulate in vapors through the air, and irrigate the land, producing springs and rivers. By them are produced all disturbances of the chemical equilibrium of the elements of nature, which, by a series of compositions and decompositions, give rise to new products, and originate a transfer of materials. Even the slow degradation of the solid constituents of the surface in which its chief geological changes consist, and their diffusion among the waters of the ocean, are entirely due to the abrasion of the wind and rain, and the alternate action of the seasons."

* "Theon of Smyrna."
† Humboldt, "Cosmos," V.
‡ Sir John Herschel.

Thus, then, to solar influence may be traced all the great phenomena which affect the surface of the earth,—day and night, heat and cold, atmospheric and oceanic currents, and the vicissitudes of the seasons, and extending even to the oxygen of the atmosphere, which to man is "the breath of life."

EXPLANATION OF THE MAP.

PLATE I.

1. The map shows the relative areas, on each Continent, of Forest, Prairie, and Desert.

2. The distribution of some of the Great Families of Plants.

3. The different Zones of the Winds, and the barriers, in the form of mountain-chains, which they encounter in their sweep over the land.

The Rain-Chart of the World would be identical with the Wind-Chart, with a substitution of names, viz., for "Zone of Variable Winds" read "Zone of Periodical Rains," which has a range north and south of nearly a thousand miles during the year; for the "Zone of Southwest Currents," read "Zone of Constant Precipitation." The deeply-shaded portions occupied by the Palmæ and Deciduous and Coniferous types, are well-watered; while the slightly-shaded portions, occupied by the Cacti and Grasses, are either deficient or unequally supplied.

CHAPTER V.

FOREST-CULTURE AND IRRIGATION.

HOW PLANTS GROW — EFFECTS OF FORESTS ON HEALTH — ON ANIMAL LIFE — EFFECTS OF DISROBING A COUNTRY OF FORESTS — RAPID DESTRUCTION OF FORESTS IN THE UNITED STATES — FORESTS, THEIR LESSONS — THEY MODIFY CLIMATE — THEY RETAIN MOISTURE — TREE-PLANTING — IRRIGATION — PRACTISED AT AN EARLY DAY, ON BOTH HEMISPHERES — SUCCESSFULLY INTRODUCED ON THE ROCKY MOUNTAIN SLOPES — FEASIBILITY OF ITS APPLICATION IN CALIFORNIA, THE COLORADO DESERT AND THE WESTERN PLAINS.

How Plants Grow. — Plants extract inorganic substances from the soil, which are essential to their perfection; but the ligneous portions, together with the sugar, starch, and acids, are derived, for the most part, from the air. The cerealia, or edible grains, require both potash and phosphate of magnesia; they also require silica, to give hardness to the stem, and to the seed-envelope. This substance enters largely into the structure of those grasses known as canes, bamboos, and scouring rushes. The oak extracts iron; and those vegetables comprehended in the term *Cruciferæ*, such as cabbages, turnips, mustard, etc., contain sulphur. The rains are the solvent power by which the salts are brought within the reach of their rootlets, by which they are taken up, assorted, and assimilated, and such parts as are useless rejected, as the human system casts off the exuviæ after the nutriment has been extracted. Hydrogen, resulting from the decomposition of water, is also absorbed, and forms an element in the composition of wood, as well as of the fruits, flowers, and seeds of plants. Ammonia, the result of the decay of animal matter, is volatilized, and passes into the atmosphere; but, returned to the earth in descending showers, it is absorbed by the soil, and enters into the pores of the plant, where it is separated into its constituent parts, hydrogen and nitrogen. The latter enters into the albumen of wood and the gluten of the cerealia, which is the nutritive part. It also enters into the composition of the esculent roots, such as potatoes and beets; and of the climbing plants, such as peas and beans.

From the air, plants derive carbonic acid, a substance which, where it exists in excess, is destructive to animal life. This is not a simple element, but a compound of oxygen and carbon, and is diffused throughout the air in about the proportions of $\frac{2}{1000}$ parts. This supply is maintained by every exhalation of air-breathing animals, by the steam poured out from every active volcano, and by every fire artificially kindled. It is also given off in the decay of animal and vegetable life, where oxygen, though by a less rapid combustion, performs the same office as fire. The leaves of plants, on the other hand, constantly absorb carbonic acid by day, decompose it, restoring the oxygen to the atmosphere, and converting the carbon into ligneous fibre. Solar influence seems to be essential to effect this result, for at night, and in gloomy weather, almost all of the carbonic acid is returned to the air unchanged.

Thus, it may be said that the trees and grasses which clothe the surface of the earth, as well as the immense accumulations of coal stored beneath the surface, are but the condensation, by solar rays, of those gases destructive to animal life, into forms which are essential to its support and comfort. The black mould in soils known as humus, is the result of the decay of vegetable matter, such as the leaves of the forests, the grasses of the meadows, and the mosses of the peat-swamps. When brought in contact with the oxygen of the atmosphere, an equal volume of carbonic acid is evolved. The effect of ploughing or stirring up the soil, is to bring fresh portions of humus in contact with the air, and thus create a fresh supply of carbonic acid. In applying animal manure to soils, we seek mainly to furnish this substance to the growing plant.

Although soils of pure lime and sand are barren, yet, if they contain two per cent. of vegetable matter, the fir and pine tribes will flourish, but oaks and other deciduous trees require ten times as much.

Such is the order which prevails throughout the realms of Nature. Inorganic substances act and react in accordant harmony, to give support to that infinite diversity of organic life, both animal and vegetable, which is found on the surface of our planet; and one series of elements which is destructive to animal life, is essential to the growth and perfection of vegetable life. Thus intimate is the connection, thus mutually dependent. Thus is constituted a great system of vital forces, by which the surface-covering of continents is perpetually maintained, and the wants of its inhabitants provided for.

Effects of Forests on Health.—We have seen that a beautiful harmony exists between animal and vegetable life,—that while the former consumes oxygen and exhales carbonic acid, the latter assimilates carbonic acid and gives out oxygen; and that the noxious effluvium arising from the decomposition of animal matter, is converted into ammonia, and elaborated into seeds, grains, and fruits, which become the essential food of man. Thus, the forests perpetually renew the purity of the air, and fit it for the respiration of the higher orders of animals.

Forests absorb to a far greater extent than mere flowering plants, the noxious gases which are continually thrown into the air from a variety of sources;—from the breath of animals, from the smoke of chimneys in densely-populated cities, and from the decay of organic matter. Few people are aware of the extent of such emanations. It is rendered probable that the peculiar principle of the atmosphere known as ozone, is a most efficient disinfectant; and yet, as stated by Angus Smith, a wind blowing over a manufacturing city, like Manchester, at the rate of fifteen miles an hour, after having passed less than a mile, is deprived of this principle. A single individual exhales, in a day, twenty cubic feet of carbonic acid, and therefore contaminates 20,000 cubic feet of air. The addition of one-tenth of one per cent. may be perceived. The rain that falls in a populous city is so acrid that a drop will redden litmus paper. Blood shaken in the air of towns takes a different shade from that shaken in pure air. A method has been devised by Dr. Smith for measuring the amount of impurity in the air, by means of dilute permanganate of potash poured in a bottle, and noticing the degree of decolorization of the liquid, when exposed to the light. The oxidizable matter in the air over a pig-sty was represented by 109 measures, in the centre of Manchester by 58, and over Lake Lucerne (Switzerland) by 1.4.* Thus, people closely huddled together are surrounded by emanations both of organic and inorganic matter, which may be injurious to health, even when the effluvium is not apparent to the senses.

The winds, in their mechanical power to transport and dissipate these exhalations, and in their chemical power to oxidize them; the sunlight, in hastening decomposition, and causing new combinations; the soil, in its power of absorption; and, lastly, the vegetation, in its power of consolidating the most abundant of these exhalations into innocuous forms, are the great natural disinfectants. Hence, then, tree-planting along crowded thoroughfares and in parks amidst dense cities, can not, as a measure of sanitary economy, be too strongly recommended. The practice, however, of surrounding a house with dense shrubbery, is far from commendable. It is desirable, so far as can be attained, that the sunlight should strike all portions of the wall during the day. Where, in-doors, there is a lack of sunlight and air, the whole surface of the rooms, and even of the furniture, becomes coated with a film of organic matter, on

---

* Dr. R. Angus Smith, in Ure's Dic. Sup.; Art. "Sanitary Economy."

which fungi germinate, giving off unpleasant odors. Books, even, become thus invested. Rubbing with water does not destroy the vegetable growth, but the application of any of the essential oils, like turpentine, benzine, etc., is effectual.

Malaria may also originate in wooded belts, particularly in conditions of the weather which cause vegetation to putrefy instead of to grow. On the other hand, deltas at the mouths of rivers, marsh lands, and lands alternately flooded either by salt or fresh water, generate malaria, resulting in fevers, which do not travel far from the places of their origin. It has been found that a forest-belt interposed to the leeward of such malarious marshes afforded an efficient protection against these diseases,—the canopy of foliage acting both mechanically and chemically, in the one case to intercept the current of miasmatic vapors, and in the other to decompose and recombine them into harmless elements. And yet, as to the relative salubrity of the forest and prairie, as evidenced in the settlement of the Western States, the preponderance is greatly in favor of the latter.

Sunlight is essential both to animal and vegetable life. It undoubtedly exercises a chemical action upon the organic tissues of both; and we know that, in the case of plants, they become bleached and sickly where it is feebly exerted; and that man, during the long and cheerless night of an Arctic winter, is peculiarly liable to scorbutic diseases. Darkness is his worst enemy. We know, too, the vivifying action which the sun brings, after his long exclusion from the heavens. Kane, with his little party, wintering at Renssellaer Harbor, describes the depressing effects of the "long, intense darkness," extending not only to man, but even to the dogs, some of whom died of epilepsy, resulting from "long-lost daylight." We read with what joyful feelings he greeted "the first distinct orange tint" indicative of the returning sun, observed on the southern horizon, at noon, January 21; and he records how different it was "from the cold light of the planets." *

Forests exclude the sunlight and obstruct the circulation of the air, and, therefore, generate and retain dampness,—conditions which are prejudicial to health, and which do not exist on the prairies. The first stirring-up of the soil, whether of the forest or the prairie, generates malaria, probably from the liberation of carbonic acid; but it is far more malignant in the former region than in the latter. The pioneers who planted themselves in Western New York, Ohio, and Michigan, suffered far more from intermittent fever than those who first subdued the soil in Illinois, Iowa, and Wisconsin. The history of those who colonized the Holland Land-

* "Arctic Explorations," Vol. I., p. 155.

Purchase, in Western New York, is one of privation and suffering from disease. A prominent physician of Chicago, whose early career was passed in Michigan, informed me that there would be hardly a family within the circuit of a day's ride, but had some member of it afflicted with chills and fever. So prevalent was this disease, that at length it came to be understood that it was necessary to build the cabin to the windward of the farm to be subdued. The partial destruction of the forest in the Middle States, by letting in the sunlight and permitting a free circulation of air, has improved, without doubt, the sanitary condition of the country. On the prairies of Illinois and Wisconsin, cases of intermittent fever occur, but it is of a mild type, and readily yields to appropriate treatment; and at this day, it is far less prevalent than on Staten Island, or along the shores of New Jersey and Long Island, where, under the action of the ebbing and flowing of the tide, large muddy flats are alternately exposed to the rays of the sun and the wash of the ocean.

The Effects of Forests on Animal Life.—The depths of the forest are almost as destitute of animal life, as the interior of deserts. Throughout the Mississippi Valley, there are abundant monuments, in the form of high circular mounds, of parallel roads and far-reaching embankments, laid out in mathematical forms, of a race who possessed a higher degree of civilization, and different manners and customs, from those who occupied the country when first known to the European. These monuments are restricted to the valleys. They are neither found in the densely-wooded region, nor on the open prairie. The banks of lakes and rivers were selected by the Indians, as the sites of their lodges; for these gave them the most easy and expeditious highways of communication. To a race unacquainted with the use of iron, the forest would present an insurmountable barrier, except so far as marking it by trails.* Even European settlements followed the same course. Colonies were planted at the mouths of rivers, or in places accessible to the sea. They extended themselves up the valleys, and at last resorted to the highlands. But, in the case of the Aborigines, there was a reason why their lodges should be restricted to the valleys. Here the sunlight could gain access. Here grew the spontaneous fruits of the earth, which could be appropriated as food. The waters furnished fish, and the quadrupeds and birds, such as furnish food to man, here found their feeding-grounds. The

---

* Perhaps it is necessary to explain what is meant by a "trail." It has, however, a specific meaning with every backwoodsman. It is the path beaten through the forest, by men moving in Indian-file — or a column of men following in the footsteps of a leader.

beasts and birds of prey followed in their wake. Every explorer in a North American forest must have remarked the absence of game remote from lakes and water-courses, and how rarely its solitude is broken by the song of birds.*

Humboldt, in his "Aspects of Nature," has devoted a chapter to the nocturnal life of animals in the primeval forests of South America. At night, all resort to the rivers. "The jaguar pursues the peccaries and the tapirs, and these, pressing against each other in their flight, break through the inwoven tree-like shrubs which impede their flight; the apes on the tops of the trees, being frightened by the crash, join their cries to those of the larger animals; this arouses the tribes of birds, who build their nests in communities; and thus the whole animal world becomes in a state of commotion."

---

* To this general rule, there is a notable exception. Those who have camped in the forests of Lake Superior, have often heard, issuing from its deepest recesses, not only by day, but in the darkness of night, the song of a small bird, of which at times he may catch a glimpse, as it flits among the branches.

Richardson, in his "Arctic Expedition," thus records: "The song of the *Fringilla leucophrys* has been heard day and night, and so loudly, in the stillness of the latter season, as to deprive us at first of rest. It whistles the first bar of 'Oh, dear, what can the matter be!' in a clear tone, as if played on a piccolo fife; and though the distinctness of the notes rendered them at first very pleasing, yet, as they haunted us up to the Arctic Circle, and were loudest at midnight, we came to wish occasionally that the cheerful little songster would time his serenade better."

So, too, in the northern forests, the deer at night resorts to the lake or running stream, tracked by his remorseless foe, the wolf. Hardly have the shades of evening fallen, when the panther, rousing himself from his lair, sets up a howl preliminary to starting on his predatory tramp, and the beaver and other aquatic animals begin their nocturnal tasks.

Effects of Disrobing a Country of Forests.— Vast areas of the prairie-region now deemed too arid for cultivation, are as well-watered and possess as productive a soil as those regions adjacent to the Mediterranean which were formerly the sites of mighty cities in the midst of a densely-populated country. If, therefore, the desolation of these regions has been brought about by the agency of man, it becomes an interesting inquiry whether that agency, beneficially exerted, can not restore their former fruitfulness. If so, can not the area of the cultivable prairies be enlarged by an application of the same means?

Mr. George P. Marsh, in a late work entitled "Man and Nature," has collected a vast body of facts tending to show the influence of man upon the material world. That influence has been beneficially exerted in the conversion of the desert into a garden, in draining marshes, in cutting canals and roads, in clearing at one point a portion of the forest and letting in the sunlight, and in planting forests at another. That influence has been injuriously exerted by disrobing a country entirely of its forests, thereby creating a more arid climate by drying up the sources of the springs, and by giving the local winds an unresisted passage over the land, thereby communicating to it a more continental character. I shall refer to this storehouse of facts to illustrate my text:

"If we compare," says he, "the present physical condition of the countries [around the borders of the Mediterranean] with the descriptions that ancient geographers and historians have given of their fertility and general capability of ministering to human uses, we shall find that more than one-half of their whole extent * * is either deserted by civilized men and surrendered to hopeless desolation, or at least greatly reduced both in productiveness and population. Vast forests have disappeared from mountain spurs and ridges; the vegetable earth, accumulated beneath the trees by the decay of leaves and fallen trunks, the soil of Alpine pastures which skirted and indented the woods, and the mould of the upland fields, are washed away; meadows, once fertilized by irrigation, are waste and unproductive, because the cisterns and reservoirs that supplied the ancient canals are broken, or the springs that fed them dried up; rivers famous in history and in song, have shrunk to humble brooklets; the willows that ornamented and protected the banks of the lesser water-courses are gone, and the rivers have ceased to exist as perennial currents, because the little water that finds its way into their old channels is evaporated by the droughts of summer, or absorbed by the parched earth, before it reaches the lowlands; the beds of the brooks have widened into broad expanses of pebbles and gravel, over which, though in the hot season passed dry shod, in winter sea-like torrents thunder; the entrances of navigable streams are obstructed by sand-bars; and harbors, once marts of an extensive commerce, are shoaled by the deposits of the rivers at whose mouths they lie."

The architectural ruins and other monuments attest that these regions, now almost withdrawn from human occupancy, must formerly have been tenanted by a dense population who derived their support from a soil of great productiveness. The causes of this decay, as traced by him, apart from the tyranny and misrule of the governing classes, are mainly found to be due to the destruction of the forests. Van Lennep states that one can not for a moment doubt that the parched region which lies between the Red Sea and the Persian Gulf, was once a fertile garden, " before the forests which covered the hill-sides were cut down, before the cedar and the fir-tree were rooted up from the sides of Lebanon." To this cause, Sir John Herschel attributes the aridity of Spain; while, on the other hand, rain has become more frequent in Egypt since the palm has been more vigorously cultivated. *

Bolander, in speaking of the power of certain trees to condense moisture, particularly the Redwoods (*Sequoia sempervirens*), which are restricted to the foggy regions of the Coast Ranges of the Pacific and the underlying meta-

* Marsh, *ibidem.*

morphic sandstones, both of which conditions are required for their growth, uses this language:

"It is my firm conviction that if the Redwoods are destroyed (and they necessarily will be, unless protected by the wise action of our Government,) California will become a desert, in the true sense of the word. In their safety depends the future welfare of the State; they are our safeguard. It remains to be seen whether we shall be benefitted or not by the horrible experience which such countries as Asia Minor, Greece, Spain, and France, have made, by having barbarously destroyed their woods and forests. But with us here, it is even of a more serious nature. Wise governments would be able to replace them in those countries; but no power on earth can restore the woods of California, when once completely destroyed." *

Rapid Destruction of the Forest in the United States.—In the United States, the destruction of the forest is going on at an accelerated rate. The lumber trees of Maine, in accessible positions, are nearly exhausted, and twenty years will accomplish the same result with regard to the extensive pineries of Michigan and Wisconsin. The White pine is the most valuable lumber tree of America. The ease with which it is wrought; its freedom, as compared with most trees, from shrinking, swelling, and warping; and its durability, when properly protected by paint; make it the principal tree employed in the construction of a vast majority of houses and even fences and sidewalks. To one

* Bolander, Henry N., "Remarks on California Trees," "Pro. Cal. Acad. Nat. Sciences."

who realizes how rapidly the sources of supply are becoming exhausted, and the prodigality with which it is used, it can not but be disheartening. It is a tree of slow growth, and the surface on which it grows, when disrobed, is unfitted for profitable agriculture. The annual receipts at Chicago alone (a city which has sprung up within the life-time of a generation) are in excess of 730,000,000 feet of lumber, 400,000,000 of shingles, and 24,000,000 of lath. Possessing a material within easy reach, and on the banks of a canal, known as the Athens limestone—a double compound of carbonate of lime and magnesia—unequaled for flagging and building, and having a river whose dredgings are capable of conversion into brick, it is a singular fact which strikes every stranger within her gates, that Chicago should exhibit such an extent of plank-walks and wooden tenements,—structures of the most superficial character, which must soon give way to those more solid and enduring. The products of the lake pineries are distributed over nearly half a continent. From them are built the farm-houses of the pioneers upon the solitary prairie, and the bridges which span the waters of the Kansas and the Platte.

The destruction of hard-wood timber is going on at a pace equally rapid. The railways require, annually, in construction and maintenance, at least

10,000,000 of ties. Nothing strikes the emigrant from the Atlantic Slope, on returning after years of absence, so forcibly, as to see those hills which, in his youth, were forest-crowned, now bare and desolate, and the streams which he was accustomed to fish, dwindled to mere trickling rills. The Pacific railroads which traverse, for long distances, the valleys of the Kaw and Platte, have consumed in their construction nearly every stick of timber, and in four years will have consumed nearly all the fire-wood. Transportation is economized by stripping each tie of its bark, and allowing it to undergo the process of seasoning, before its conveyance to the place where required. The beautiful Black walnuts of the Kaw Valley, fit for gun-stocks and cabinet-ware, have been remorselessly sacrificed to these base purposes. Public policy requires that this wholesale destruction of the forest be arrested. As a sanitary measure, in thronged cities, the sidewalks should be firmly laid in stone or brick, instead of plank, which serve as coverings to reservoirs of stagnant waters, screened from the evaporation of the sun. A "balloon" house, as proverbially known throughout the West, can be hastily thrown up, but one of brick or stone is, in the end, far more durable and economical. Ties can be treated, at an inconsiderable expense, with kreosote or coal-tar, so that their durability shall be protracted for a quarter of a century; but we have yet to learn the name of the corporation that has resorted to the process. The managers of such roads, particularly, as the Union Pacific, where transportation is so far and so expensive, would have consulted the true interests of their stockholders if they had placed the iron on ties thus prepared.

In the first settlement of the country, so far as relates to the Atlantic Slope, the Appalachian Region, and the Ohio Valley, the forest was the great obstacle to be encountered. The settlers attacked it as though it were a common enemy. To fell, to girdle, to "log," and to burn, those noble forms of vegetation whose origin stretches back to remote ages, was a preliminary work to that of planting, sowing, reaping, and harvesting. But that necessity no longer exists.

Our people find themselves possessed of a country vast in resources, but imperfectly developed. On every side, they see avenues leading to the exertion of human skill and energy. They are restless, eager in the pursuit of gain, and bound by few local attachments. In their investments, they look for immediate returns. If they build a house or subdue a farm, it is in reference to its market value, should they desire to migrate. If they plant trees, say they, two generations must elapse before they attain their growth. If appealed to, that their acts will be commended by posterity, they will probably answer, in the language of the bluff English statesman, "Confound posterity! what has it ever done for us?" But this is a narrow, selfish spirit. The future has claims upon the present generation,—that they shall not despoil the fair heritage which is entrusted to them as an usufruct, but transmit it to future generations, not only unimpaired, but beautified and adorned.

Forests—Their Lessons.—They Modify Climate.

> "The groves were God's first temples; 'ere man learned
> To hew the shaft and lay the architrave.'"

No one can wander "through the dim vaults and winding aisles" of a primeval forest, amid the "venerable columns" which support the "verdant roof," and listen to the sound of the "invisible breath" that "sways at once all their green tops," without acknowledging, with all-reverent spirit, that here he verily is in the sanctuary of Nature.

Trees are the noblest manifestations of vegetable life. Like men, they flourish best in communities, and are dependent on one another for support. Their infancy must be sheltered beneath the outstretching arms of the parent, until they acquire the strength and vigor to shoot into the upper air, and become self-supporting.

They modify climate, in breaking the force of the winds, in sheltering the earth's surface from the intensity of the sun's heat, and in serving as the perpetual reservoirs for the supply of streams. The transitions of temperature on the plains of Kansas are very great. In the spring the winds may blow for several days from the southwest, bringing with them an almost summer temperature, under whose influence the buds of fruit-trees expand and burst; when, suddenly veering to the northwest, the blast sweeps down from the snow-clad peaks of the Rocky Mountains, in cold and blighting frosts, the thermometer often dropping 15° or 18°.*

The interposition of a forest belt, or even of hedges of Osage orange, a shrub which flourishes on a prairie soil, would obviate these disastrous effects. It has been found, in older countries, that the effects of such a barrier extend to a very considerable distance above its own height. Becquerel states that, in the Valley of the Rhone, a simple hedge two metres (a little more than 5½ feet) in height, is a sufficient protection for a distance of twenty-two metres (72 feet) in length.

* "Geological Report Kansas," 1866.

"From the experience," says he, "in older countries, there is no doubt that the effects of these cold blasts can be greatly mitigated; and observation teaches that, while the tops of the trees are swayed by their violence, the surface air will be found calm and warm. Certain districts which have there been stripped of their forests, are now exposed to loss of harvests by tempests, droughts, and frosts. Hurricanes, before unknown, sweep unopposed over the regions thus denuded, conveying terror and devastation in their track." *

Forests Retain Moisture. — The continuous existence of moisture in the forests, and its constant evaporation, modify the heats of summer. The leafy canopy of trees naturally condenses the floating vapors of the air, and causes them to descend in fertilizing showers. It retards the circulation of the atmosphere, and consequently retards evaporation. The leaves shed during the autumnal frosts, not only protect the ground, but serve as a sponge to absorb and retain a portion of the moisture which would otherwise find its way at once into the streamlets.

On the other hand, the roots constantly draw from the earth moisture, which passes through the trunks and branches, as through a mass of capillary tubes, and this is given off through the leaves; a process by which the humidity of the air is increased and its temperature lowered.

* Marsh, "Nature and Man."

"In wooded countries," according to Schacht, "the atmosphere is generally humid, and rain and dew fertilize the soil. As the lightning-rod abstracts the electric fluid from a stormy sky, so the forest abstracts to itself the rain from the clouds which, in falling, refreshes not it alone, but extends its benefits to the neighboring fields. * * The forest, presenting a considerable surface for evaporation, gives to its own soil and to all the adjacent soil an abundant and enlivening dew. There falls, it is true, less dew on a tall and thick wood than on the surrounding meadows, which, being more highly heated during the day by the difference of insulation, cool with greater rapidity by radiation. But it must be remarked, that this increased deposition of dew on the neighboring fields is partly due to the forests themselves; for the dense saturated strata of air which hover over the woods, descend in cool, calm evenings, like clouds, to the valley, and in the morning, beads of dew sparkle on the leaves of the grass and the flowers of the field. Forests, in a word, exert in the interior of continents, an influence like that of the sea on the climate of islands and of coasts; both water the soil, and thereby insure its fertility."

Tree-Planting.—Although the wooded regions, as shown by the hyetal charts, have more abundant moisture and more equally distributed than the prairies, yet there is little doubt that, under suitable conditions, tree-planting may be successfully extended over large areas which now show no evidences of ever having been clothed with arborescent forms, first removing the light pulverulent soil so rich in humus, and bedding the rootlets in the stiff loamy subsoil; and as we push our conquests further into the domain of the grasses, the trees first

---

* Schacht, "*Les Arbres,*" quoted by Marsh.

planted will have acquired the power of retaining not only the existing humidity, but of abstracting that which the winds bring from other quarters, and causing it to be precipitated. Thus, I doubt not that a century would very materially change the existing outlines between woodland and prairie.

The effect of such tree-planting would be, as we have shown, to break the force of the fierce blasts so destructive to fruit-culture; to modify the extremes of heat and cold; to check the recurrence of droughts; to fill the brooklets with running water; and, at the same time, to beautify and adorn the country.

Man appreciates these noblest types of the vegetable kingdom. He loves their symmetrical form, their spreading canopy of leaves, and their grateful shade.* His ideas of the pleasures of a country life are intimately connected with trees; and no object is more beautiful or attractive than a park with a carpet of bright greensward. Every farmer

* An ordinary observer, after viewing the long avenues of elms which line the streets of Hadley, Northampton, New Haven, and other New England villages, wonders at the dearth of shade-trees which characterizes western villages, whose sites have been reclaimed from the primeval forest; but a little reflection would convince him that trees grown in the forest are mutually dependent upon one another for support, and lack the canopy of foliage which is required for shade. In clearing a forest, therefore, where isolated trees are left, they are found to be deficient both in the spread of their roots and limbs, and are liable to be toppled over by every careering blast. Hence, then, shade-trees are the result of a second growth, and under different climatic conditions.

can commence a grove, and though he may not hope to enjoy its shade, it will be a highly-prized heritage to his children.

Our ideas of rural felicity are,—a country of sufficient relief and depression of surface to admit of perfect drainage, divided in proper proportions between woodland, pasture, meadow, and field; with springs gushing out from the shaded recesses of the forest, and furnishing perennial water to the streams which flow through the lowlands; with the rising knoll crowned by a neat painted farm-house and ample barns, protected by locust groves or fruit-bearing orchards, alike from winter winds and summer heats; with fields enclosed by well-trimmed hedges, and pastures dotted with clumps of trees, to which cattle can resort for shelter from the midday sun or the drifting storm; while, as a conspicuous feature in the landscape, should stand out in bold relief, the village church and village school-house, a sign and symbol of the morality and intelligence of its inhabitants;—and such a landscape can be created almost every where in the fertile prairie-region of the West.

God bless, then, the man who plants a tree!— whether by the dusty roadside or on the grassy plain; for thereby he renders himself a public benefactor. The pedestrian, foot-sore and weary, as he pauses beneath its shade, shall bless him; the patient ox, with lolling tongue, shall bless him; his children and his children's children, as they gather in sportive group beneath its sheltering boughs, shall remember him. Not to the wandering Arab is the recollection of the solitary palm on the desert, overhanging a fountain, more grateful than is to us the village elm, associated with childhood's sports. These associations touch a chord in the memory of every one, which shall cease to vibrate only with life itself. The Charter Oak, the Big Elm of Boston Common, the Willow of Pope, and the Mulberry of Shakespeare, each has become historical. Again we say, God bless the man who plants a tree!

IRRIGATION.

Another method by which the aridity of the plains can be modified, under favorable conditions, is by irrigation,—an art practised by the early inhabitants of both continents, who represented the highest civilization then attained. The plains which contain the sites of Nineveh and Babylon, were irrigated by the surplus waters of the Tigris and Euphrates, distributed in a series of canals through the cultivated fields. Layard describes the ruins of an immense artificial mound erected in the heart of the Assyrian capital, built up with terraces, planted with the choicest flowers, and irrigated by fountains,—a work constructed by one of the monarchs as a tribute of respect to the queen-consort, who had been born in a mountainous region, and desired some reminiscence of her youthful home. From the earliest ages, too, this system has been practised in the valley of the Nile, and the area thus cultivated, as indicated by the abandoned and nearly filled-up canals, was far more extensive under the Pharaohs than at this day. In Armenia, Palestine, India, and China, in fact throughout most Oriental countries, there is evidence that this practice prevailed; and, without supposing an abandonment of it, we can not account for the diminished fertility of the soil, and the decimation of the population.

When the Spaniards invaded Peru, they found the country developed by a great system of internal improvements;—an artificial road more than a thousand miles in length, forming a line of communication through all the different provinces of the empire, the road-bed either macadamized or paved with flat stones; ravines and rivers spanned by bridges of stone, or wood, or rope; distances marked by mile-stones; station-houses of well-cut stone at convenient intervals; aqueducts for bringing water to the caravansaries; and cisterns for retaining water to irrigate the cultivated fields. As the Peruvians used no wheeled vehicles, the mountain steeps were scaled by long flights of steps, with resting-places at proper intervals. Humboldt remarks that nothing he had seen of the remains of Roman roads in Italy, in the South of France, or in Spain, was more imposing than these works of the ancient Peruvians; and Hernando Pizarro, the brother of the Conqueror, exclaimed: " In the whole of Christendom, there are no where such fine roads as those which we here admire." * Not the least of the evils inflicted on the country by the more warlike and, we might add, less civilized Spaniards, was the destruction of the aqueducts and cisterns by which the supplies of water were regulated.

In Piedmont and Lombardy, according to Marsh, irrigation is bestowed on almost every crop, and the amount of water each day distributed over the plains would equal the entire volume of the Seine.

This system has been successfully introduced along the slopes of the Rocky Mountains. The farming operations of the Mormons exhibit a degree of thrift, and are attended with results, which it would be difficult for the prairie farmer of Illinois to parallel. The same results have been achieved in Colorado. The wheat thus grown is of the choicest kind, and the yield is far beyond

* "Aspects of Nature."

that known in the most favored regions of the Mississippi Valley. When it is ripened, the water is withdrawn, and the farmer may gather the crops at leisure, secure against blight or rains. The prices of wheat and beef at Denver are less than at Chicago.

California has astonished the world by becoming a wheat-exporting region, but whether she will maintain this position, is a matter of doubt. Colton, who resided there during the early occupation by the Americans, says:

> "Some of the largest crops that ever rewarded the toil of the husbandman, have been gathered in California; and yet those very localities, owing to a slender fall of winter rains, have next season disappointed the hopes of the cultivator. The farmer can never be certain of an abundant harvest, till he is able to supply the deficiency of rain by irrigation." *

Antisell states that—

> "The annual fall of rain in the central counties is about 20 inches. In the south, it ranges from 10 to 12 inches. As this quantity does not suffice to keep the rivers running throughout the year, or to soak the soil thoroughly with moisture, irrigation is necessary during the summer months. In the latter period of the year, every thing languishes for drought, and the valleys that blossomed like the rose in March and April, with every wild flower, rare, beautiful, or fragrant, becomes from July to August, brown, parched, fissured, and the abode of the grasshopper and reptile. During October, sooner or later with the latitude, comes the first rain, and vegetation starts afresh into life and variety." †

---

* "Three Years in California.'

† "Pacific Railroad Survey," Vol. VII.

During the rainy season, all of the agricultural operations are carried on. "The whole of the rain," he continues, "does not come at once, but at intervals, like the former and the latter rain of Judea."

In the Valley of the Santa Clara, the varieties known as "California bearded" wheat and the "Chile" are cultivated. The seed is of good size and white, and the yield is from forty to fifty bushels to the acre. Barley yields seventy-five bushels, and oats one hundred.

The Colorado Desert is inhospitable, not so much by reason of the poverty of the soil, as absence of moisture, only requiring the presence of this condition to quicken vegetation into life, and secure to the cultivator abundant crops. The barometrical measurements carried over the valley, show that it is so much lower than the stream that it may be successfully irrigated. Capt. Humphreys gives the area as 4,500 square miles, or four times greater than that of the cultivated land of the Mississippi, between the mouth of Red River and the Balize, that may be rendered cultivable.

The Colorado Plateau, or the *Mesa* formation of New Mexico, consists of broad uplands, abruptly terminated, according to Parry, by steep mural declivities, bounding narrow valleys of erosion, or presenting isolated buttes and fantastically castellated rocks. The uplands are almost bare of detrital materials, while the valleys afford strips of land adapted to agriculture. The Pueblo Indians are enabled to cultivate the soil, availing themselves of the inundations of the rivers, and to pasture their flocks by shifting them at different seasons to different exposures, which involves a nomadic life.

The region to the east of the Rio Grande presents a far different aspect, and an increase of moisture alone is required to render it fertile beyond compare. Newberry thus describes it:

"For seventy-five miles after leaving Santa Fé, and proceeding east, we were involved in the spurs of the Rocky Mountains, and were passing through a remarkably picturesque and beautiful region, in which the surface is nearly equally shared between rocky, ragged, and pine-covered Sierras, and open, grassy valleys, through which flow streams of the purest water, fed by the melting of the snows. In this interval, we crossed the rim of the Great Mississippi Valley and began to descend its western slope. * * * The soil became more fertile, the vegetation more varied. The summer showers by which we were drenched, were for a time so refreshing a novelty that we scarcely cared to avoid them. By all these and other signs, we saw that we were emerging from the vast arid area [the Colorado Plateau], in which many preceding months had been passed, where sterility was the rule and productiveness the marked exception, and were approaching the region where a flowing stream is not a wonder, and where an unbroken sheet of vegetation covers the soil. * * The contrast of physical features presented by the plains east and west of the mountains is not merely of abstract interest. It involves all of the economical differences between a nearly uninhabitable desert and perhaps the best agricultural region of the Continent." *

* "Pacific Railroad Surveys," Vol. XI.

So far from Providence having doomed these plains to everlasting sterility, they will be cultivated whenever population shall press on the means of subsistence; and the waters of the Platte, Kansas, Canadian, and Arkansas, will be gathered in reservoirs and distributed by canals through cultivated fields, like those of the Tigris and Euphrates, as in olden time. On the banks of the Euphrates was founded a city which the prophet pronounced "the glory of kingdoms," and the plains of Shinar sustained another city of nearly equal magnificence, whose "merchants" were "multiplied above the stars of heaven."

CHAPTER VI.

CLIMATE.

DEFINITION OF CLIMATE—ATMOSPHERIC CURRENTS — RAINS AND WINDS—CLOUD-BURSTS — ISOTHERMAL LINES — GULF-STREAM—EVAPORATIVE POWER OF WINDS—ISOTHERMS OF THE UNITED STATES—CLIMATE OF THE PACIFIC AND GREAT BASIN—PHENOMENA OF THE SEASONS—TABLE OF TEMPERATURES—OF RAIN PRECIPITATION.

Definition of Climate.—Climate, in its most extended sense, embraces a great variety of phenomena; such as the ever-varying changes of the atmosphere, the direction of the winds, the precipition of rains, the distribution of temperature, the organic development of plants, and the conditions of animal life. Each of these branches, properly illustrated, would comprise a treatise; but we must content ourselves with announcing general results which have been recorded by numerous explorers in this domain of nature. Much information as to the distribution of winds and rains, which properly belongs to this subject, has already been anticipated in the preceding Chapters.

Atmospheric Currents.—We may regard the earth as surrounded by two oceans,—one aerial and the other aqueous. The height of the atmosphere has been assumed at fifty miles; but, owing to the difference of temperature at the Equator and at the Poles (as 80° to 0), it is unequal, amounting to a difference of about four miles. Owing, also, to the rapidly-decreasing density of air, as we ascend into celestial space, one-half of the mass is compressed into a limit of three and one-half miles, which is less than the height of the culminating points of several of the great mountain chains, such as the Himalaya and the Andes; and hence it may be inferred, that those tremendous perturbations, as manifested in the tornado or hurricane, whose track is marked on the surface by indiscriminate ruin, extend to no great height in the region of space.

Henry, in his "Contributions to Meteorology," has so well explained the complex system of winds that we shall avail ourselves of his explanation, but with some condensation.

If the earth were at rest, he remarks, it is obvious that the air, expanded by the sun's heat at the Equator, would rise up and flow over, descending, as it were, an inclined plane towards the poles, where it would reach the earth's surface, and flow back to the Equator, and thus a perpetual circulation would be maintained. It is further evident that, since the meridians of the earth converge, all the air that rose at the Equator would not flow along the upper surface entirely to the Poles, but the greater portion would proceed no further north and south than latitude 30°, for the surface of the earth, contained between the parallel of this degree and the Equator, is equal to that of half of the whole hemisphere. Portions, however, in the Northern Hemisphere would flow on, to descend at different points further north; and of these portions, some probably would reach the pole, and there sink to the surface of the earth, and from that point diverge in all directions in the form of a northerly wind. Between the two ascending currents near the Equator there would be a region of calms, or variable winds. The currents which flow over towards the poles would descend with the greatest velocity at the coldest point, because there the air would be densest.

Now, the earth is in rapid motion on its axis, from west to east; and every particle of air, therefore, flowing from the north to the Equator, would partake of the motion of the place at which it started, and would reach in succession lines of latitude moving more rapidly than itself. It would, therefore, lag behind continually, and appear to describe on the surface of the earth a slightly curvilinear course towards the west; and hence the Northeast Trades in the Northern Hemisphere, and the Southeast Trades in the Southern Hemisphere, where the conditions are reversed, but both blowing towards the belt of greatest rarefaction.

The particles of air approaching the equator will not ascend in a perpendicular direction, but will rise continually as they advance towards the west along an ascending plane, and will continue for a time their westerly motion in the Northern Hemisphere. After they have commenced their return towards the north, and until they arrive at parts of the earth moving more rapidly than themselves, they will gradually curve towards the east, and finally descend earthward, to become again a part of the surface Trade Winds from the northeast. The atoms will move westward as they ascend: 1. On account of the momentum in that direction; and, 2. Because, as they reach a higher elevation, they will have less easterly velocity than the earth beneath. They will also be affected by another force, first pointed out by Mr. Ferrell, due to the increase of gravity which a particle of matter experiences in traveling in a direction opposite to that of the rotation of the earth. The last-mentioned cause of deflection will operate in an opposite direction on atoms when they assume an easterly course. The result of the complex conditions under which the motive-power acts in such a case, would be to produce a system of circuits inclined to the west, the eastern portion of which would be at the surface, and the western portion at different elevations, even to the top of the atmosphere.

The greater portion of the circulation would descend to the earth within 30° of the equator, giving rise to the Trade Winds; another portion would flow further north, and produce the Southwest Winds; and another portion, flowing still further north, would descend to the earth as a Northwest Wind. The air which descends in the region of the North Pole would not flow directly southward; but, on account of the rotation of the earth, would turn towards the west, and become a northeasterly current. It might appear, at first sight, that the north wind which descends from the polar regions would continue its course along the surface, until it joined the Trade Winds within the tropics; but this could not be the case, on account of the much greater western velocity which this wind would acquire from the rapidly-increasing rotary motion as we leave the pole.*

Thus it is that we have different belts of air encircling the earth with girdles, divided, as it were, by impenetrable walls. In the circumpolar region of the North, we have the girdle of Southwest Currents, bounded by the Calm Belt of Can-

---

* Professor Joseph Henry, "Patent Office Report," 1856.

cer; in the circumpolar region of the South, the girdle of Northwest Currents (at right-angles to the former), bounded by the Calm Belt of Capricorn. Within the tropics, we have, north of the Equator, the girdle of Northeast Trades, and south (at right-angles), the girdle of Southeast Trades, with the Movable Belt of Variable Winds and Constant Precipitation, whose action is regulated by the advance and recession of the sun, during the progress of the seasons. (*Vide* Plate I.) This gives rise to the periodicity, in the tropics, of winds and rains. The breadth, too, of the several belts varies, being contracted into a smaller space towards the poles during the winter, and expanded into a wider space during the summer.

If the earth were a sphere perfectly smooth, the flow of the winds, as thus defined, would be uniform; but it is crested with ridges, the culminating points of which in some instances pierce, as we have seen, at least one-half of the mass of the aerial envelope, and hence interrupt that uniformity of flow, giving force and direction to local winds.

The inclination of the earth's orbit to the Equator ($23°\ 27'\ 54.8''$), and the inclination of its axis to its orbit ($66°\ 32'$), give origin to a great variety of changes which exert a marked influence on animal and vegetable life. If the earth's Equator coincided with the Ecliptic, the sun would pursue an unvarying round, and to the inhabitants of the Poles it would never appear, except on the verge of the horizon. The days and nights would be of equal duration, the winds would blow constantly in one direction, and the difference between summer and winter temperature would be unknown. Instead of the vicissitudes of the seasons,—spring, with every valley and plain covered with new-born verdure; summer, with its maturing fruits and harvests; autumn, with its rustling and shriveled leaves; and winter, with its ice-bound streams and mantle of snow;—we should have at the Equator, eternal summer; at the verge of the Tropics, eternal spring; and within the Arctic Circle, which now, during the short-lived summer, is made verdant by a covering of Alpine blossoms, would reign eternal ice.

Rains.—The ocean receives into its abyss the superabundant moisture of the land, and at the same time is the great source from which it emanates. The heated air which ascends from the Equator up into the regions of space, is saturated with moisture gathered in its passage across these wide expanses of water. The ocean may be compared to an enormous sponge, whose capacity for absorption is in direct proportion to its power of expansion. As the heated column ascends, it constantly encounters a diminished temperature, which condenses its volume, and causes it to part with a portion of its moisture, which descends under the form of fog, or dew, or hail, or rain, or snow, or ice.

This action is more energetic under the direct rays of the sun than in the cold glare of an Arctic night; and hence it is, *theoretically*, that the greatest precipitation takes place within the tropics, and the least within the circumpolar regions. Humboldt estimates that the average rain-fall at the Equator is 96 inches; at latitude 19°, 80 inches; at 45°, 29 inches; at 60°, 17 inches. But there are disturbing causes, such as the configuration of the country by reason of lofty mountain chains, vast sandy plains, oceanic expanses, etc., as we have before shown, which modify the flow of atmospheric currents; so that these speculations are nearly valueless.

There are two conditions of the atmosphere under which precipitation ordinarily takes place: 1. Where two equal portions of air at different temperatures, completely saturated with moisture, are mingled together, so as to partake of the mean temperature of the whole mass; and, 2. As in thunder-storms, due to the electrical action of the clouds, where the hygrometric moisture of the air is held in suspension by the mutual repulsion of the particles, until the electricity, which is the sustaining power, is withdrawn, when the particles coalesce and descend by the force of gravitation. To enter into an explanation of all these complex phenomena would lead to a wide digression from the objects of this Chapter; but it may be said that, through the ocean, with its connecting springs and rivers, a harmonious circulation of moisture is perpetually maintained over the whole of our planet, which may be compared to the flow of blood from the heart, through the arteries and veins of the human system, each pulsation of the great centre communicating a vital force to the very extremities.

In making an application of these general principles to the Great Valley, it may be said that its configuration is such as to show marked peculiarities, both in reference to temperature and the distribution of moisture, which separate it in some degree from the Atlantic Slope, and widely from the Great Basin and the Pacific Slope. Walled in, as we have seen, both on the east and west, by two diverging mountain chains, and presenting between the Gulf of Mexico and the Arctic Sea no elevation much to exceed 2,000 feet, there is no great barrier to arrest the flow of the hot southerly winds of summer, or the cold northerly winds of winter; in this respect presenting far different structural relations from those of the northern portion of the

Eastern Hemisphere. Though included mainly in the Belt of Southwest Winds, yet, owing to the configuration of the country, as before shown, it draws its supplies of moisture from the Northeast Trades, which, during one-half of the year, traversing the Caribbean Sea and the Gulf of Mexico before striking the land, bear the warmth of those waters far inland, and communicate to the region the peculiar semi-tropical character of its summers; while, during the other half of the year, the cold blasts of the north sweep down unopposed into the lower latitudes, producing all of the rigors of an Arctic winter. We have already adverted to the effects of these extremes of temperature upon the forest-growth, and shall have occasion to describe their influence in determining the range of those plants which are cultivated for human food.

The phenomena often attending the summer precipitation are these: Day after day, under the influence of a southwest wind, the thermometer will mark a temperature of 90° or even 100° F., and however violent the wind, it brings no refreshing coolness, but rather increased languor. The sun glows with a fierceness and intensity unknown in the tropics, and the air itself seems to be deprived of ozone, or that principle of oxygen which communicates life and energy to the system. But at length there comes a change. A cloud is seen to gather in the north or northwest, which gradually unrolls its murky folds as it advances against the wind. The sky becomes overcast, and almost the darkness of night succeeds. Then there is a lull. The wind suddenly veers to an opposite point, and sweeps down with careering force. The air is filled with dust, and the foliage of the trees sways to and fro. The rain descends in torrents, accompanied by loud peals of thunder and intense flashes of lightning. Gradually the rain abates, the clouds disperse, the sun comes out, a rainbow spans the sky, new life is infused into the air, and every organism, whether animal or vegetable, is refreshed and invigorated.

There are ordinarily two or three of these heated terms in the course of the summer season, terminated by abrupt changes of temperature. The prairie region, having no forest-belts to break the force of these thunder-gusts, suffers from their visitations; and each year there are recorded instances from this cause, of the loss of life and the destruction of property. In the great northern forests, even, are to be seen wide tracks where every tree is prostrate, provincially known as "windfalls."

Cloud-Bursts.—Standing at Denver, in a clear summer's afternoon, and looking west at the long range of mountains in whose gulches snow is perennial, a cloud may often be seen to rise up in a straight column, like the smoke of a volcano, and gradually spread out like the covering of an umbrella. Another cloud will rise up in another quarter and assume the same shape, until at length there is a mingling of vapors with electrical explosions, when there falls a gentle shower, extending often to a region which, but for these local phenomena would be nearly rainless. Soon the sun shines out, and the sky is cloudless. But these manifestations of electrical phenomena are not always equally harmless. Explorers in the Great Basin describe wide washes of coarse gravel, which bear unmistakable evidence of the action of violent torrents, which occasionally pour down the valleys and involve every thing in a common ruin.

These phenomena are known as "cloud-bursts," and are frequently of such violence as to endanger life. The appearance is described by Mr. Harrison "as if an inverted whirlwind was drawing from the cloud immense quantities of water, which it dashed in floods against the mountain sides." By these floods, he had known trees to be uprooted, and rocks transported to considerable distances. On one occasion, the water in the cañon was thirty feet deep. These storms are in the nature of a water-spout, and occur when elsewhere the sky is clear and cloudless.*

In the region of Texas, and extending far up the Plains, there is a peculiar wind, experienced in the first months of the year, known as "a norther." The wind will blow from the Gulf for many days, bringing with it a summer heat. Man, under its influence, feels an oppressive languor, while vegetation quickens into life; but almost instantaneously the weather-cock veers to the north, and a cold blast succeeds. Instances are recorded where the temperature has suddenly dropped from 84° to 36°.

During the winter, in Canada, the cold winds are northwest; in the Middle States, west; and in Texas, north. The winter storms are usually preceded by southerly winds, and are attended with great fluctuations of the barometer. To these succeed cold westerly winds, during which the mercury occasionally drops to −20°.

Of all the storms, however, in the temperate region, the most cheerless and tantalizing to him, particularly, who is sensitive to rheumatic twinges, are those known as "northeasters." They are long-continued, and are accompanied by a chilling sensation not characteristic of rains from other quarters. These storms are rare in the Gulf region, but are felt, though in diminished force and fre-

* W. J. Young, of Boise City, in "Smithsonian Report," 1867.

quency, west of the Mississippi. The general cloud-movement, north of latitude 30°, is from west to east, whatever may be the direction of the surface current. The fact that a northeast storm may originate at Pittsburg or Washington, when a west wind is blowing at Boston, is pretty conclusive that the saturation of the under current is not derived from the Atlantic. This fact, first observed by Franklin, is recognized by men engaged in the practical pursuits of navigation.*

Without further detail as to the atmospheric movements, we submit the following summary:

1. That the Northeast Trades, deflected in their course to south and southeast winds, in their passage through the Caribbean Sea and the Gulf of Mexico, are the warm and moist winds which communicate to the Mississippi Valley and the Atlantic Slope, their fertility.

2. That the prevalence of these winds from May to October, communicates to this region a subtropical climate.

3. That, in the region bordering on the Gulf of

---

* Mr. Prescott states that the owner of a line of steamers plying between Boston and Portland, employs an agent in New York to transmit to him daily reports of the weather. If foul, he sends a message at 8 A.M.; if a storm comes up, he sends another at noon; and another at 3 o'clock P.M., giving a full statement of its progress. If violent, the owner then orders the Portland boat to remain in harbor; and next determines whether the Boston boat can reach Portland before the storm can overtake her. ("History Electric Telegraph.")

Mexico, the atmospheric disturbances are propagated from south to north; but in the Northern and Middle States, owing to a prevailing upper current, from west to east.

4. That while this upper current is cool and dry, and we have the apparent anomaly of rain-storms traveling from west to east, at the same time the moisure supplying them comes from the south.

5. That, in the winter, the south and southeast winds rise into the upper current, while the west and northwest winds descend and blow as surface winds, accompanied by an extraordinary depression of temperature, creating, as it were, an almost Arctic climate.

6. That the propagation of the cold winds from west to east, is due to the existence of a warmer and lighter air to the eastward.

7. That in summer the westerly currents seldom blow with violence, because, in passing over the heated plains, they acquire nearly the same temperature as the southerly currents; but in winter, these conditions are reversed.

Isothermal Lines.—Before the laws of climatology were understood, it was customary to judge of the mean temperature of a place by its distance from the Equator; but with the progress of physical geography, it was found that the influence of radiation was essentially modified by the presence of large oceanic or continental areas. Humboldt was the first to connect together, by certain lines, those places which possessed the same degree of temperature; and he extended the application, by lines uniting places where the summer temperature was the same, and the places where the winter temperature was the same. The lines of mean annual temperature were termed *Isothermal;* those of mean winter temperature, *Isochimenal;* and those of mean summer temperature, *Isotherial.*

The lines of mean winter and summer temperature, when traced around the earth, are not parallel, but exhibit convex and concave summits, and often describe sharp curves. The mean annual temperature of two places may be equal, and yet the summer and winter temperatures may present the most abrupt contrasts. Compare, for instance, Dublin, Ireland, with West Point, New York:

	Lat.	Mean.	Winter.	Spring.	Summer.	Autumn.
Dublin	53° 23'	49.1	40.2	47.1	59.6	49.7
West Point	41° 23'	50.7	29.7	48.7	71.3	53.2
Difference	12°	1.6	10.5—	1.6	11.7+	3.5

We are first struck with the difference in latitude, Dublin being 12° further north; and next, while the mean temperature of the year is about the same, the winters are more than 10° colder, and the summers more than 11° warmer, thus making an extreme difference of nearly 22° in the yearly variation between the two points. And yet Ireland, with her equable climate and moist skies, where the orange may remain out-doors unfrosted, all the year round, can not mature those fruits and grasses which fully ripen on the banks of the Hudson. The deflection of the isothermal lines to the south, in passing from the western coast of Europe to the eastern coast of the United States, is equivalent to about 11° of latitude, or nearly 700 geographical miles. The reason of this, when we come to comprehend all of the phenomena, is obvious.

The Gulf-Stream.—This current, with a mean temperature of 80°, sets over from the coast of Africa, into the Caribbean Sea and the Gulf of Mexico, then abruptly curves around the extreme peninsula of Florida, and conforms in its course to the trend of the Atlantic Slope as far north as latitude 40°, when it is deflected northeast, and spreads itself in a fan-like shape over the cold waters of Western Europe, from Spitzbergen to the Bay of Biscay; throwing upon those shores the warmth and moisture gathered in the tropics, and communicating an equable climate unknown to the eastern portion of the United States.

The Arctic Current. — The Arctic Current which, setting from Baffin's Bay, flows along the coasts of Labrador and Newfoundland, interposes a zone of cold water between the Gulf-Stream and the land, which refrigerates the region far inland. The winds, too, which prevail on the land, are cold westerly winds, and off-shore, thus bearing the warmth and moisture of the Gulf-Stream away from the United States. This is evident from the fact that a vessel often in approaching the coast, in mid-winter, finds her shrouds and decks encased in ice, so much so as to render her nearly unmanageable. Reversing her course, a few hours' run brings her into a summer heat; the ice drops from her shrouds, the frosted crew are warmed by the soft breath of the Gulf-Stream, and are reinvigorated to encounter again the perils of a winter's sea.

The harbor of St. John has been known to remain closed until June, while that of Liverpool, two degrees further north, is never obstructed by ice. A native of the British Isles, taking up his abode in New York, finds a climate almost the reverse of that to which he has been accustomed; a summer as hot as that of Rome, and a winter as cold as that of Copenhagen.

We can conceive of changes in the relative level of the land and sea, by which Western Europe would assume climatic conditions such as prevailed during the Drift epoch. A German physicist (Harwig) has remarked:

"If we suppose the narrow isthmus of Central America to be sunken in the ocean, the warm equatorial current would no longer follow its circuitous route around the Gulf of Mexico, but pour itself through a new opening directly into the Pacific. We should then lose the warmth of the Gulf-Stream; and cold Polar currents, flowing further south, would take its place, and be driven on our coasts by western winds. The North Sea would resemble Hudson's Bay, and its harbors would be free from ice only in summer. The power and prosperity of its coasts would shrivel under the breath of winter; commerce, industry, fertility of soil, and population, would disappear; and the vast waste — a new Labrador — would become a worthless appendage of some clime more favored by nature."

Between the eastern coast of the United States and the western coast of Europe, there is a similarity in the equable precipitation of rain, but a marked dissimilarity in the temperature of the seasons. Between the western coast of the United States and the western coast of Europe, there is a marked similarity in the temperature of the seasons, but a marked dissimilarity in the distribution of rains.

Evaporative Power of the Winds. — While the annual fall of rain in the British Isles averages 36 inches, that of the Atlantic coast is 44 inches. The air of the latter region is dryer, notwithstanding this excess of rain, for the reason that its evaporative power is greater. This arises from two causes:—the greater proportion of cloudless skies, and the higher temperature of the summers. Comparing Cambridge, Massachusetts, with Whitehaven, England,— one of the most copiously watered points in the British Isles,—we find that the annual precipitation is nearly the same (44.48 inches and 45.25 inches), and that the annual evaporation is as 56 to 30.03 inches.

The United States enjoy a serenity of sky unknown to Great Britain. While in one country the crops are subject to drought with a great summer precipitation, in the other they are liable to be injured by excess of moisture; while in the lower latitudes of the United States the grasses shrivel up and die, under the heats of a summer's sun, in Ireland they preserve a perennial green. These examples show that the dryness of a climate does not depend upon a mere deficiency of rain, but upon heat which expands the air and increases its absorbing capacity, and upon the serenity of the skies which permits evaporation to take place. The air is the dryest in the hottest months, when evaporation is the greatest; it contains the greatest dampness in the coldest months, for the reason that the moisture is condensed and thus rendered apparent.

Isotherms of the United States. (See Plate II., at the end of the Chapter.) — In comparing the climate of the Atlantic Slope with that of the Great Valley, where it assumes the character of treeless plains, it is found that, as we advance into the interior, the summers become warmer and the winters cooler. Great as are the extremes on the sea-board, they become greater on the prairies, — thus showing the effect of the earth's radiation over vast surfaces remote from internal seas, and deprived of forest-belts. The presence of the ocean tends, in some degree, to mitigate the excessive temperature of the Atlantic Slope, and the same effect is produced by the forests which clothe not only the crests but the slopes of the Alleghanies. The Great Lakes also exercise a similar influence over the adjacent regions. Hence, as we trace the isotherms of spring and summer, say from New York as a geographical point, they are found to pursue a pretty uniform direction westerly until they reach the western shore of Lake Michigan, when they abruptly curve to the northwest, and at longitude 105° are found to have deviated about 8° from the corresponding parallel of latitude. Capt. Mullan, who was engaged in the Pacific Railroad Surveys of this region, and was subsequently detailed to open a wagon-road from Fort Benton to the Columbia, gives several citations of mean temperature. That of Walla-Walla, in latitude 46°, corresponds to that of Washington, latitude 38°; that of Clark's Fork, 48°, to that of St. Joseph's, Mo., 41°; and that of Bitter-Root Valley, 46°, to that of Philadelphia, 40°.

In reference to the climatology of this region, he remarks:

"As early as the winter of 1853, which I spent in these mountains (the Upper Missouri Valley), my attention was called to the mild open region lying between the Deer-lodge Valley and Fort Laramie, where the buffalo roamed in millions during the winter, and which, during that season, constituted the great hunting-grounds of the Crows, Blackfeet, and other mountain tribes. * * * The meteorological statistics collected during a great number of years, have enabled me to trace an isochimenal line across the continent, from St. Joseph's, Missouri, to the Pacific; and the direction taken by this line is wonderful, and worthy the most important attention in all future legislation that looks towards the travel and settlement of this country. This line, which leaves St. Joseph's, in latitude 40°, follows the general line of the Platte to Fort Laramie, where, from newly-introduced causes, it tends northwesterly between the Wind-River Chain and the Black Hills, crossing the summit of the Rocky Mountains in latitude 47°; showing that in the interval from St. Joseph's, it had gained 6° of latitude. Tracing it still further westward, it goes as high as 48°, and develops itself in a fan-like shape, on the plains of the Columbia. From Fort Laramie to Clark's Fork, I call this "an atmospheric river of heat," varying in width from one to one hundred miles. On either side, north and south, are walls of cold air, which are so clearly perceptible that you always detect when you are on its shores." *

* Captain Mullan, "Guide to Oregon," etc., 1865.

Captains Paliser and Blackstone, of the English Army, accompanied by Dr. Hector as Geologist, in their report of the Saskatchawan country, and of the region lying between Lake Winipeg and the Rocky Mountains, which are embraced in this warm belt, state that there is an area of 11,000,000 acres of fertile soil, where the winters are mild, and where the Hudson Bay Company have produced every crop grown in the Northwestern States. In the Pembina Settlement, we know that for years agriculture has been successfully prosecuted.

In explanation of these phenomena, it may be said that the Rocky Mountains, as we have before shown, attain their highest elevation south of the South Pass, in the parallel of 39° north, and as prolonged northward, they drop down and become merged in hills of moderate elevation. Through this depression, it is believed that the warm breath of the Pacific, brought by the southwesterly winds, flows, until it is met by the cooler currents which prevail over the eastern slope of the Great Valley. The effect of this flow is to modify the rigor of the climate on the eastern slope of the Rocky Mountains as far up even as Athabasca and the Assiniboin, and to render subservient to agriculture a region corresponding in latitude, on the Atlantic Coast, with the inhospitable wastes of Labrador.

Along the Gulf Coast, the isothermal lines pursue a nearly uniform parallelism with those of latitude, until they strike the high table-lands of Western Texas, when they are rapidly deflected south; but in their passage across the Great Basin, are rapidly deflected to the north.

The upper portion of the Mississippi Basin is more directly exposed, in spring and summer, to the warm, moist breath exhaled from the Gulf, than the sea-board; and its effect is seen in the increased duration of tropical heat, and the quickening power communicated to vegetation. The profuse rains which characterize this portion of the year, deprive the climate largely of its continental features, and dispense their fertilizing effects far towards the base of the Rocky Mountains.

Climate of the Gulf Coast.—Along the Gulf Coast, the climate assimilates in its features to that of the tropics,—clear blue skies in the morning, starlight nights, gentle showers at midday, and a luxuriant vegetation, with large spreading leaves,—unlike the vegetation of the Plains, where the dry air concentrates the saps, and often communicates to the plants an aromatic odor. But even here, the fluctuations of temperature occasioned by the change of air-currents, are very great. The south winds sweeping over the Caribbean Sea and the

Gulf of Mexico, are moist and warm, while the north winds, meeting with no barrier to arrest their progress, and being overland, are dry and cold; and hence the changes of temperature are abrupt. At New Orleans, snow occasionally falls, and for a short time whitens the ground. The frosts which accompany the "northers" are of sufficient intensity to destroy the sugar-cane and cotton-plant; but at the same time, while they do not strip the trees of their leaves, they hardly admit of a perpetually-verdant vegetation. The processes of fructification and foliation are arrested, and the distinctions between summer and winter are faithfully preserved.

The effect of these two differences which we have pointed out, between the climate of the Upper Mississippi Valley and the Atlantic Slope,—to wit, excess of moisture and warmth during the summer, and deficiency of moisture during the fall and winter,—are conditions highly favorable to the growth of the grasses, and unfavorable to the growth of arboreal forms; a fact which nature seems to have written in legible characters on the features of this region. If the conditions of equally-distributed rains over the four seasons, which characterize the climate of the sea-board, as before shown, existed west of the Mississippi, it would greatly restrict the area over which the cerealia can be cultivated, and render uninhabitable a region which will hereafter afford a vast range of pasturage to the domestic herds.

In tracing the isotherms for the fall and winter seasons, a depression of the lines, so far as relates to the Upper Mississippi region, begins to manifest itself during the autumnal months, which becomes more marked as the season advances. Thus, St. Paul's, which has the summer temperature of West Point, has the winter temperature of Montreal; and Fort Riley, which has the summer temperature of Washington, has the winter temperature of New York.

The Gulf Coast exhibits no marked deflections of temperature until the Llano Estacado is reached. The interposition of the Rocky Mountain Chain, many of whose peaks are snow-clad, and many of whose sheltered valleys retain the drifted snows during the entire year, causes a local refrigeration of the air which is exhibited in a series of abrupt curves, like the plications of strata in a highly metamorphic mountain range.

Climate of the Pacific Slope.—Notwithstanding the equable temperature which characterizes the immediate Pacific Coast, the foot-hills of the Sierra Nevada and the Colorado Valley exhibit an intensity of heat seldom indicated by the thermometer in other parts of the world, whether on the

Neva, the Senegal, the Ganges, or the Orinoco. Humboldt has remarked that on no part of the earth's surface, if the observations be properly made in the shade, at a distance from all solid bodies which radiate heat, and with thermometers not filled with spirit which absorbs light, do the readings range higher than between 93° and 104°; and that those excessive heats of 122° and 133°, recorded by Ritchie, in the oasis of Mourzouk, must be ascribed to hot particles of sand floating in the air.

At Ringgold Barracks, in the Rio Grande Valley, the mean of the observations, at 3 o'clock P.M., for the entire three summer months of 1850, was 101.2°, and the single extremes reached 107° for each month. Still higher readings are recorded in the Colorado Valley, at Fort Yuma, and in the San Joaquin Valley, at Fort Miller, reaching at the former point 121°, and at the latter 116°.* Now, when we reflect that the mean temperature of the tropics, the region of the palms, is between 78.2° and 85.5°, we see that, for continuous periods, the Pacific Slope, and also the Colorado Valley, have a climate where the heat is as excessive as within the torrid zone; and occasionally the thermometer marks as high a temperature on the borders of Lake Superior, and even at Methy Lake (latitude

* Blodget, "Climatology of the United States."

56° 36' 30" N., and longitude 109° 52' 54" W.,) as beneath the vertical rays of a tropical sun.

Oregon has an equable climate. The rains, as in California, assume a periodic character, and winter is the rainy season. As early as the middle of February, the grounds are ploughed and planted.

Sitka lies in the region of constant precipitation, and the annual rain-fall reaches 90 inches,—an amount equal to that which ordinarily falls at the Equator. While here the winter temperature is about the same as that of Washington City, or St. Louis, the summer temperature is that of the northern shore of Lake Superior. British Columbia and the southern slope of what were lately the Russian Possessions, now added to our domain, partake of these equable features.

To account for these climatic conditions, it is only necessary to study the topography of the country in connection with the prevailing winds and currents. The peninsula of Alaska juts far into the Pacific, and is separated from Asia by Behring's Straits, whose channel in the narrowest part is only thirty miles broad and twenty-five fathoms deep. Through these Straits, no icebergs from the Polar Sea escape into the Pacific, but a warm current, setting in an opposite direction, enters these regions of ice, while a cold current strikes the Californian coast as low down as San Francisco. This region, too, is in the belt of Southwest Winds which traverse a vast expanse of waters, warmed by a tropical sun, before they strike the shore. The country sinks down so as to permit their flow inland, warming up the Athabasca and Saskatchawan regions, as before shown, until their influence is destroyed by the continental conditions which prevail in the interior.

Thus, then, it may be said that the conditions of climate on the Atlantic Slope are continental, on the Pacific Slope oceanic, while those of the Great Interior Plain are of a mixed character, resulting from the conflict of these two systems.

PHENOMENA OF THE SEASONS.

Lake Superior Region.—That portion of the region occupied by the great Coniferous forest, has but two seasons, summer and winter. About the middle of September, heavy gales sweep over the lake, and hoar-frosts fall, nipping the leaves of the deciduous trees, of which the maple is conspicuous, and dyeing them with many-colored tints. Large flocks of geese, arranged in a V-like form, are seen winging their way southward, filling the air with discordant notes, and the lesser water-fowl follow in their track. By the middle of October, the snow begins to fall, and to this succeeds an interval of calm, lasting two or three weeks, when winter sets in in earnest. The interior lakes are closed with a thin covering of ice, and land and water are wrapped in a mantle of snow, so that the ground becomes frozen to no great depth. The dense forest prevents the drifting of the snows, and the warmth of the soil is retained until the opening of spring. The thermometer occasionally drops to $-30°$, followed by a dry, cold, and elastic northwest wind, which seems to rob the temperature of its intensity, so far as relates to its effects upon the human system. The trapper, amid these intense colds, and shod with snow-shoes, pursues his accustomed round, camping at night with his feet towards the log-built fire, with no other covering than a Mackinac blanket.

During the long winter nights, the northern sky is frequently illumined with brilliant streaks of variously-colored light, which reach to the zenith, and then dissolve in luminous waves. So intense are they at times as to communicate a crimson tint to the snow, and clothe every object with an unnatural hue. The Northern Lights increase in number and intensity in September and March, as though there was an intimate connection between these phenomena and the changes of the equinoxes.

The animal tribes are in various ways affected

by these protracted winters. The bear and hedgehog remain in a state of hybernation; the ermine and the hare put on a robe of white; the beavers, living in communities, erect houses several stories in height, putting on the exterior coat after the frosts have set in, that it may freeze hard, and thus resist the attacks of their natural enemy, the wolverine. The fur-bearing animals are now in perfection, and in man they find their most remorseless foe.

Towards the end of April, the streams become released from their icy fetters. When the weather has become so far mollified, as it ordinarily does by the middle of March, to thaw at midday and freeze at night, the sap of the maple begins to flow, and then commences the sugar-harvest. This tree, as far north as the shores of Lake Superior, clothes most of the ridges, and the bird's-eye and curled varieties are the most abundant. By the beginning of May, when the sun's rays have acquired sufficient power to dissolve the snows, the trees start from their winter's sleep, and commence the process of foliation with an activity unknown in lower latitudes; the air is vocal with the hum of insects; the birds resume their accustomed haunts; and all nature seems roused from a lethargic sleep.

In June, the thermometer often rises to 90°, and the sun's rays have a scalding effect. In reference to the heat of these northern latitudes, Richardson, when on the Mackenzie River, entered on his journal that the irritability of the human frame is either greater, or the sun, notwithstanding its obliquity, acts more powerfully than near the Equator; for he had never felt its direct rays so oppressive within the tropics, as he experienced in these sub-Arctic regions. The luxury of bathing, even, is not without alloy; for if you choose the midday, you are assailed in the water by the *Tabani* (moose-flies), who draw blood in an instant with their formidable lancets; and if you select the morning or evening, clouds of mosquitoes, hovering around, fasten on the first part that emerges.* But these are not the only foes. The black fly on the high ridges is so abundant that the wood-chopper has to go masked; and on the sand-beeches, the midges, although nearly microscopic, inflict a sting that burns like the point of a glowing coal of fire. Thus, nothing can be more uncomfortable than summer life in a northern forest. The explorer is assailed by day and night, whether by the lake-shore or on the mountain-top, by myriads of insects thirsting for his blood, who seem to make up in activity for the brief period of their summer's existence.

The presence of so large a body of water as is contained in the Great Lakes, modifies the range

* "Arctic Journey."

of the thermometer, lessening the winter's cold and the summer's heat. Lapham has given a map, illustrating in an accurate manner the effects of this action, so far as relates to the State of Wisconsin.* In freezing, the water evolves a large amount of heat, and during the summer the winds are tempered in passing over its surface. When the unclouded sun sinks behind the western horizon, a cool breeze commences blowing toward the heated surface of the land; so that, however hot the day may have been, the night is rarely sultry. In the winter, the ice accumulates around the shores, drifting with the prevailing winds, and it is rare that the blue water is not seen beyond. When the thermometer suddenly drops below zero,—the air becoming far colder than the water,—vast columns of vapor roll up from the surface, like the steam from some great geyser; or, if a wind prevail, it is drifted like the smoke from a burning prairie. This scud, when driven inland, invests every tree and shrub with ice which, in the clear sunlight, flashes back the rays like so many surfaces of the purest crystal.

Climate of the Plains.—The climate of the Plains exhibits some peculiarities deserving of notice,—such as the purity of the air; the cloudless

* "Chicago Academy of Sciences," Vol. I.

skies during certain seasons, giving to the landscape such sharply-defined outlines; the dewless nights; the illusive phantoms of the mirage; and the feeling of vastness which impresses every beholder as he stands on some high swell, and in every direction, sees the surface stretched out like a hemisphere.

As in the distant north there is a mingling of spring and summer, so here the summer is protracted far into autumn. This is the most delightful season of the year, characterized by an absence of severe rain-storms, with a cool, bracing atmosphere, so gratifying to the physical system that man exults "in the intense consciousness" of his existence.

That delicious season known as "Indian summer" is often prolonged into December, when a calm, soft, hazy atmosphere fills the sky, through which, day after day, the sun, shorn of his beams, rises and sets like a globe of fire. This peculiarity is observed as far north as Lake Superior, but is more conspicuous and protracted in Kansas and Missouri, but does not extend south, into the lower latitudes of the United States.

Thus it will be seen that the Mississippi Valley possesses a great diversity of climate; and this is naturally to be inferred, when we consider that it extends through twenty degrees of latitude, and that its western rim, at many points, rises into the region of perpetual snow, so that the traveller may elect whether to breathe the pure and difficult air of the mountains, or the soft and balmy air wafted from the tropics.

TABLE OF TEMPERATURES IN THE UNITED STATES.

Compiled from Blodget's "Climatology."

STATIONS.	ALT. Feet.	SPRING °	SUMM'R °	AUT'MN °	WINTER °	YEAR °
Toronto, Canada,	341	41.1	64.8	46.6	24.5	44.3
Portland, Me.,	20	42.8	65.2	48.1	24.7	45.2
Portsmouth, N. H.,	20	43.2	64.4	49.0	26.6	45.8
Cambridge, Mass.,	71	44.3	68.6	50.1	26.2	47.3
Amherst, "	267	45.0	68.6	48.7	24.7	46.7
New York City	23	48.7	72.1	54.5	31.4	51.7
Albany, N. Y.,	130	46.7	70.0	50.0	26.0	48.2
Rochester, "	506	44.6	67.6	48.9	27.0	47.0
Philadelphia, Pa.,	60	50.6	71.0	52.1	32.6	51.6
Gettysburg, "	600?	50.0	71.6	51.1	30.1	50.7
Washington City,	78	54.2	73.1	53.9	33.9	53.8
Charleston, S. C.,	20	65.8	80.6	68.1	51.7	66.6
Pensacola, Fla.,	20	68.6	81.6	69.8	54.9	68.7
Vera Cruz, Mexico,	∞	78.0	81.5	78.7	71.9	77.5
Mobile, Ala.,	25	70.1	82.7	71.0	57.3	70.3
New Orleans, La.,	10	70.0	82.3	70.7	56.5	69.9
Galveston, Texas,	∞	71.0	82.5	70.2	53.8	69.4
Fort Towson, I. T.,	300?	62.4	79.1	61.3	43.9	61.7
St. Louis, Mo.,	450	54.1	76.2	55.4	32.3	54.5
Cincinnati, O.,	550	54.3	73.0	55.0	32.9	53.8
Hudson, "	1,131	49.1	70.2	48.4	28.8	49.1
Ann Arbor, Mich.,	700?	45.5	66.3	48.4	25.3	46.4
Fort Wilkins, Lake Superior,	627	38.5	60.8	43.0	21.8	40.1
Fort Brady, "	600	37.6	62.0	43.5	18.3	40.4
Milwaukee, Wis.,	591	42.3	67.3	50.1	26.0	46.4
Chicago, Ill.,	591	44.9	67.3	48.8	25.9	46.7
Fort Madison, Iowa,	550?	50.5	73.2	53.1	26.3	50.8
St. Paul's, Minn.,	820	45.6	70.6	49.5	16.1	44.6
Fort Scott, Kansas,	1,000?	54.8	74.9	55.3	33.0	54.5
Fort Leavenworth, "	896	53.8	74.1	53.7	29.6	52.8
Fort Riley, "	1,147	56.5	77.2	60.2	32.4	56.6
Fort Kearney, Neb.,	2,360	46.8	71.5	49.3	23.0	47.7
Fort Laramie, "	4,519	46.8	71.9	50.3	31.1	50.1
Great Salt Lake	4,351	51.7	75.9	....	32.1	...
Fort Benton, Upper Mo.,	2.663	49.9	72.8	44.5	25.4	48.2
Fort Union, Texas,	6.418	48.3	67.3	48.3	32.6	49.1
Santa Fé, New Mexico,	6,846	49.7	70.4	50.6	31.6	50.6
Fort Yuma, Col.,	120	72.1	90.0	75.7	56.8	73.6
San Francisco, Cal.,	50	57.0	60.1	60.1	51.5	57.2
Sacramento, "	50	59.2	72.8	61.3	46.3	59.9
Fort Miller, "	402	62.8	85.5	66.4	49.3	66.0
Dalles of Columbia	350	53.0	70.3	52.2	35.6	52.8
Astoria, Oregon,	50	51.1	61.6	53.7	42.4	52.2
Sitka, Alaska,	50	40.0	54.2	43.9	32.2	42.6

ANNUAL PRECIPITATION OF RAIN AT SEVERAL STATIONS IN THE UNITED STATES.

Compiled principally from Blodget's "Climatology."

STATIONS.	SPRING.	SUMMER.	AUTUMN.	WINTER.	YEAR.
Toronto, Canada,	7.16	9.57	10.33	4.29	31.35
Portland, Me.,	12.11	10.28	11.93	10.93	45.25
Portsmouth, N. H.,	9.03	9.21	8.95	8.38	35.57
Cambridge, Mass.,	10.85	11.17	12.57	9.89	44.48
Amherst, "	10.23	11.84	11.39	9.70	43.16
New York City	11.55	11.33	10.30	9.63	42.23
Albany, N. Y.,	9.79	12.31	10.27	8.30	40.67
Rochester, "	6.62	8.86	9.38	5.38	30.44
Philadelphia, Pa.,	10.97	12.45	10.07	10.06	43.56
Gettysburg, "	9.74	10.20	9.77	9.10	38.81
Pittsburg, "	9.38	9.87	8.23	7.48	34.96
Washington, D. C.,	10.45	10.52	10.16	11.07	41.20
Charleston, S. C.,	8.60	18.68	11.61	9.40	48.29
Vera Cruz, Mexico,	31.90	116.80	51.40	5.50	183.20
Pensacola, Flor.,	12.86	18.69	13.71	11.72	56.98
Mobile, Ala.,	14.24	18.00	13.91	18.27	64.42
New Orleans, La.,	11.29	17.28	9.62	12.71	50.90
Jackson, Miss.,	10.90	14.20	9.50	18.40	53.00
Fort Jessup, La.,	13.68	10.94	9.74	11.49	45.85
Fort Towson, I. T..	15.55	14.36	12.23	8.94	51.08
St. Louis, Mo.,	12.30	14.14	8.94	6.94	42.32
Cincinnati, O.,	12.14	13.70	9.90	11.15	46.89
Hudson, "	9.76	8.87	6.16	8.00	32.79
Ann Arbor, Mich.,	7.30	11.20	7.00	3.10	28.60
Mackinac, "	4.67	8.88	7.01	3.31	23.87
Fort Brady, "	5.44	9.97	10.76	5.18	31.35
Milwaukee, Wis.,	6.60	9.70	6.80	4.20	27.20
St. Paul, Minn.,	6.61	10.92	5.98	1.92	25.43
Fort Madison, Iowa,	15.30	15.90	14.50	4.70	50.50
Fort Scott, Kansas,	12.57	16.37	8.39	4.79	42.12
Fort Leavenworth, "	7.97	12.24	7.33	2.75	30.29
Fort Riley, "	7.91	7.15	5.58	1.26	21.90
Fort Kearney, Neb.,	10.80	12.05	3.82	1.31	27.98
Fort Laramie. "	8.69	5.70	3.96	1.63	19.98
Fort Union, Texas,	2.47	9.62	5.12	2.03	19.24
El Paso, New Mexico,	0.70	3.56	5.25	1.70	11.21
Santa Fé, "	2.83	8.90	6.02	2.08	19.83
Fort Yuma Cal.,	0.27	1.30	0.86	0.72	3.15
San Francisco, "	7.56	0.09	2.96	11.34	21.95
Sacramento, "	7.01	0.00	6.61	12.11	25.73
Fort Miller, "	9.57	0.02	2.80	9.79	22.18
Astoria, Oregon,	16.43	4.00	21.77	44.15	86.35
Steilacoom, Wash. Ter.,	11.19	3.85	15.83	22.62	53.49
Dalles of Columbia	2.63	0.42	3.78	6.98	13.81
Sitka, Alaska,	18.32	15.75	32.10	23.77	89.94

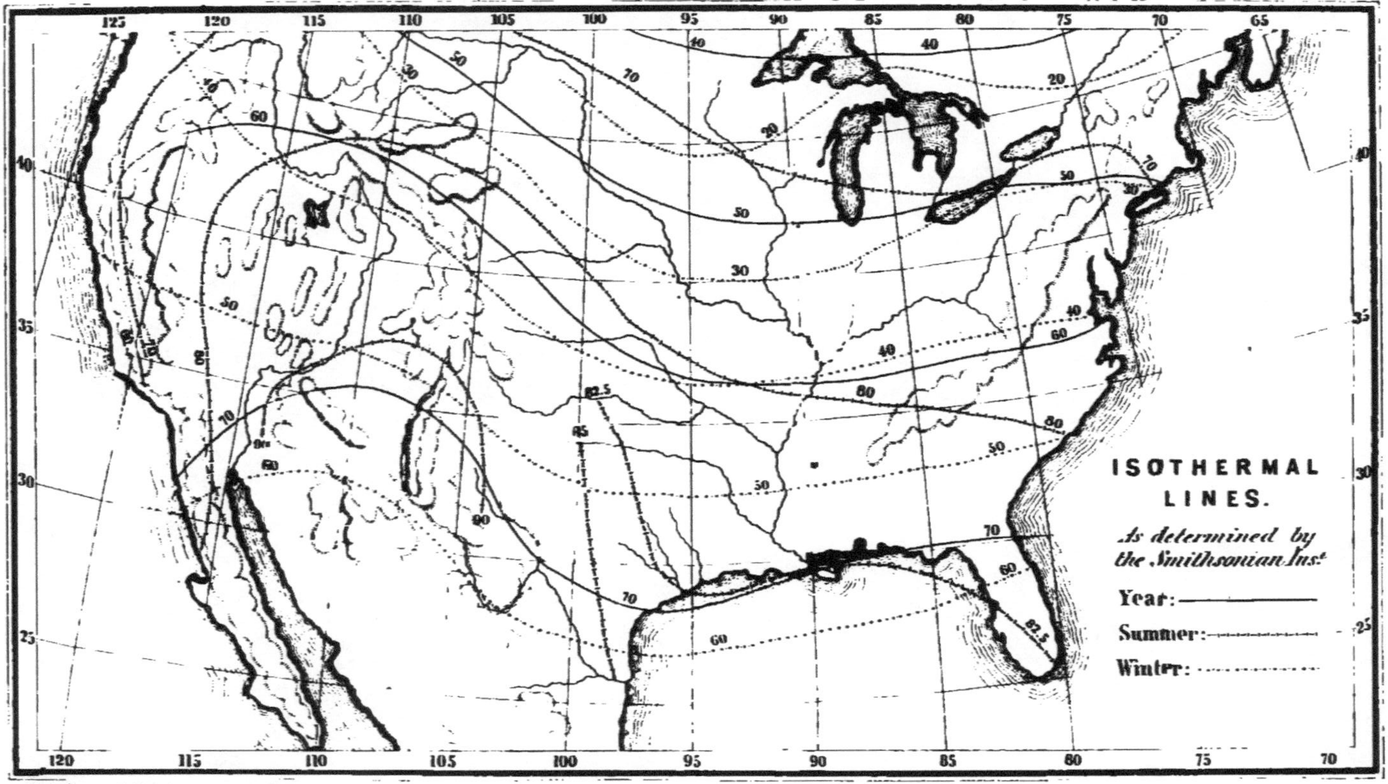

Plate II.

ISOTHERMAL
LINES.

*As determined by
the Smithsonian Inst.*

Year:
Summer:
Winter:

CHAPTER VII.

CULTIVATED PLANTS.

CONDITIONS OF CLIMATE AND SOIL, RESTRICTING THE RANGE OF PLANTS—OF THE SOIL IN REFERENCE TO THE GROWTH OF PARTICULAR PLANTS — MAIZE — WHEAT — OATS, RYE, AND BARLEY, NATIVES OF THE PLAINS OF CENTRAL ASIA— RICE — SUGAR-CANE — SORGHUM — POTATO — COTTON — TOBACCO—GRASSES FOR PASTURAGE—EXHAUSTION OF THE SOIL—FACILITIES FOR CULTIVATION—TABLES OF POPULATION AND PRODUCTION.

Conditions of Climate and Soil.—The range of plants is dependent on two causes:—climatic conditions, such as temperature and moisture, and the chemical and mechanical composition of the soil. We have pointed out the extreme range of temperature which is characteristic of the climate of the Great Valley, as compared with that of Western Europe; we now propose to inquire into the effect of this range upon the growth of food-producing plants.

The newly-arrived immigrant may be disposed to deprecate a climate so different from that to which he has been accustomed; but the experience of a single year will convince him that it is to this extreme range, during the growing season, that we owe the cultivation of many of the kindly fruits of the earth, and of many of the plants most useful to man. The tropical element in our summers enables the peach and apple to ripen, and the corn and tobacco-plant to mature, which they will not do in England, although the mean temperature of the year be considerably higher. Thus, the history of vegetation shows that a high temperature for a short season produces a different effect upon plants than a moderate temperature long continued.

With regard to the conditions of soil, it may be said that its character is largely influenced by the subjacent formation. The different classes of rocks have a physiognomy as distinct as the features of the different races of men. The granites rise up in dome-shaped masses, or as pinnacles; the metamorphic rocks stretch out in serrated ridges; the traps assume a precipitous or stair-like form; the volcanic cones are generally isolated; the limestones are often cliff-like; the sandstones exhibit rounded outlines, except where undermined by running streams; while the shales of the slightly-metamorphosed strata, and the detrital materials of the Drift, are spread out, forming extensive plains or savannas. Now as the soil results from the abrasion or decomposition of these rocks, mingled with organic matter, it is not surprising that it should exhibit great diversity, and partake of the character of the underlying rock, both in chemical composition and mechanical texture. We thus speak of a soil as argillaceous, calcareous, arenaceous, etc., as expressive of the source from which it has been derived. Each of these soils has its appropriate vegetable covering, and each contains certain elements adapted to the nourishment of peculiar plants. Its agricultural capacity is also undoubtedly influenced by the extreme state of subdivision in the particles, by which the rootlets of plants are enabled readily to appropriate such elements as are fitted for their growth. The cotton-plant shuns the sandy soil of the Tertiary, but thrives in the mellow loam of the Cretaceous; the sweet potato luxuriates in the dry, sandy plain, but shuns the damp clayey soil of the meadow; Indian corn grows best in the prairie-soils rich in nitrogen, with a period of sixty or ninety days of high temperature; while wheat flourishes best in a cooler climate and on a soil less fertile.

Many of the useful plants, too, have improved by being transported from their habitats to a different climate. Cotton is a plant which grows, in the tropics, with a perennial growth, where it has a tree-like, woody stem. Transplanted to a temperate climate, it becomes a delicate annual, with an herbaceous growth. Indian corn is of tropical origin, where it grows with a rank stock, and produces little seed. Perhaps none of the cerealia show so great a susceptibility to adapt themselves to a modified climate, as this plant; for every few degrees of latitude exhibits a different variety. The potato has a still more diversified range, and is characterized by a still greater number of varieties.

In the domestication of plants, then, as in that of animals, there is a strong tendency to run into varieties, resulting from altered conditions of temperature, soil, and moisture. The New World is indebted to the Old for many of the most useful and widely distributed plants, such as wheat, barley, rice, and coffee; and many of the most luscious fruits, such as oranges, lemons, peaches, and apples. The sugar-cane is probably indigenous to the West Indian Isles. On the other hand, the New World has contributed to the Old, potatoes, which form so important an article of food; Indian corn, perhaps the most valuable of the cereals; and tobacco, now consumed the world over. It is proposed to give a brief sketch of the principal plants cultivated for the use of man in the Great Valley, and to inquire how far their cultivation, in each instance, is restricted by the conditions of soil and climate.

Maize (Zea mays).—Of all crops, where the conditions of soil and climate are favorable, there is none, with perhaps the exception of rice, which affords so great an amount of nutriment in proportion to the labor bestowed, as this. The cheap food derived from this source was the origin of the ancient Peruvian civilization, which enabled the surplus labor to be expended upon those immense structures which excited the admiration of the Spanish conquerors and all subsequent observers. So, too, we can trace the ancient Egyptian civilization to the abundance of the date, and that of India to the ease with which rice was grown,—the chief food of most people living within the tropics. Maize is emphatically the great food-producing plant of the Great Valley; not so much, perhaps, as contributing directly to human sustenance, as in those modified forms of beef, pork, etc., which constitute the bulk of the animal food of the people of the temperate zone. In a congenial climate, it is rarely cut off by drought, or frost, or blight. It can be harvested at leisure, as it receives no injury from exposure, whether cut or uncut. A man and boy can tend forty acres, besides devoting a portion of their time to other crops, which, with good management, may be made to yield from sixty to eighty bushels to the acre. This would give all the way from 2,400 to 4,800 bushels of grain; and the yield would furnish rations to between 120 and 240 able-bodied men for an entire year. The estimate of the western farmer is that, in feeding swine, every ten bushels of corn produces one hundred pounds of pork.

The northern limit of corn-culture may be represented by the summer isotherm 65°, which would exclude a considerable portion of Maine, the region north of the immediate Valley of the St. Lawrence, the Azoic region of Lake Superior, the higher slopes of the Rocky Mountains, and the immediate coast of the Pacific. It attains its full perfection in the region between the isotherms 72° and 77°, which would include the central and southern portions of Ohio, Indiana, Illinois, and Iowa, nearly all of Kentucky, Tennessee, Missouri, and Kansas, and the great plains north and south between the Canadian and the sources of the Missouri; but limited on the west by a line running east of Fort Laramie and west of Fort Atkinson.

As to the conditions of moisture, it is probable that its limits would be restricted, except in the immediate valleys, to about longitude 100°. It is to the presence of the two elements,— a period of intense heat during the summer, and a virgin soil rich in nitrogen,— that the great geographical range of this plant in the United States is due; and to their absence in Western Europe, which has there rendered its cultivation unprofitable.

Wheat. — There are two principal varieties recognized: — *Triticum hibernicum*, or winter wheat; and *T. æstivum*, summer or spring wheat. The geographical range of these varieties is not coincident. Wheat requires a cooler climate and a less nitrogenized soil than corn, and has a wider geographical range. It is a reliable crop east of the Rocky Mountains, as far north as the Saskatchawan Valley, latitude 54°; and on the Pacific Slope as high as latitude 60°. Along the flanks of the Rocky Mountains, from British Columbia to the limits of Mexico, where sufficient moisture can be obtained from the melting snows, it arrives at a perfection and development of grain unknown to the region east of the Mississippi; and the Californian Coast, cooled by the breezes of the Pacific, seems to be well adapted to its growth, and produces an amount far beyond the wants of its inhabitants. The tropical element in our climate so favorable to the growth of Indian corn, is unfavorable to the perfection of wheat. Winter wheat is not successfully cultivated in the immediate Valley of the Mississippi above the parallel 40°, for the reason that the plant is not sufficiently protected during the cold season by a permanent body of snow, so as to exclude the direct action of the air. Even if there was not a deficiency of snow, the prairies are so wind-swept that it seldom lies to a great depth, and the young wheat is liable to be winter-killed. In the partly-wooded regions of Southern Indiana, Illinois, and Missouri, where there is a clay subsoil of considerable tenacity, winter wheat is successfully cultivated. It is sown as early as the middle of September, so that it may ripen in the spring, before the hot suns of July strike it. The harvest-time is late in May or early in June.

The great bulk of the wheat grown in the Mississippi Valley is the spring or summer variety. It requires to be sown as soon as the frost leaves the ground, which should be prepared for its reception the preceding autumn. The danger to which this crop is exposed, is the stimulating nature of the soil, producing a too rapid growth of the stalks, which causes the vesicles to burst, and at the same time prevents the ear from filling. Hence, the high rolling knolls are generally selected for its cultivation. The ingredient, lime, would consolidate the stock, and check the tendency to a rank growth. Hence, I infer that the conditions of soil for the cultivation of this plant are highly favorable in Eastern Kansas and the Cherokee country, provided the conditions of climate—hot summer suns — are obviated by early sowing; and the reports as to the results of wheat-culture in that region, confirm these views.

Minnesota, while not prolific in corn, is the best wheat-growing region in the Northwest; but, without exact knowledge, it is believed that in the region of Pembina and Assinaboin there is a belt of country, vast in extent, where this class of cerealia can be successfully cultivated. *

The finest specimens of wheat on exhibition in the Agricultural Bureau at Washington, are from New Mexico; and it would seem that the dry climate which there prevails during the ripening of the plant, develops the grain at the expense of the stalk. Dr. Le Conte speaks of the yield of the Sonora wheat in the Purgatoire Valley as being eighty bushels to the acre.

The irrigated region of Utah and Colorado pro-

---

* Col. Whittlesey, who, as a practical geologist, has had a large experience in the Northwest, furnishes the following testimony, in a note to Captain Mullan:

"In the fall of 1848, I was at Red Lake, in Northern Minnesota, when Mr. Ayres, a very intelligent missionary, came in from the British Settlements on the Red River. He brought some unbolted flour, from wheat grown on the banks of that river, at the Pembina Settlements. It was the sweetest and most nutritious flour I ever ate. He stated that the employes of the Hudson Bay Company had for a quarter of a century produced all the wheat needed; that it was a sure crop, the grain sound, and that it would yield forty bushels to the acre. The result of my examinations at that time, on our northern frontiers, was a conviction that the true wheat-growing region of the United States lies north of the St. Peter's River, and west of the Mississippi."

duces wheat of a far greater yield and of a far better quality than the most favored region of the prairie, the yield reaching sixty bushels to the acre. The Californian wheat, as we have before shown, is abundant in yield and excellent in quality.

The best conditions, then, are a cool and rather dry climate, and a clayey soil, not too rich in nitrogen, with the presence of lime.

Oats, Rye, and Barley.— These are hardier plants than wheat, and are successfully cultivated to the northern limits of the United States. Wheat, rye, and oats, are probably native to the dry plains of Central Asia, which as we have shown, partake in soil and climate of the character of the prairies, where they have been cultivated from the earliest historical period. Herodotus, the earliest of profane historians, describes the Scythian husbandmen as dwelling on the borders of the Black Sea, in the country extending on the south to Taurica (the Crimean Coast from Sevastopol to Kaffa); on the east to the Trench of the Blind Slaves (the mart of Palus Mærotis) called Cremni (the Cliffs); and in part to the River Tanais, now the Don.* Thus it will appear that, in the provinces of Kherson, Kiev, and Ekaterinoslav, in the fifth century B. C.,

---

* "Herodotus," Book IV., Ch. 16, 20.

the Scythians cultivated corn,* "not for their own use, but for sale." This trade was chiefly carried on with the Greeks, and gradually extended to the

---

* Corn is a generic term, comprehending the seeds of certain grasses which may be ground into meal, and fitted for the food of man or animals. In the United States, the term "corn" is restricted to maize or Indian corn.

"All bread corns are annual plants, and from that circumstance far better adapted for universal cultivation than if they had been perennials, or even biennials. An annual plant may indeed be said to belong to no country in particular, because it completes its existence during the summer months; and in every part of the world there is a summer. Hence, we find the same corns ripening their seeds within the Frigid and Torrid Zones; and though the quality of the grain of barley and wheat grown in Lapland is far inferior to that grown in the south of Spain or on the plains of India, yet it is still such as to be made into wholesome bread and invigorating fermented liquor. Had the bread corns been perennials, they must necessarily have required to live through the winter in every country in which they are grown, as well as through the summer; and such of them as might have been adapted to the winters of cold climates, when taken to warm climates, have been so far weakened by being kept in a growing state throughout the year, as in a few years to have ceased to exist; while the perennials of warm climates, such as the south of Spain and Italy, could not have lived through a single winter in Russia or Lapland. For the same reason that they are annuals, and require little more than to be sown and reaped, bread-corns are in an especial manner the domestic plants of man in an early stage of civilization. A people like the wandering Arabs, who live in tents, and change their encampments annually or oftener, may conveniently reap their crops, raise their tents, and carry their seed-corn about with them, till they find a suitable spot where they can pitch their tents, and take their next crop. This, however, could not be done by a people who, in addition to corn and pulse, depend for the food of themselves and cattle, on the production of roots, such as the turnip and the potato; and these accordingly are plants characteristic of a settled people, in a higher degree of civilization and a greatly-advanced state of agriculture. The capacity of any country for growing corn, may be said to be according to the flatness of its surface, provided it be neither too hot nor too cold. too wet nor too dry; and hence the immense plains of Russia and Tartary are eminently calculated for raising food for man." (Brande's Dictionary, Art. "Corn.")

east of the limits assigned by Herodotus; and between B. C. 400 and B. C. 300, the princes of the Bosphorus drew from the shores of the Sea of Azov and the Crimea, supplies to an enormous amount.

According to Strabo, Leucon, who reigned from A. C. 393 to B. C. 353, sent on one occasion 2,100,000 medimini (3,150,000 bushels) of corn to Athens, from the single port of Theodosia. Demosthenes states that, of the whole foreign importation of grain into Attica, almost one-half came from the Euxine; and estimates its amount in ordinary years at 400,000 medimini, or 600,000 bushels. ("Orat. in Leptin.") *

The fertility of the country and the habits of the people remain nearly the same as when Herodotus wrote. The trade of the Mediterranian ports with those of the Black Sea is nearly the same as was carried on twenty-three centuries ago; the Hylea still deserves the name of the "Woodland," and the multitudinous channels of the Dneiper still wind through the forests of oaks and poplars, seldom touched by the axe; while beyond, the Panticapes stretch out in treeless steppes, as in the days of old. The fertility of the soil is not renewed by a system of rotation of crops, or by the application of manures; but when it shows signs of exhaustion, it

* Rawlinson, Note to "Herodotus," B. IV., Ch. 17.

is suffered to lie fallow until it reimbibes those elements from the atmosphere which have been abstracted, or creates a fresh supply of humus by the decay of its own vegetation. These facts have a significant bearing upon the ultimate productiveness of our own prairies. They show that, while they may be deficient in the equably-distributed moisture essential to tree-growth, they possess superior advantages for the cultivation of the food-producing plants, and that these advantages remain constant.

The modes of transportation to the markets of Odessa and Kertch, are such as formerly prevailed in Illinois and other Western States. The carts, laden with grain, move in long lines, like an army train, and the oxen at night are unyoked and allowed to feed upon the open plain. In modern times, the exports of wheat from Odessa in some years have reached nearly 7,500,000 bushels; and it is a singular fact that, while the flour in the Mediterranean marts is esteemed above all others; in the English market, when British wheat commands 60s., wheat from this source only brings 52s. The route between Liverpool and Odessa is circuitous, and quite as much time is consumed in making it as in crossing the Atlantic. It is almost essential that the voyage be made in winter, as the summer heats are almost sure to damage the wheat.

The expense of importing a quarter is from 16s. to 18s. The price free on board at Odessa considerably exceeds 40s. per quarter. It is, therefore, evident that England can draw her supplies cheaper from other sources than this.*

Rice (*Oryza sativa*) is a plant of intertropical range, which heretofore has formed a large item in southern exports. It was introduced, according to McCulloch ("Com. Dictionary"), into the Carolinas from Madagascar, late in the seventeenth century; and the thorough adaptation of the soil and climate to its growth, is evidenced by the fact that the Carolina rice commands a higher price in the English market than that grown in the Indies. This cereal constitutes the principal food of the inhabitants of a warm climate. It is the most nutritive of all the cerealia, and contains about eighty-five per cent. of starch. As, in a cold climate, a highly-nitrogenized food is required to replace the waste of the tissues; so, in a hot climate, where that waste is less rapid, the system requires a food in which there is an excess of oxygen,—and rice and vegetables fill this requirement. The facility of irrigating the fields during the progress of its growth, seems to be all-important; and hence it is, in those Oriental countries where, by

---

* *Vide* "Encyclopædia Brittanica," Art. "Wheat."

chance, the annual flood of the rivers is withheld, the people are subject to deplorable famines.

On the delta of the Mississippi, between New Orleans and Fort Jackson, rice is grown in small plantations, and its culture is said to be not unhealthy, for the reason that the water is not allowed to stagnate. The river begins to swell in February, and does not subside until June. In its overflow, it deposits a layer of sediment on its banks, leaving the clear water to flow into the swamps of the interior, and to find other channels to the ocean. This process, continued for ages, has raised its banks above the level of the surrounding country.

Rice-culture is accomplished in this way: A sluice is cut through the river-bank, and the fields, being first enclosed in a levée, are flooded. The land is ploughed and sown in March, and as soon as the young plants appear, they are submerged in water, so regulated as to keep their heads just above the surface. When the grain has matured, the fields are laid dry, and the crop is gathered; and the yield is from thirty to sixty bushels to the acre.

These small plantations, before the Rebellion, were cultivated by white labor, and there is no reason why that culture may not be maintained. The rice-swamps along the Savannah River and the Carolina coasts were formerly cultivated by slave-labor, and so unhealthy were they, that they were regarded as the synonym of disease and death. The acclimated white man dreaded to be detained in the region over night, so sure and deadly were the effects of the miasmata,—effects clearly traceable to the stagnant water. The rice product in 1860, was in excess of 187,000,000 pounds, of which the Carolinas furnished the great bulk.

Sugar-Cane (Saccharum officanarum).—This is a tropical plant which has been domesticated on the verge of the Gulf Coast, and is so sensitive to frost that, if its juice becomes frozen, its saccharine matter will not crystallize into sugar. As it does not mature until October, and the frosts set in late in December, the whole labor of gathering, grinding, and boiling, is compressed within a space of sixty days, during which, under the system of compulsory labor which formerly prevailed, the strength and endurance of the slaves were tasked to the utmost. In Cuba, this plant is perennial; but in Louisiana, the crop is propagated by rattoons, one-third of which is renewed each year. The rattoons consist of stock-cuttings, eighteen inches long, which are planted at a shallow depth. Shoots spring up from every joint, which are cultivated like Indian corn. The plant grows to the height of twelve feet or more, but about three feet of the upper portion are too watery to pay for crushing and evaporating. Sugar-culture has not extended farther north than the mouth of the Red River. Since the Rebellion, some of the estates have passed into the hands of northern men, who find no difficulty in securing all the labor which they require. The annual product of sugar formerly exceeded 300,000 hogsheads of 1,000 pounds each, and 16,300,000 gallons of molasses.

Sorghum saccharatum.—The immense consumption of sugar in the United States has led our farmers to attempt the domestication of this plant, to supply at least a portion of that consumption; and while, perhaps, it has not succeeded as a sugar-producing plant, it has repaid for the cultivation, in yielding a much-prized syrup. The sorghum is a native of China, while the imphee is a native of South Africa. The cultivation of both varieties can be maintained up to the isotherm 67°. Like corn, it requires a loose, deep soil, and one rich in nitrogen. The dry autumns of the West are favorable to its culture, as the elaboration of the saccharine principle is more effectually accomplished under such conditions than where the plant receives an excess of moisture. The product in syrup in

1860, was in excess of 7,000,000 gallons,—grown, for the most part, in the Mississippi Valley.

The Potato (*Solanium tuberosum*).— The germ of this most useful of all vegetables was first found on the flanks of the Andes, some 4,000 feet above the sea-level; and it is the most valuable contribution which America has made to the food-producing plants of the world. Its culture has extended to all the temperate climates; it forms the principal part of the food of many nations; and every table,— whether spread in the palaces of kings, or the cottages of the poor,— is incomplete without the presence of this esculent. It has even a wider geographical range than wheat; and, like that cereal, it has a tendency to run into varieties. It is cultivated in Bermuda, and as far north as Iceland. The short summers of Lake Superior, and even of Hudson's Bay, give to it a perfection which it does not acquire in the mild latitude of St. Louis or Southern Illinois. The potato degenerates rapidly in a warm climate; and if the tubers are allowed to remain in the ground, they undergo a second germination, which is at the expense of their size and nutritive properties. Hence it is, that those regions lying south of the parallel 40°, derive their supplies for winter use from colder climates, while the stock in Bermuda is kept up by transmitting annually northern varieties, and cultivating them only during the winter season.

Cotton (*Gossypium herbaceum*).—The upland varieties have been cultivated nearly as far north as latitude 40°, but only under favorable circumstances. Cotton-patches are to be seen in Southern Illinois and Southern Missouri, where the plant is grown for domestic use; and in many a family the hand-loom is yet in vogue.

As a great commercial staple, however, its culture embraces a belt of country 100 miles or more in width—underlaid by the Cretaceous formation—which starts near the northern line of the State of Mississippi, and, sweeping round the base of the Alleghanies through Alabama, Georgia, South Carolina, and North Carolina, extends as far north as Raleigh and even Richmond, Virginia. The southern limit of this belt is where it comes in contact with the region of Pine Barrens, whose soil consists of Pliocine-Tertiary sands. Its culture extends up the Mississippi to Memphis, and up the lower valleys of the White, Arkansas, and Red Rivers.

The cotton-soils are of moderate fertility, and when stripped of timber, are exceedingly liable to wash into gullies and ravines. After a few croppings, they are very difficult to renovate, since they do not admit of a rotation of crops. The climate is unfit for the growth of the nutritious grasses, and hence, where the ground lies fallow for a few years to recover its productive powers, it ceases to be profitable. The grasses which spring up are coarse, and afford little nutriment to cattle. The forage of the planter is derived from corn-stalks, cut before maturity; and hence, throughout the region, we find no herds of cattle or swine, nor can any course of industry render stock-raising profitable. Formerly the shipments of breadstuffs and provisions from the North into this region were enormous,— sufficient almost to sustain the entire population. This interchange of products was found to be profitable to both sections, the labor of each being applied to the cultivation of those plants requiring a peculiar soil and climate for their full development. The Rebellion operated as an effectual bar to all interchange; and since the restoration, the South, owing to her disorganized industry, rendered more deplorable by successive failures of crops, has not established to the full extent, those ties of commercial intercourse which formerly prevailed; and, in the absence of credit, has been forced to devote a portion of her labor, under disadvantageous circumstances, to the cultivation of those crops which are absolutely essential to the support of human life. Let us hope that this state of affairs is not long to continue.

The sea-island variety is restricted to the islands and a narrow belt on the immediate coast of the Atlantic, extending from the Great Pedee River, in North Carolina, to Cape Canaverel, in Florida. It has a length and strength of fibre unequaled, and is therefore well adapted to thread or spool-cotton. These qualities give it a commercial value five or six times greater than that of ordinary upland cotton.

So far as relates to the sanitary conditions of soil and climate, there is nothing to prevent the cultivation of this plant by free labor; but it is doubtful whether this crop will recover the commercial importance which it enjoyed before the outbreak the Rebellion; since the effect of that act was to divert European capital, which was formerly employed in moving this crop, to opening new sources of supply, and abstracting a portion of Oriental labor from its accustomed channels. The product of cotton in 1860, was in excess of 5,000,000 bales, and showed an increase of more than 100 per cent. in ten years.

It is only within the last century, that cotton-manufacture became so important a branch of national industry; and this importance is due to the inventions and discoveries of a few men in the

United States and Great Britain. Owing to the difficulty of separating the fibre from the seed by hand, the labor was great, and the price was so high, that cotton would never have come into general use; but this difficulty was obviated by Whitney, in the invention of the cotton-gin. The invention of the jenny, by Hargreaves, enabled one person to spin one hundred and twenty threads, in the same time that a single thread could be spun by the methods before in use; and the subsequent inventions of the spinning-frame by Arkwright, and of the power-loom by Cartwright, may be regarded as among the greatest achievements of inventive genius, which have conferred the most lasting blessings on the race, giving employment to many millions of people, affording cheap clothing to all, and forming a principal item in the commerce and industry of more than one nation.

Tobacco (Nicotiania tabacum).—This plant is indigenous to America, and to Sir Francis Drake and Sir Walter Raleigh is ascribed the honor of having first introduced it into England, more than three centuries ago. Perhaps there is no habit which has taken so strong a hold upon mankind, as the use of this weed, nor one which, when acquired, is so difficult to eradicate. It is smoked "from Indus to the Pole," alike by civilized and savage races, and by men in every walk of life. Its culture, too, has extended from America to every part of the civilized world, where the conditions of soil and climate are favorable to its growth. It was in universal use among the Indians when this country was first known to the European; and from the pipes found in the mounds, it is evident that that mysterious race who built them, knew its virtues,— or rather, perhaps, its vices.

Tobacco requires a warm, light, silicious soil to develop its peculiar aroma in all of its perfection. Where grown on an argillaceous soil, or one rich in organic matter, the leaf is rankly developed, and is lacking in the finer qualities. Tobacco-culture is carried on as far north as the Connecticut Valley, and south to the tropics; but here it becomes necessary to cultivate it only during the winter, as the summer heats and rains are unfavorable to its profection. The States of Missouri, Illinois, Kentucky, Indiana, and Ohio, are far better adapted to its culture than those bordering on the Gulf. Of the entire product of the United States, in 1860,—a little more than four and one-fourth million pounds,— these five States furnished about two hundred and seventy-three and one-half millions.

Grasses for Pasturage.—The natural grasses of the prairies east of the Mississippi, do not put forth their leaves until May, and they wither in August. The treading and cropping of the turf by cattle, cause them at first to become thin, and then die out. They are supplanted by white clover which in turn is rooted out by the Kentucky blue-grass (*Poa compressa*). The latter is destined to become the most valuable grass of the prairies. It bears the heat of the summers, and affords a rich pasturage in the winters. A rapid change is going on in the cultivated prairie. The native grasses are retreating before the cultivated grasses, as the Red man retreats before the White man. Wherever a wagon-track is made or a path beaten, the white clover comes in; wherever a tract is appropriated to pasturage, the blue-grass becomes dominant.

The English grasses, as a general thing, do not flourish, for they are adapted to a moist and cool climate. Timothy, however, once rooted, maintains its ground, and remains green from May to December. The yield in hay is not as great as in the meadows of New England.

West of the Mississippi, agriculture is too new to have solved the question of what grasses are best for cultivation. The Western Plains, as we have before remarked, contain several species of bunch-grass, which are highly nutritious, grow in an arid climate, and are self-curing. Frémont remarks that:

"The grazing capabilities of this region are great, and in the indigenous grasses an element of individual and national wealth may be found. In fact, the valuable grasses begin within one hundred and fifty miles of the Missouri frontier, and extend to the Pacific Ocean. East of the Rocky Mountains, it is the short, curly grass on which the buffalo delight to feed (whence its name of *buffalo grass*), and which is still good when dry and apparently dead. West of the mountains, it is a larger growth, in clusters, and hence called *bunch grass*. This has a second or fall growth. Plains and mountains both exhibit them, and I have seen good pasturage at an elevation of ten thousand feet. It is upon this spontaneous product, the trading or traveling caravans can find subsistence for their animals; and in military operations, any number of cavalry may be moved, and any number of cattle may be driven; and thus men and horses supported on long expeditions, and even in the winter, in the sheltered situations." *

Governor Bross, who has traversed the western region extensively, in a late communication to the Chicago Academy of Natural Sciences, described the agricultural capacities of Colorado as being very great, and so rapidly developing that the people would soon be independent of supplies from the

---

* "Report of Exploring Expedition."

NOTE.—" Captain Croft, U. S. A., recognizes four principal varieties of grasses in Arizona: 1. Lowland Grama (*Pleuraphis jamesii*), which grows in great profusion in the Valley of the Gila. 2. Highland Grama (*Aristida purpurea*), growing on the sandy 'mesas.' 3. Black Grama (*Muhlenbergia pungens*), growing on the highlands, in sandy, arid soil. 4. *Sporobolus airoides*, growing in the valleys. ("Proc. Cal. Acad. of Natural Science," 1865.)

Mississippi Valley, and even compete in the provision-market of the world. He described the cattle as superb in form, and clean in limb; and anticipated the time when herds would be driven eastward, moving afoot by easy stages, and grazing on the rich grasses of the prairies, until they were brought within the lines of railroad transportation. There is no doubt that, while much of the region between the Missouri and the base of the Mountains, is not adapted to agriculture, it will afford an almost unlimited range of pasturage.

Exhaustion of the Soil.—Rich as are the prairie-soils in organic matter, they are treated as though inexhaustible. The products, so far as relate to corn and wheat, are for the most part exported to distant regions, where, after entering into the animal economy, they recombine, and contribute to fertilize the soil. Even the exuviæ of the cattle and the straw of the grain, are allowed to accumulate in heaps, and rot on the ground, without any attempt on the part of the farmer to restore them to the sources from which they have been derived. Thus, each year the farmers of the Northwest are sending off millions of tons of organic matter, in a highly concentrated form, — impoverishing their own fields to enrich those of distant regions. Such a drain upon the fertility of the soil, though apparently imperceptible now, will ultimately manifest itself in diminished production, and will involve the necessity of adding organic matter to the soil, or of allowing it to remain fallow until it shall have reimbibed, from the decay of its own vegetation, or from the elements of the circumambient air, those principles which have been abstracted.

Nature, under almost every condition of soil and climate, exhibits a self-perpetuating power whereby to renew the youth and fertility of our planet. In the absorption of the gasses, whether arising from the decay of vegetation, or the volume of smoke poured out from the multitudinous chimneys of densely-populous cities — which, under other circumstances, would prove destructive to life, — and in their conversion into ligneous fibre or into food-producing seeds, she evinces a providence which ought to be appreciated by every one who, with an inquiring spirit, investigates her laws.

If man, therefore, like an honest debtor, will only restore what he abstracts, over and above the requirements of self-support, he will find that she is not an all-remorseless creditor, but a kind and beneficent parent.

Facilities for Cultivation.—Perhaps there is no region of the world where the facilities for cul-vation, and for the conversion of the natural surface into productive fields, are so great as on the western prairies; and hence their rapid development in agricultural resources. To subdue a primeval forest and render the ground fit for cultivation, is a Herculean task; and it requires the lapse of a generation before the fields, by a removal of the stumps and trunks, become entirely fit for the plough. Intercommunication is confined to highways cut out at rare intervals; trees are felled or girdled, and abandoned to fire or spontaneous decay. Hence, the settlement of a wooded country has been attended with an immense destruction of the forest, without having subserved any useful purpose. While it has required nearly two and one-half centuries to subdue and bring under cultivation the Atlantic Slope of the United States, a greater area in the Upper Valley of the Mississippi has been subdued, producing ampler supplies of human food, and sustaining a larger population, within the memory of men yet living.

This wonderful change has been wrought out by the inventive genius of an illiterate Northumbrian coal-miner, George Stephenson. When he conceived and brought out the locomotive known as the "Rocket,"—one among the few inventions that ever originated complete in all its parts, from the brain of the inventor,—he conferred an inestimable boon upon mankind, before which the labors of the most successful statesmen, or the achievements of the most renowned warriors, stand dwarfed. So far as relates to our own country, he placed in our hands a power by which to subdue a continent and revolutionize the trade of the world. Up to the time of the introduction of railways, the prairies repelled settlement. The difficulty of procuring materials for construction, such as wood and stone, restricted the immigrant to the borders of some timbered belt, while the prairie spread out before him, an almost illimitable waste. When the lines of improved communication had crossed the Alleghanies, it was found that the prairies were the appropriate field for the development of the railroad system. Their topographical features were such that almost air-lines could be constructed between given points, and at an expense which bore no proportion to that through the wooded or mountainous regions of the Atlantic Slope. Settlement followed along these lines, and as fast as villages sprang up at the stations, a rural population also sprang up to sustain them. It was found, too, that, with the great forest-belts at the north, adjacent to the shores of the Lakes and lining the tributaries of the Upper Mississippi, Nature had dealt kindly with man in spreading out these vast, grassy plains, — more so, even, than if she had robed them with forests; for it was far easier for the settler to draw his supplies of lumber from this source to fence his farm already prepared for the plough, than to doom the forests to indiscriminate destruction, as had been done in Ohio and Western New York, preliminary to cultivation.

No where on the continent is a farm so easily subdued, and no where are the processes of agriculture performed with so slight an expenditure of human strength. The spade and the hoe are seldom resorted to, and the furrow is formed by the plough. Planting, sowing, reaping, raking, binding, threshing, shelling,—all are mainly done by machinery;—processes which in many regions are impracticable by reason of the inequality of the soil, the presence of stumps, rocks, and other impediments.

The older States of the Mississippi Valley are now intersected by a net-work of railways. Their effects are seen in a rapid development of the agritural capabilities of the regions they traverse; in an enormous increase of internal commerce; in an active intercourse between widely-separated points; in the spread of civilization; and in the mingling of discordant characters, arising from local prejudices or ancestral traditions, into a harmonious whole.

The appended tables, compiled from the Census Returns of the United States, exhibit the progress of population, as well as of agriculture, in the States of the Upper Mississippi Valley, showing an increase,—unparalleled in other portions of the earth,—of two-fold, during each decade of ten years. Comparing the whole superficies of these States, 525,301 square miles, with the area cultivated, it will be seen that only about 18 per cent. has been devoted to agriculture.

The product of cereals in the eight food-producing States for the year 1859, based on a crop which was nearly one-third deficient, exceeded 550,000,000 bushels.

To convey an adequate idea of the motive power required to distribute this prodigious mass, in its crude state, it may be stated that it would employ more than 64,400 locomotives, each hauling 8,500 bushels; and, if required to deposit their freight at a given depot, a train must arrive oftener than once in seven minutes, by day and by night, throughout every working day of the year.

After feeding the existing population of those States, there remained a surplus of more than 500,000,000 of bushels, to be used as seed for future crops, as food for the domestic animals, and for exportation, either in a crude state, or in a concentrated form, as beef, pork, lard, oil, whisky, etc.

The amount of cereals which, in 1862, flowed out of the lake-region to the seaboard, was in excess of 136,000,000 bushels; since which time it has greatly augmented.

TABLE, SHOWING THE INCREASE OF POPULATION AND OF THE NUMBER OF ACRES OF IMPROVED LAND IN THE STATES NORTHWEST OF THE OHIO RIVER AND THE UPPER MISSISSIPPI BASIN, FROM 1800 TO 1860.

STATES.	1800. POPULATION.	1800. IMPROVED LAND.	1810. POPULATION.	1810. IMPROVED LAND.	1820. POPULATION.	1820. IMPROVED LAND.	1830. POPULATION.	1830. IMPROVED LAND.	1840. POPULATION.	1840. IMPROVED LAND.	1850. POPULATION.	1850. IMPROVED LAND.	1860. POPULATION.	1860. IMPROVED LAND.
Ohio	45,365	225,675	230,760	225,675	581,295	2,892,456	937,903	4,665,000	1,519,467	7,558,750	1,980,329	9,851,493	2,339,502	12,665,587
Michigan	....	....	4,762	....	8,765	....	31,639	....	212,267	....	397,654	1,929,110	749,861	3,419,861
Indiana	4,875	24,890	24,520	125,530	147,178	751,445	343,031	1,751,409	685,866	3,485,179	988,416	5,046,543	1,350,428	8,161,717
Illinois	....	....	12,282	72,692	55,162	325,272	157,445	931,860	476,183	2,818,373	851,470	5,039,545	1,711,951	13,251,473
Missouri	....	....	20,845	89,805	66,557	286,870	140,455	605,117	383,702	1,653,001	682,044	2,938,425	1,182,012	6,246,871
Iowa	....	....	....	....	....	....	....	....	43,112	184,059	192,214	824,682	674,948	3,780,253
Wisconsin	....	....	....	....	....	....	....	....	30,945	105,930	305,391	1,045,499	775,881	3,746,036
Minnesota	....	....	....	....	....	....	....	....	....	....	6,077	5,035	173,855	554,397
Kansas	....	....	....	....	....	....	....	....	....	....	....	....	107,206	372,855
Totals	50,240	250,565	293,169	513,702	858,957	4,256,043	1,610,473	7,953,386	3,350,542	15,806,752	5,403,595	26,680,332	9,064,896	52,199,050

240

STATEMENT, SHOWING THE INCREASE IN SOME OF THE PRODUCTS OF AGRICULTURE IN THE EIGHT GRAIN-GROWING STATES, FOR TEN YEARS, ENDING IN 1860.

STATES.	WHEAT—Bushels.		CORN—Bushels.		OATS—Bushels.		RYE—Bushels.		SWINE—Head.		CATTLE—Head.	
	1850.	1860.	1850.	1860.	1850.	1860.	1850.	1860.	1850.	1860.	1850.	1860.
Ohio.........	14,487,351	14,532,570	59,078,695	70,637,140	13,472,742	15,479,133	425,918	556,146	1,964,770	2,175,623	1,358,947	1,657,820
Indiana.......	6,214,458	15,219,120	52,964,363	69,641,591	5,655,014	5,028,755	78,792	400,326	2,263,776	2,468,528	714,666	1,170,005
Illinois.......	9,414,575	24,159,500	57,646,984	115,296,779	10,087,241	15,336,072	83,364	961,322	1,915,997	2,270,722	912,036	1,505,581
Michigan.....	4,925,889	8,313,185	5,641,420	12,154,110	2,866,056	4,073,098	105,871	497,197	205,847	374,664	274,497	534,267
Wisconsin.....	4,286,131	15,812,625	1,988,979	7,565,290	3,414,672	11,059,270	81,253	888,534	159,276	333,957	183,433	512,866
Minnesota....	1,401	2,195,812	16,725	2,687,570	30,552	2,202,050	125	124,359	734	101,252	2,002	119,003
Iowa..........	1,530,581	8,433,295	8,656,799	41,116,994	1,524,345	5,879,653	19,916	176,055	323,247	921,161	136,621	536,254
Missouri......	2,981,652	4,227,586	36,214,537	72,892,157	5,278,079	3,680,870	44,268	293,262	1,702,625	2,354,425	791,510	1,168,684
Totals.......	43,842,038	93,293,693	222,208,502	392,289,631	42,328,731	62,738,901	739,597	3,997,201	8,536,182	11,039,332	4,373,712	7,204,810

CHAPTER VIII.

GEOLOGY — IGNEOUS AND METAMORPHIC ROCKS.

GEOLOGICAL STRUCTURE OF THE MISSISSIPPI VALLEY — TABULAR VIEW OF THE DIFFERENT FORMATIONS — RANGE OF ORGANIC LIFE — IGNEOUS ROCKS OF DIFFERENT AGE — SYSTEMS OF ELEVATION OF MOUNTAIN-CHAINS — THE LAKE SUPERIOR SYSTEM — THE PRIMEVAL CONTINENT — THE APPALACHIAN SYSTEM — THE ROCKY MOUNTAIN SYSTEM — THE PACIFIC COAST RANGES — IGNEOUS PRODUCTS — RIVER SYSTEMS — THE AZOIC SYSTEM, ASSOCIATED WITH IRON ORES — IRON-REGION OF LAKE SUPERIOR — OF MISSOURI — THE MYTHOLOGICAL AGE OF METALS — THE PRESENT, THE IRON AGE — ANNUAL PRODUCT OF THE WORLD.

Geological Structure.—If, from an elevated position, an observer were enabled to comprehend in a bird's-eye view the entire structure of the Mississippi Valley, he would find that it was rimmed on three sides by granitic or highly metamorphic rocks; and that these rocks, while affording abundant evidences of having originated from the action of direct or transmitted heat, have at many points been invaded by products of a purely volcanic origin. He would further find that the basin had been filled in with rocks of a far different character, reposing for the most part in nearly horizontal strata, and little metamorphosed by heat,—such as limestones, sandstones, shales, and loose, detrital materials, the whole forming an assemblage many thousand feet in thickness. Descending from his elevated position, and examining the individual groups critically, he would find that, while the granitic, the metamorphic, and volcanic rocks afforded no traces of organic life, the sedimentary rocks were stored with numerous forms as delicate or massive in structure, as any that now tenant the earth or sea. He would further find that they differed not only from existing forms, but among themselves, and that there was a corresponding order of succession in the strata wherein they had been entombed; and from the constancy of this order, he would be justified in inferring that they appeared upon the earth at different intervals, and that those intervals comprehended long periods of time. Now, as this order is never reversed, these fossils have come to be regarded as land-marks in the physical history of our planet,—as so many "medals, struck by nature to commemorate her revolutions." Extending his researches to vegetable forms, he finds that the same diversity and the same order of succession prevail.

Directing his attention to those substances useful to man, he finds stored in the granitic, volcanic, and metamorphic rocks, the precious metals — gold and silver, — and the baser metals — copper, tin, zinc, mercury, lead, iron, etc., — sometimes segregated in veins, and at others in beds or sheets, incorporated with the strata.

In the limestones, sandstones, and shales, which show slight signs of igneous action, while he notes the absence of the precious metals, he finds the more useful ores, such as iron, lead, and zinc. In addition to these, he finds at various intervals, and stretching over vast areas, immense deposits of fossil fuel, stored away at accessible depths, and in positions protected from combustion and decay, to supply the wants and conveniences of man throughout all time.

When he examines the superficial materials, he finds that they repose on rocks which have been grooved and striated, and the removed parts ground up into an almost impalpable powder; but when he reflects that this impalpable powder forms the soil which supports the infinite variety of vegetation that clothes the earth and constitutes the food, directly or indirectly, of every living form that moves upon its surface or sports in its waters, and how slow would have been its accumulation if left to mere atmospheric changes, he is led to the irresistible conclusion that these are the results of a manifest design.

To investigate the structure of the globe, and the revolutions which its surface has undergone; to trace the succession of animal and vegetable life; to determine the conditions under which the precious metals and the useful ores are found; and to bring forth from hidden depths those materials which minister to the conveniences of man, is the province of geology.

Geologists, then, guided by the succession of organic remains and the superposition of the strata, have become satisfied that the earth did not come from the hands of the Creator as we now behold it; but that it acquired its present configuration after repeated revolutions, embracing the lapse of long periods of time, during which distinct races of living organisms were introduced, flourished, and died, and their remains became entombed in the rocks; from many of which we build our temples and dwellings, and out of which even we carve our monuments,— thus using the sepulchres of extinct races to perpetuate the remembrance of our own. The very dust we tread upon was once instinct with life.

The following classification may be adopted as embracing the most conspicuous groups of rocks in the Great Valley:

TABULAR VIEW

OF THE

PRINCIPAL FOSSILIFEROUS STRATA of the MISSISSIPPI VALLEY AND PACIFIC SLOPE.

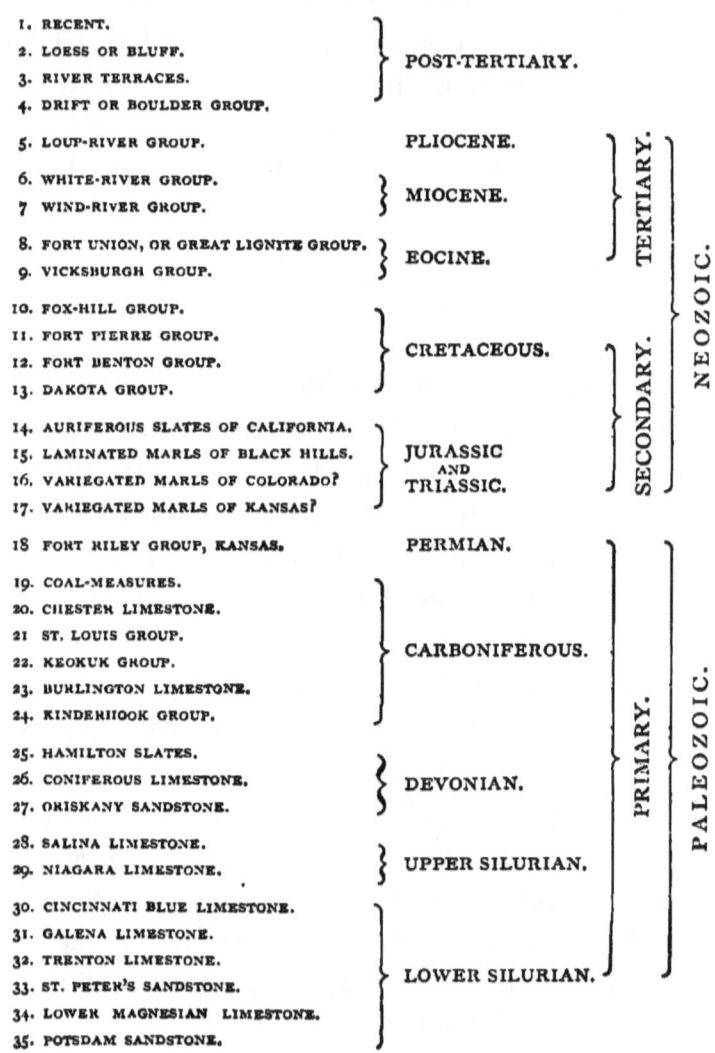

While each of these groups has its characteristic fossils, by which it can be identified over widely-separated areas, yet there are two inferences, erroneous in their results, which the geological student might draw without further examination.

1. He must not infer that these groups envelope a considerable part of the earth like the coats of an onion, for at no point do they present an unbroken succession of comforming strata. There exist gaps, indicating that while aqueous causes were active in one region in accumulating strata, they were dormant at another; but this fact is unquestioned,—the order of succession is never reversed.

And 2. That while the age of a group is determined by the assemblage of fossils, they are not in all instances restricted to a particular zone of life, but certain specific forms are found to range through several distinct formations. In such cases, they generally appear as varieties; as though the surrounding conditions had so far changed as to produce variations in their form and character.* While the extremes differ in

---

* Take, for instance, that subdivision of the Mollusks known as Brachiopods (animals with *arm-like feet*), which comprehends the four genera: *Rhychonella, Crania, Discina, and Lingula.* Davidson, the most eminent of English palæontologists, after an exhaustive investigation of the Brachiopods of the British Isles, finds that all of

these particulars, there is a series of gradations, the result of altered conditions of habitat, which link them together.

As it is not my purpose to refer, except incidentally, to the fossil fauna which characterize the several groups of strata, I will simply remark that, in the order of creation, there appears to have been a progressive development, from the simplest organic structures in the oldest formations, to the highest type of being represented in the latest creation,—man. According to the existing knowledge, the Vertebrates, represented by the fishes, first appear in the Upper Silurian; the Reptiles in the Sub-carboniferous (the *Sauropus*

---

these genera appear in the Silurian, and are continued through all the subsequent formations up to the present time, persistent in form and character; while other genera have a less diversified range, and exhibit wide deviations from the primitive type. Thus the common fossil, *Atrypa unguicularis*, appears in the Devonian, is continued in the Carboniferous, where it is known as *Spirifer urii*, and is still continued in the Permian, where it is known as *S. clannyanus*. Whether what are known as species are independent creations, and so long as they continue to exist, preserve a fixedness of character; or whether they are capable of varying indefinitely from an original type, dependent on altered conditions of climate, food, etc., are questions upon which naturalists are divided. In the breeding of domesticated animals, we certainly see a strong tendency to run into varieties; on the other hand, we find certain living species of Mollusks which are identical with the fossil forms entombed in the Tertiaries; thus showing that these forms must have remained constant through millions of years. But in reply to this objection, the believer in the transmutation of species might say that the physical conditions, such as the temperature and saltness of the water, depth of the ocean, etc., had remained constant, and that, therefore, we had no right to expect a deviation from pristine types.

primævus of Lee); the Mammalia, represented by a marsupial or pouched animal, like the opossum of America, in the Upper Oolite; and some small quadrupeds not clearly made out, in the Upper Trias; traces of birds are detected in the Upper Oolite (*Archæopteryx macrurus*), in the lithographic limestone near Solenhofen, Bavaria; and last, the evidences of man occur in the Post-Pliocine, if not in the Pliocine itself.

Igneous Rocks.—When we examine the igneous rocks of this region, we find that, like the fossiliferous strata, they are not all of the same age. For instance, if, as on the shores of Lake Superior, we find the Potsdam sandstone abutting against a great boss of granite, with all of its projections worn off,—like rocks at the present day on the sea-shore exposed to the action of a heavy surf,—while the sandstone reposes in horizontal beds, and shows few signs of metamorphism, we infer, and justly too, that the granite was upheaved and assumed its present relative position before the deposition of the sandstone.

If, on the other hand, we go to the Rocky Mountains, and observe granite in the form of domes or crests, constituting mountain masses, flanked by Triassic strata reclining at a high angle; and if we find that, where such contact takes place, sandstone is metamorphosed into quartz, shale into gneiss, and limestone into marble, we infer that the granite has been protruded through the yielding strata, and that this change in the sedimentary rocks, is due to the action of direct or transmitted heat. As this is the usual form in which granite appears, and never in the form of a lava-overflow, it is inferred that it is not a volcanic product, but that it was elevated in a pasty condition, and under circumstances which permitted it to assume a crystalline form.

We also observe another class of rocks, occupying narrow apertures in the pre-existing strata in the form of dykes, or diffused over the surface, sometimes in aspect compact and close-grained, at others glassy or scoriaceous. These rocks intermingle with the fossiliferous strata of all ages, and resemble so much the product of modern volcanoes that geologists have not hesitated to ascribe their origin to this source.

Systems of Elevation. — It has been found, too, that the structural features of the earth — the outlines of continents and the shore-lines of the ocean — have been mainly determined by the upheaval of these crystalline rocks. These again have influenced the destinies of the human race, in the migrations of men, in the distribution of languages, and in the modification of climate. Hence, then, the study of mountain chains, their range and extent, is one of absorbing interest. They form the grandest and most imperishable record of the great cycle of events through which the earth has passed.

It has been found, too, as first observed by Steensen, and subsequently elaborated in the comprehensive work of Elie de Beaumont, that the great lines of fracture and uplift, instead of being fortuitous, pursue certain determinate lines of direction, conforming to the great circle of the earth; and that, instead of a single line of fracture and uplift, there are parallel lines which appear to have been formed simultaneously over vast areas of the earth's surface. Mountain chains of different ages intersect one another at different angles; and thus, while to the superficial observer, such an assemblage as the Rocky Mountains, the Alps, the Himalayas, or the Caucasus, may appear as a confused and discordant mass, yet by patient study of the strata which repose on their flanks, the geologist may determine the several systems of upheaval, and evoke order out of apparent confusion.

While the outlines, then, of continents have been determined by mountain chains, the result of paroxysmal action, the area of continents has been determined in many instances by the gradual oscillations of the crust, such as are now taking place over the northern portion of the hemisphere. That these oscillations have been going on during the whole progress of the earth's history admits of no doubt; for, *e. g.*, in the strata of the Coal-Measures, and of the Cretaceous, we meet with repeated alternations of marine and terrestrial life; and in the Tertiaries, we see that fresh and salt-water have alternately held dominion over the surface. The Drift-terraces and ancient sea-beaches, high above the present water-level, point to the same conclusion. The earth, therefore, to the geologist, is not an emblem of stability. He sees, in the displacement and plication of the strata, that its foundations have been repeatedly broken up, and that its crust is but an oscillating mass.

It is customary to speak of the *elevation* of mountain chains, as though it were a bodily lifting up of the strata, by a force operating directly from beneath; but in this respect the term is misapplied. If we suppose that the earth was once in a fluid state, and that the present condition of its surface is due to a process of refrigeration, there must have been a time when a solid crust was formed, composed wholly of crystalline rocks. As the process of refrigeration went on, the earth's sphere would gradually contract to accommodate itself to the diminished nucleus. Such contraction would be attended with ruptures of the crust, which would pursue certain determinate lines, represented by mountain chains; so that the word *elevation*, as applied to mountain ranges, really means *subsidence*. If the interior of the earth is an incandescent mass, as is supposed, the pasty matter would rise up and fill the fissures thus created, and appear under the form of granite; or if this matter were in a fluid condition, it would appear under the form of porphyry, basalt, trap, etc., filling pre-existing fissures in the crust as dykes, or flowing over the surface in long lines like lava-currents. Earthquake and volcanic action belong to this class of phenomena, and the reason why their manifestation is less striking now than at former periods, is, that the earth is supposed to have arrived at that stage when the radiation of heat into space is about equal to that received from the sun.

No American physicist, perhaps, has investigated the structural relations of continents so thoroughly and so ably as Dana. He has brought to bear upon this subject extensive observation, made in various parts of the world, united to close analytical reasoning; and the conclusions in which such a mind rests are entitled to all respect. He recognizes two great systems or trends applicable to the whole world:—A *northwestern* and a *northeastern*, transverse to one another; and he claims that the islands of oceans, the outlines and reliefs of continents, and the oceanic basins themselves, alike exemplify these systems.

In the application of these principles, it may be said that there are three grand systems of upheaval, different in age and direction, which have determined the structural features of the Mississippi Valley, viz.:

1. *The Lake Superior System*,—which ranges N. 80° E., S. 80° W., from Labrabor to the sources of the Mississippi: northward it extends to near the shores of the Arctic Sea. The rocks composing this system consist of granites, traps, and porphyries, undoubtedly of igneous origin; together with quartzites, marbles, and chlorite and talcose schists, of aqueous origin,—the whole highly metamorphosed. On both sides of the axis, the Silurian groups are found resting uncomformably. This, as we long ago pointed out, is the oldest system in America, forming, as it were, the Primeval Continent, which stretched east and west in a low, narrow belt, from the sources of the Mississippi to Labrador; and north and south, from the northern borders of Michigan to the Arctic Sea. Its culminating points no where attained an elevation of more than 2,000 feet above the old Silurian ocean. At that time, the Alleghanies and Rocky Moun-

tains had not assumed their form and direction, and the only objects which rose above the barren waste of waters to break the monotony of the scene, were a few isolated islands, like the Iron-Mountain region of Missouri, Magnet Cove of Arkansas, and perhaps the Washita Mountains of Texas, the Black Hills of Nebraska, and the Central Plateau of Colorado. No forms of vegetable life, at that time, clothed the slopes of the hills, no forms of animal life roamed through the valleys, and even the waters were tenantless. It was emphatically a petrified continent, rigid and stony.*

2. *The Appalachian System.*—This system, as we have seen, extends from Alabama to the River St. Lawrence, where it intersects the Azoic belt of Lake Superior, pursuing for 1,200 miles a general direction of northeast and southwest, and presenting a nearly unbroken succession of conforming strata; and yet the strata at many points are traversed by a series of faults, particularly observ-

---

* This generalization was made by the writer as far back as 1851, and was communicated to the American Association for the Advancement of Science, at the Cincinnati Meeting of that year. Agassiz, who was present, endorsed it as among the most important that had been made in American Geology. In some miscellaneous papers published in the "Atlantic Monthly," and subsequently collected into a volume, this eminent naturalist has substantially repeated my views; and while many ascribe to him the merit of this generalization, he himself, if questioned, would be the first to acknowledge the source from which it was derived.

able in Southern Virginia and Northern Alabama, by which rocks of the Silurian era are brought to a level with those of the Carboniferous. These vertical displacements in some instances amount to 20,000 feet. It was at the close of the Carboniferous epoch that the Appalachian chain became folded, plicated, and metamorphosed. The force by which these changes were produced, appears to have been a lateral one, and to have operated from the Atlantic side, since the steepest and most abrupt acclivities invariably face in that direction, and as the strata are traced westward, they unfold in a series of gentle undulations until they come within the influence of N. N. W. system of Illinois and other western States, where all further traces become obliterated.

The Triassic and Jurassic series of the Atlantic Slope repose upon the upturned edges of the Appalachian System; and, while having the same general direction, and disturbed by an elevatory movement of their own, in no instance do they appear to have crossed the Alleghanies and invaded the valley of the Mississippi. On the other hand, the region of the Pacific opposed no barrier to the Triassic and Jurassic seas, since deposits of this age are found on both sides of the Rocky Mountains.

Thus then, at this early epoch, we find evidences

of ancient shore-lines conforming to those which give configuration to the whole Atlantic Slope.

3. *The Rocky Mountain System.*—This system has a general trend of N. N. W. and S. S. E. (though subject to minor deviations where invaded by the purely volcanic rocks), through the whole territory of the United States. This assemblage, view as a whole, may be regarded as a vast sea of mountains, sometimes rising in isolated summits above the snow-line, sometimes in ranges, either serrated or dome-shaped, often overlapping, and often sending out lateral spurs, as buttresses to the main wall. Whether called Sierra Madre, Sierra Blanca, Washtash, Wind-River, Black Hills, etc., they are but parts of one stupendous whole.

With regard to the age of their elevation, much doubt has hitherto prevailed. Our own views, expressed as far back as 1851, based on the observations of Humboldt and Von Tschudi among the Andes of South America, was that their elevation was as late as the Cretaceous age. The observations of those attached to the Pacific Railroad Surveys, seemed to point to the Carboniferous period, making their elevation contemporary with that of the Alleghanies; but the more exact observations of Whitney in California, and of Rémond in Northern Mexico, would indicate beyond a doubt that their elevation to their present relative position, took place at or near the close of the Triassic period. Between the Rocky Mountains and the Sierra Nevada, we see no reason to draw a line of demarcation. They are parallel in direction, are charged with the same metallic contents, and are invaded by the same volcanic products.

Whitney, in summing up the results of the California Survey, remarks:

" The sedimentary portion of the great metalliferous belt of the Pacific Coast of North America, is to a large extent made up of rocks of Jurassic and Triassic age, with a comparatively small development of Carboniferous limestone, and these formations are so folded together, broken up, and metamorphosed in the great chain of the Sierra Nevada, that it will be immense labor, if indeed possible at all, to unravel its detailed structure. While we are fully justified in saying that a large portion of the auriferous rocks of California consists of Triassic and Jurassic strata, we have not a particle of evidence to sustain the theory which has been so often brought forward, that all, or even a portion of the auriferous rocks are older than the Carboniferous, not a trace of a Devonian or Silurian fossil ever having been discovered in California, or indeed any where to the west of the 116th meridian. It appears, on the other hand, that no inconsiderable amount of gold has been obtained from metamorphic rocks, belonging as high up in the series as the Cretaceous.*

While such are the generalizations of Whitney as to the age of the auriferous rocks of the Sierra Nevada, Rémond arrives at the same results as to

* "Palæontology of California," Vol. I.

the metalliferous rocks of Northern Mexico, embraced in the ranges known as the Sierra Madre, which may be regarded as the southern extension of the Rocky Mountain system.

"The oldest sedimentary rocks which I have observed belong to the Carboniferous series; this is represented in the eastern part of Sonora, by heavy masses of limestone, forming very high and rugged ridges, running a little west of north. * * Argentiferous veins occur throughout this formation. The next group of rocks in order is the Triassic, * * made up of heavy beds of quartzites and conglomerates. * * Wherever metamorphosed, the Triassic rocks are auriferous, and contain veins of silver ores. * * The Cretaceous period is also represented at the foot of the Sierra Madre. * * The strata belonging to this series are chiefly argillaceous shales, and these rest upon porphyries and Carboniferous limestones. They have been disturbed and elevated since their deposition. * * The veins cut all the rocks older than the Cretaceous, whether igneous or sedimentary." *

These facts clearly indicate that the Sierra Nevada and Rocky-Mountain Chains were uplifted, metamorphosed, and infiltrated with the precious metals at or about the close of the Tri-

* "Proc. Cala. Academy Nat. Sci." Vol. III.

It would seem that the Carboniferous and Triassic series exist in intimate relation through the whole range of the Rocky Mountains in the United States. The Triassic has been recognized in the Colorado Basin (Newberry); in the region of Washoe (Whitney); east of the Rio Grande, and in the vicinity of the Raton Mountain (Le Conte); in the Black Hills, Big Horn Mountains, and about the sources of the Missouri (Meek and Hayden). The Carboniferous series exists in great force in the region of Santa Fé (Newberry); Salt Lake (Hall); and in the Great Basin east of longitude 116° (Whitney).

assic age; and yet they must have subsequently undergone great subsidence, for we find the Cretaceous strata reposing undisturbed upon both slopes, and imposed on these, a series of Tertiary beds, some marine and some fresh-water, which appear to have been unaffected by the elevatory movements which gave form and direction to the Rocky-Mountain System. Subordinate systems are known to exist, and others will undoubtedly be determined; but it is to these three great lines of upheaval that the Mississippi Valley owes its configuration.

The Coast Ranges. — The elevation of the Coast Ranges of the Pacific, as determined by Antisell and others, is as recent as the Miocine-Tertiary, which has brought up strata over 2,000 feet in thickness, containing fossils differing from those of the Mississippi Valley, and indicating a difference in the waters of the two oceans.* Later observations by Whitney show, that while the Cretaceous strata repose undisturbed on the flanks of the Sierra Nevada, they partook of the movement by which the Coast Ranges were made to assume their present form and direction; and are, therefore, far more modern in age. Their range is from the extremity of the peninsula of California to the

* "Pacific Railroad Surveys." Vol. III.

British Possessions, and their bearing about N. 70° W.

Volcanic Products.—This class of rocks is observed in the form of basalts, greenstones, and amygdaloids, protruded among the grits and conglomerates of the Silurian age, in the Lake Superior district; but their grandest display is in the Rocky-Mountain region, and on the Pacific Slope. Mt. Hood, Shasta, and Lassan's Peak, on the one side, and the Raton Mountain, Long's Peak, and the Three Teutons, on the other, with San Francisco and San Mateo on the Colorado Plateau, are, as we have seen, but volcanic craters, whose fires have but recently been extinguished. All over this region there are crested ridges and isolated peaks that have been thus lifted up, and from their orifices have flowed lava, peperino, scoria, and ashes, so copiously as to cover the fundamental rocks over large areas. These overflows will probably be found to be of various ages, but some of them are of extremely modern origin. Perhaps the most conspicuous example of recent action is exhibited at Table Mountain, California, as described by Whitney, where the summit consists of basaltic lava nearly 150 feet thick, and elevated 2,000 feet above the Stanislaus River. The stream of once molten matter is traceable for forty miles up to its source in the High Sierra; and, as it must have sought the lowest depressions, at the time of its overflow, it is inferred that the country has since been denuded to that extent. Beneath the basalt are about 200 feet of slightly-coherent sandstones, and argillaceous shales and clays, containing silicified wood and impressions of leaves, which Newberry refers to the later Pliocine epoch; and quite recently Silliman has obtained the fragmentary bones of a mastodon from the same locality.

Gabb describes the occurrence of Post-Pliocine deposits on the peninsula of Lower California, made up almost of casts or shells of Molusca still living in the adjoining waters, which are often capped by volcanic products to the depth of 100 feet; and Rémond states that, scattered along the whole Pacific coast of Northern Mexico, volcanic products are found in positions which clearly indicate that they have been poured forth since the elevation of the formations which constitute the fundamental rocks of that region.

These facts would indicate that man has probably been witness to some of the most stupendous events which have modified the physical geography of the continent,—the lifting up of long lines of coast, the formation of volcanic cones 12,000 feet or more in height, and the denudation of the country to the depth of 2,000 feet. Accustomed as we are, at this day, to witness the calm operations of nature, rarely interrupted by catastrophes, it is almost impossible to conceive that such tremendous changes in the physical aspect of these regions, are to be ranked among the most recent of events in the world's history.

River-Systems.— In comparing the Mountain-systems with the River-systems of the Great Interior, we find that the direction of the Saskatchawan, the Churchill, the Athabasca, and other affluents of Hudson's Bay, together with those great fresh-water lakes,—Great Bear, Slave, and Athabasca,—almost rivaling in dimensions the Laurentian Chain, has been determined by the Lake Superior System; the Ohio and the St. Lawrence, including Lakes Erie and Ontario, by the Appalachian System; and the Upper Mississippi, the Missouri, together with Lake Winipeg, and Mackenzie's River, by the Rocky-Mountain System.

The line of greatest depression on the continent would be represented by about longitude 90°, which cuts the Mississippi River, Lake Michigan, Lake Superior, and Hudson's Bay. That these features which make up the architecture of the Continent are not fortuitous, but are the result of the operations of fixed laws, will be apparent to every careful student of physical geography.

CLASSIFICATION OF THE FORMATIONS.

Within this valley, though at no one point exhibiting an unbroken succession, have been deposited the principal groups of formations observed elsewhere, as constituing the crust of the earth.

Azoic System.— From the entire absence of all vestiges of organic remains in these rocks, and lying inconformably beneath that group which exhibits the first traces of such remains, this system has been called the AZOIC (without life). It is inferred that the very condition of our planet at that epoch — an incandescent body gradually cooling, its crust subject to volcanic paroxysms, mephitic vapors constantly escaping through wide fissures communicating with the interior, and the waters heated to a high temperature,— would be highly unfavorable to the existence of animal or vegetable life. The rocks consist of igneous products, such as granites, greenstones, and porphyries; and of metamorphic products, such as talcose and chlorite slates, quartzites, and saccharoidal marbles.

In the Lake Superior region they are largely developed; and while the metamorphic strata are tilted at high angles, the Potsdam sandstone, which contains the earliest forms of organic life, reposes upon their basset edges, slightly metamorphosed, and in nearly horizontal strata.

The crystalline belt which forms the crest and eastern slope of the Appalachians has, by some, been referred to this system, while others regard it as a portion of the Silurian system highly metamorphosed; but the discussion of this question does not come within the purview of this work.

In Missouri and Arkansas there are isolated patches of these rocks, which appear to have been islands in the old Silurian sea, and it would seem that portions of the region occupied by the Rocky Mountains served as the floor of the Azoic ocean, on which the purely sedimentary deposits were formed; for Newberry, in the Cañon of the Little Colorado, saw in one magnificent section, over 4,000 feet in depth, an unbroken succession of sedimentary rocks, conformable in dip, and extending from the Potsdam sandstone, reposing on granite, up to and including the Carboniferous series; and Meek and Hayden have detected the Potsdam sandstone, with its characteristic fossils, in the Black Hills of Nebraska.

Iron Ores.—The Azoic rocks are the repositories of vast deposits of specular and magnetic oxide of iron. They range through the region of Lake Superior; they occur in Canada, in the Adirondacks of New York, in New Jersey, Missouri, and Arkansas.

IRON REGION OF LAKE SUPERIOR.—As intimately connected with the commerce and manufactures of the Mississippi Valley, the ores of iron, occurring at two of the points above enumerated, deserve a more extended notice, both by reason of their purity, and the magnitude of the deposits; viz., those of Lake Superior and of Missouri.

There is no region of the earth where the ores of iron are developed on a scale of such grandeur, or concentrated in a state of such purity, as on the southern shore of Lake Superior. Nijny Tagilsk, Dannemora, and Elba, may contain isolated deposits equally rich; but these combined would occupy a mere patch on the surface over which the ores of this region are known to be distributed.

This area is somewhat irregular in outline. Its length, east and west, is about one hundred and fifty miles, with a variable breadth, north and south, from six to seventy miles. The greatest concentration of the ores, however, is in the vicinity of the Jackson, Cleveland, and Lake Superior mines. For many years these ores were worked in open quarry; but, with the vast demand, it has become necessary to sink upon them below the drainage of the country. This demand now exceeds one-half million of tons a year. In the furnace, the ores yield about 65 per cent. of pig metal, which, when properly puddled, gives an iron of great strength and tenacity. The principal market for these ores is in the Mahoning and Shenango Valleys, Detroit, Buffalo, and Pittsburgh.

IRON REGION OF MISSOURI. — In this region, embracing the counties of Iron and St. François, in the State of Missouri — about eighty miles south of St. Louis, — occur large deposits of specular and magnetic iron-ores, known as Iron Mountain, Pilot Knob, and Shepherd's Mountain. The Iron Mountain rises to the height of about 200 feet above the surrounding country, and, while so far as revealed by the uncovering, it contains a vast amount of ore of the purest quality, it is traversed north and south by one or more porphyritic dykes. The ore, externally, has the appearance of an erupted mass. Pilot Knob rises to the height of 581 feet, in a symmetrical form. The mass is porphyry to the height of 450 feet. Then succeeds a layer of banded ore, resembling a metamorphic product, about 60 feet in thickness, which is capped by a lean, jaspery ore, 70 feet in thickness, forming the summit of the hill. At Shepherd's Mountain the ores are magnetic, and occur in two veins, respectively eight and fourteen feet in width, traversing porphyry. These ores give, in their working, about 60 per cent. of pig iron, and are known to ironmasters as "neutral" in the quality of bar-iron. In Dent County there is said to exist a mountain-mass of iron-ore still larger than any described.

Owing to the supposed remoteness of a proper fuel to smelt these ores, the greatest product of the mines in no one year has exceeded 25,000 tons; but there has lately been developed an iron-making coal in the counties of Randolph and Perry, adjoining the Mississippi River, in the State of Illinois, so that a union between the materials for iron-making can be easily effected, and these ores will hereafter play a more prominent part in the manufacturing industry of the Mississippi Valley.

In Missouri, the granite associated with this series of rocks is traversed by numerous veins of tin — a discovery which, at the time of its announcement, was received with much distrust by the scientific community. Like tin veins in other parts of the world, they are not rich, but specimens have been assayed which gave as high as eight per cent. of metal.

Gold has been found sparsely distributed in the Azoic rocks throughout their entire range; and the baser metals, copper and lead, are by no means rare. The true Golden Age of the world, however, was of far more recent date.

The igneous and metamorphic rocks are the principal repositories of metallic wealth. This wealth is concentrated in the form of veins, or in beds running parallel with the formation. The accuracy of the opinion almost universally entertained in the early investigation of mineral veins, that they had been filled by injections from beneath, may well be doubted. Their filling, where they exhibit a comb-like structure, must have been the result of successive infiltrations, and their gangues, particularly where they consist of the zeolite minerals, would indicate that water, or superheated steam, rather than heat, had been the solvent power. It will probably be found, too, that some action like that of galvanism, has abstracted the metallic particles from the enclosing rocks, and concentrated them in fissures and beds. The theory of injection has led to the delusive idea, justified by no mining experience, that veins become enriched in proportion to the depth penetrated.

According to the Mythology of the Ancients, there were Four Ages, symbolized by the four metals — gold, silver, brass (copper), and iron. The geologist, while recognizing the fact that certain periods in the earth's history were prolific in certain metals, fails to recognize this order of succession. The Azoic series is characterized by the abundance of iron; copper is associated with the first-formed sedimentary rocks, or rather their igneous products; lead predominates in the Lower Silurian and Sub-carboniferous series; silver is of the Carboniferous age, and even of that of the Tertiary volcanic rocks; gold appertains to the Triassic; and mercury to the Cretaceous.

The Golden Age, according the poets, was one of unmixed delight, when man,

"Vindice nullo,
Sponte suâ sine lege fidem rectumque colebat."

Ours is emphatically an age of IRON. The use of this metal is intimately associated with the whole history of the progress and civilization of man. In every thing relating to the production, transformation, and distribution of material wealth, whether extracted from the sea, the soil, or the deep recesses of mines, iron performs an all-important part. No other metal could be successfully substituted for the axe, the plough, or the spade; or for the loom, the steam-engine, the locomotive, or the railroad track.

"Every one," says Ure, "knows the manifold uses of this truly precious metal. It is capable of being cast into moulds of any form; of being drawn into wires of any desired strength or fineness; of being extended into plates or sheets; of being bent in any direction; of being sharpened, hardened, and softened at pleasure. It accommodates itself to all our wants, our desires, and even our caprices. It is equally serviceable in the arts, the sciences, to agriculture, and war; the same ore furnishes the sword, the ploughshare, the scythe, the pruning-hook, the needle, the graver, the spring of a watch, or of a carriage, the chisel, the cannon, and the bomb. It is a medicine of much virtue, and the only metal friendly to the animal frame." *

The amount of iron consumed by a nation may be regarded as an unerring index of its progress in civilization. In Great Britain the annual consumption is about the combined weight of the whole population; in the United States and France, it is a little less; and in Prussia, Austria, and Russia, it is still less.

The following is the annual product of pig and wrought iron in the several countries of the world, in tons of 2,240 pounds each: †

	Pig Iron.	Wrought Iron.
ENGLAND,	4,530,051	3,500,000
FRANCE,	1,200,320	844,734
UNITED STATES,	1,175,000	882,000
BELGIUM,	500,000	400,000
PRUSSIA,	800,000	400,000
AUSTRIA,	312,000	200,000
SWEDEN,	226,676	148,292
RUSSIA,	408,000	350,000
SPAIN,	75,000	50,000
ITALY,	30,000	20,000
SWITZERLAND,	15,000	10,000
ZOLLVEREIN,	250,000	200,000
	9,322,047	7,005,026

* "Ure's Dic." Art. Iron.

† Hewitt's "Report," etc. (Paris Universal Exposition), 1867.

CHAPTER IX.

GEOLOGY (*Continued*)—SEDIMENTARY ROCKS.

SILURIAN SYSTEM — FIRST EVIDENCES OF ORGANIC LIFE — AREA OF THE SILURIAN — LOWER SILURIAN — POTSDAM SANDSTONE — PICTURED ROCKS — COPPER REGION OF LAKE SUPERIOR — LOWER MAGNESIAN LIMESTONE — LEAD-BEARING VEINS OF MISSOURI — ST. PETER'S SANDSTONE — CINCINNATI BLUE LIMESTONE — LEAD-BEARING ROCKS OF WISCONSIN — UPPER SILURIAN SYSTEM — NIAGARA LIMESTONE — ONONDAGA SALT-GROUP — DEVONIAN SYSTEM — CARBONIFEROUS SYSTEM — FLUOR-SPAR VEINS WITH GALENA — GALENA DEPOSITS — SILVER ORES OF MEXICO — COAL-MEASURES — THEIR AREA — THICKNESS — CHARACTER OF THE COALS — PERMIAN SYSTEM — TRIASSIC AND JURASSIC SERIES — GOLD-DEPOSITS OF CALIFORNIA — COPPER DEPOSITS — CRETACEOUS SYSTEM — COAL DEPOSITS.

IN treating of the vast assemblage of rocks of a purely sedimentary origin which fills the connected basins of the Ohio, the Missouri, and the Mississippi, we shall begin with a description of the lowest, and, therefore, the first-formed, and proceed in an ascending order to the most recent. And that the reader may fully comprehend the order of succession, so far as relates to the Lower Silurian groups, and their relation to the igneous

Plate III.

GEOLOGICAL SKETCH
of the
UNITED STATES.

1. Azoic.
2. Silurian
3. Devonian
4. Carboniferous.
5. Coal-measures
6. Permian.
7. { Triassic &
     Jurassic.
8. Cretaceous.
9. Tertiary
10. Recent.
● Volcanic Peaks.

The Cretaceous and Tertiary
(widows deeply-shaded)

rocks, we append the following ideal section, extending from the Copper-region of Lake Superior to the Lead-bearing region of the Mississippi Valley:

1. AZOIC rocks of Lake Superior, bearing iron.
2. TRAPPEAN rocks of Lake Superior, bearing copper.
3. POTSDAM SANDSTONE.
4. MAGNESIAN LIMESTONE, including ST. PETER'S SANDSTONE, the Lead-bearing rock of Missouri.
5. TRENTON LIMESTONE.
6. GALENA LIMESTONE, Lead-bearing rock of Wisconsin.
7. CINCINNATI BLUE LIMESTONE.
8. NIAGARA LIMESTONE, capping mounds.

The Silurian System.—The term SILURIAN was first applied to a series of fossiliferous strata lying below the Old-Red sandstone, and occupying a part of Wales, and some contiguous counties in England, which were once inhabited by the SILURES, a tribe of ancient Britons; but so universally has this series of rocks been recognized, the world over, that the term has passed into the nomenclature of every text-book on geology. In this region, this system is divisible into not less than eight distinct groups, characterized alike by fossil remains and lithological characters.

In the lowest member of this system—the POTSDAM SANDSTONE—we detect the first traces of organic life,— not of those complicated and highly-organized forms which now inhabit the earth, but low in the scale of creation,— trilobites, with crescent-shaped head and jointed body, allied to the crab and lobster; graptolites, or sea-pens, so closely resembling certain vegetable forms that zoologists long hesitated to which kingdom to assign them; encrinites, which were permanently attached to the sea-bottom, and sent forth their branches like vegetable forms; and chambered shells of the least ornate structure. It is no part of this treatise to describe the succession of organisms introduced upon the earth,— beginning with the simplest forms, and terminating in man, the most complex in organization, and far-reaching in his capacities. To this succession incidental reference only will be made. The economic materials, however, furnished by these several groups, will be dwelt upon more in detail.

The greatest area occupied by the Silurian System (See the Geological Sketch of the United States appended to this Chapter, p. 271), lies south of the Azoic belt of Lake Superior and stretches west to near the Missouri River, comprehending portions of Michigan, Illinois, Wisconsin, Minnesota, and Iowa. In this area are to be found all of the groups from the Potsdam sandstone up to the Niagara limestone. In Ohio, a circular area of thin-bedded limestones occurs in the vicinity of Cincinnati, which has received the name of the Blue limestone, as typical of that member of the system. The Silurian rocks flank both slopes of the Alleghanies; they occupy a large area in Southeastern Missouri, extending into Southern Illinois, and Northeastern Arkansas. They have been recognized in the Black Hills of Nebraska, and in the Black Cañon of the Little Colorado.

Lower Silurian System.—THE POTSDAM SAND-STONE finds its greatest development in the region of Lake Superior, and it is probable that the bed of this lake, whose area is 32,000 square miles, is mainly excavated in this rock. Here, where it has been invaded by trappean overflows, it is highly metamorphosed, often containing jaspery materials and large pebbles of greenstone and amygdaloid, derived from the immediate vicinity, but no pebbles like granite or quartz, which are foreign to the region. So energetic were the igneous and acqueous causes, that they have been accumulated to the thickness of more than 3,000 feet, while 250 feet would represent the general thickness of this member, remote from this telluric activity. South of the Azoic belt, the sandstone is so slightly coherent that it may be crushed in the hand, and is characterized by the presence of

Lingulæ and *Trilobites*. It extends south to the Wisconsin River, and west to the Mississippi, in Minnesota. In this region the strata repose horizontally upon the irregular surface of the Azoic series.

PICTURED ROCKS OF LAKE SUPERIOR.—The best natural section of the Potsdam sandstone in the Northwest, is afforded by the famous Pictured Rocks of Lake Superior. Commencing at Grand Island, and extending eastward for about five miles, this group of strata lines the shore, rising from the water's edge, in mural-like faces, from 50 to 200 feet in height, not in an unbroken line, but in a series of projections and recessions. It is not the mere height of these cliffs, or the bold sweep of their lines, which constitute the charm of this landscape, and impress so profoundly the beholder; but it arises from two other sources,— the brilliant hues with which they are dyed, and the fantastic shapes into which they have been excavated. While the general tone of the rock is a light-yellow, at particular points there are broad vertical stripes extending for thirty or forty feet above the water, variously-tinted umber, yellow, and grey, together with bright-blue and green, the two latter tints being less frequent. All the colors are fresh, distinct, and brilliant, as in a fresco painting; and, embracing the whole scene in a *coup d'œil*,— the deep-blue waters of the lake at the base, the canopy of bright-green foliage above, and still beyond the over-arching sky,—the effect is grand and beautiful. These colors result probably from the percolation of the water through the strata, taking up various mineral oxides, and depositing them on the nearly vertical walls. Adverting to the second conspicuous feature, it may be said that the action of the lake-waves upon the slowly-yielding strata, continued through an indefinite period of time, has excavated them into many grotesque forms. As approached from Grand Island, in the distance they resemble the ruins of some fortified city,—ramparts formed into bastions and curtains, solitary towers, and long lines of wall, with arched entrances, or portals; and hence, the early voyageurs gave to this assemblage of rocks the name of *Les Portails.* Coasting in a small boat, along the verge of the water and beneath the overhanging cliffs, the observer passes a succession of scenes each one of which is of rare and exquisite beauty:—"Miner's Castle," with its turrets and portals; the "Amphitheatre," with its smooth walls and its symmetrical curves; "Sail Rock," where a tabular mass of sandstone, detached from the cliffs above, stands nearly vertically in the water, presenting the similitude of a sloop under full sail; and the "Grand Portal," where a quadrilateral mass of strata 200 feet in height, projects into the lake for 600 feet, and is pierced with an arched opening 100 feet high and 168 feet broad, leading through high vaulted passages into the great dome, 300 feet from the face of the cliff. Nor must it be forgotten that the effects of this scenery are heightened by occasional cascades, which descend in a sheet of foam from the brow of the cliffs, and mingle with the waters of the lake.

The whole line of cliffs presents a succession of wonderful and constantly-varying scenes, and amply repays the tourist who pauses sufficiently long to contemplate the details.*

This group of rocks is recognized as flanking the Alleghanies in Tennessee, always disturbed, and sometimes in nearly vertical strata. Traces, too, are observed in the vicinity of the Iron Mountain, Missouri, where it is nearly horizontal. It appears in Burnet County, Texas (Shumard); in the Black Cañon (Newberry); and in the Black Hills of Dakota, the Laramie, Big Horn, and Wind-River Ranges of the Rocky Mountains (Hayden). It would thus seem that the Potsdam sandstone was deposited in a sea whose confines were as extended as those of the Great Valley, and that it

---

* For a more minute description of the "Pictured Rocks," see Foster and Whitney's Report, "Geology of Lake Superior Region." Vol. II.

rests at the base of the whole fossiliferous series. Thus far, throughout its range, we are not aware of its having proved metalliferous, except in connection with the igneous products, in the region of Lake Superior.

THE COPPER-REGION OF LAKE SUPERIOR commences at the head of Keweenaw Point, where the trappean rocks, with their associated conglomerates, rise up in bold, stair-like cliffs, and afford many scenes of picturesque beauty. This peculiar physiognomy is characteristic of the whole trappean region. From this point, in a variable belt, from two to ten miles broad, the associated traps, conglomerates, and sandstones, range in a southwestern direction for 130 miles, conforming to the trend of the shore, when they sink down, and their presence is only indicated at times by an isolated knob. Those portions of the range most productive in copper, are in the vicinity of Portage Lake, the Cliff, and Copper Falls locations, and the Ontonagon River. Native copper is almost exclusively found. On Keweenaw Point it occurs in a system of veins bearing about north $21\frac{1}{2}°$ west. In the early mining, it was supposed that the productive deposits were restricted to these veins; but, in the progress of development, it was found that certain intercalated beds of amygdaloid and volcanic ash were sufficiently impregnated with copper to render its extraction profitable; and it is from the latter sources that the bulk of the copper is now derived.

The annual consumption of refined copper in the United States is about 12,000 tons, of which these mines furnish about 9,000 tons; Tennessee, 100 tons; and California, and Vermont, 2,500 tons, leaving a small surplus for exportation.

THE MAGNESIAN LIMESTONE, the equivalent of the CALCIFEROUS SANDSTONE of the New York Survey, is nearly as persistent in its range as the Potsdam sandstone; but in the Lake Superior region it assumes an arenaceous character, while in Wisconsin and Missouri it becomes a gray, calcareous rock (an almost pure dolomite), with more or less embedded chert. The Magnesian limestone series in the latter State, as determined by Swallow, is divisable into four members, numbered in a descending order: 1. (190 feet); 2. (230 feet); 3. (350 feet); and 4. (300 feet); separated by bands of sandstone, saccharoidal in character, varying from 50 to 125 feet. While the Second Magnesian limestone contains galena in economical quantities, the well-known mines of Washington, Franklin, and St. François Counties, are in the third member of the series.

THE LEAD-BEARING VEINS OF MISSOURI appear under different forms. In Franklin County, there is a series of vertical fissures, bearing nearly north and south, which penetrate indefinitely downwards, filled in with sulphate of barytes and associated with galena. Where they pass through a soft mineral plane they become enlarged and enriched; and where they enter a close, cherty rock, they become pinched and impoverished. Like other classes of veins, they have their "chimneys" or cavernous openings, where the "mineral" is concentrated. Galena also occurs in flat sheets in the soft arenaceous bands of Magnesian limestone, which weather into a yellowish sand. At Mine la Motte and St. Joseph's, the lead is deposited at the base of the individual layers of limestone, which are separated by well-defined lines of stratification, as though the metal had been held in solution with the lime, and precipitated, and accommodated itself to this position by reason of its greater specific gravity. At Mine la Motte, also, occurs nickel in paying quantities, in connection with cobalt and copper.

THE ST. PETER'S SANDSTONE is the line of separation between the Lower Magnesian and Trenton groups, and is readily recognized in Illinois, Iowa, Wisconsin, and Minnesota. Its thickness rarely exceeds 100 feet. It is a soft, friable rock, often pure-white, and is employed for glass-making, at Chicago.

The Trenton-limestone group is widely distributed. It is recognized along the southern shore of Lake Huron, and amid the islands of the St. Mary's River. It crosses the Escanaba River just above the head of Bay de Noquet, and thence is protracted into Wisconsin, Iowa, and Illinois, where it rests at the base of the lead-bearing rocks. It forms the crest of the Falls of St. Anthony, reappears on the Missouri River, in Franklin County, and on the Mississippi, below St. Louis, and is developed in the interior of Kentucky and Tennessee, where it is known as the Stone's-River group.

The Galena limestone may be regarded as an intercalation in the series, and is locally developed in the southwestern part of Wisconsin and the adjacent parts of Iowa and Illinois, embracing an area of about 3,000 square miles. Its thickness is about 250 feet. Its tone is light-grey or yellowish, and the rock itself, a compound carbonate of lime and magnesia (dolomite), often weathers into fantastic forms, leaving at the base a coarse, meagre, ochre-colored sand. It is by no means rich in fossils, but there is a peculiar sun-flower-like form, the *Solenoides iowensis* of Owen, which, when once seen by the casual observer, is ever afterwards recognized. With regard to the occurrence of galena in this limestone, it may be said that the upper fifty feet are unproductive. The middle is characterized by gash veins, which are crevices with no polished walls or well characterized gangue. These crevices, as followed, often expand into "openings" or caves, which again close up to a mere seam. As traced downward to the Trenton or Buff limestone, the "mineral" spreads out in a flat sheet, or bed-like form, with a considerable pitch to some angle of the horizon. The ore is almost invariably a sulphuret of lead (galena), except where decomposition has partially taken place, when the cubes are often studded with pearl-colored crystals of carbonate of lead. Sulphuret of zinc (black-jack), carbonate of zinc, iron pyrites, and occasionally carbonate of copper, accompany the galena, together with calc-spar, and rarely heavy spar.

THE CINCINNATI BLUE LIMESTONE, the equivalent of what was formerly regarded as the Hudson-River group of the New York Reports, occurs at the typical locality, in thin-bedded strata of limestone, profusely filled with fossils, with interlaminated marls and shales. It is also traced along Drummond's Island in the St. Mary's River and the northern slope of Lake Michigan to Green Bay, and through Lake Winnebago. It reappears in the lead-region of Wisconsin and Iowa, in isolated mounds, often capped by the Niagara limestone. Here it is about fifty feet thick, and the layers consist mainly of calcareous shales, in which the *Nucula* forms the predominating fossil, while *Orthoceratites* and *Lingulæ* are not wanting. This group is recognized in Missouri, by Swallow, where it is 220 feet in thickness, and by Worthen in Southern Illinois, adjacent to the Mississippi River.

Upper Silurian System.—THE NIAGARA LIMESTONE series is a most important one in the Lake region, inasmuch as the shore-lines for many hundred miles have been determined by its range. It is an enduring rock, and furnishes a building material of an agreeable color, and easily-wrought. From Niagara Falls, it ranges through Canada, forming the ridges near Hamilton and Dundas, and the conspicuous promontory known as Cabot's Head on Lake Huron; and thence through the Manitoulin Islands, and along the northern shore of Lake Michigan and the eastern shore of Green Bay; thence through Wisconsin to Chicago and the head of Lake Michigan. In this vicinity it is known as the "Athens marble," and in chemical composition is almost a pure dolomite. It is of a light-grey, or cream-colored tint, and forms one of the best and most easily-wrought materials for architectural purposes to be found in the United States. The thickness of the series is about 250 feet. Traced westward, it becomes the fundamental rock over a large space in Northwestern Illinois, rises in continuous bluffs along the Mississippi, and caps, in many instances, the mounds of the Lead-region. Near the town of Hampton, according to Worthen, it sinks below the bed of the Mississippi, but reappears along the southwestern border of the State, and in Jersey County, forms perpendicular cliffs from 50 to 100 feet high, along the Illinois and Mississippi Rivers. The quarries at Grafton furnished the material for that noble structure, now in ruins, the Lindell Hotel of St. Louis.*

THE ONONDAGA-SALT GROUP forms the base of the island of Mackinac, is developed in the interior of Michigan, and is recognized by Hall,† in Wisconsin and Iowa. It is not improbable that the bed of Lake Michigan has been in part excavated in this group. That portion of the series in which originate the salt-springs in the vicinity of Saginaw, has been designated by Winchell as the SALINA GROUP, and is estimated to cover an area of 17,000 square miles. The annual product

* "Geology of Illinois." Vol. I, p. 136.

† "Geology of Iowa.' P. 76.

of the salt-wells of Michigan reaches 1,300,000 bushels.

Devonian System.—The rocks consist of sandstones, limestones, and shales. In their range, they occupy nearly the whole area of Lower Michigan, Western Ohio, and Eastern Indiana, and are protracted southerly into Kentucky and Tennessee. A narrow belt, running northwest and southeast, skirts the northern rim of the coal-field in Iowa, and a limited area also occurs in Northeastern Missouri. Among the fossils collected by Stansbury in the vicinity of Salt Lake, Hall recognized Devonian types, and Meek has described their occurrence in the Great Basin, near the base of the Sierra Nevada.

These rocks are the reservoirs of the copious petroleum springs of Western Pennsylvania, which have added so much to the national wealth, the exports of which now exceed ninety-four and one-half millions of gallons.

To illustrate the order of succession in the groups which make up the interval between the Silurian and Cretaceous formations, the following ideal section, from the Smoky-Hill River, west of Fort Riley, Kansas, to Callaway County, Missouri, is appended:

SECTION FROM KANSAS TO MISSOURI.

1. **DEVONIAN**, the equivalent of the Hamilton, Onondaga, and Oriskany groups of the New York Reports.

2. **SUB-CARBONIFEROUS**, including the Ferruginous sandstone, Upper Archimedes or Kaskaskia limestone, Prairie du Rocher sandstone, Middle Archimedes or Ste. Geneviéve limestone, St. Louis limestone, Lower Archimedes or Keokuk limestone, and Encrinital limestone of the Missouri Reports.

3. **COAL-MEASURES** of Missouri and Kansas.

4. **PERMIAN**, embracing the variegated marls and soft magnesian limestones of Kansas.

5. **TRIASSIC?** along the western border of the Permian.

6. **CRETACEOUS.**—Reddish and whitish sandstones of the Dakota group, widely distributed over Western Kansas.

Carboniferous System—(*a*). SUB-CARBONIFEROUS.— In the States of Iowa, Illinois, and Missouri, the Sub-carboniferous limestones are developed on a scale of unbroken succession, and are stored with a variety and profusion of organic forms such as are not elsewhere observed. To the palæontologist they afford materials of absorbing interest, and the splendid illustrations which have already been given in the Geological Reports of these States, convey to us a pretty complete knowledge of the conditions of organic life during this period in the history of our planet.

Taking Illinois as typical of these groups, we

have between the base of the Coal-Measures and the Devonian, the following subdivisions, as determined by Worthen:

CHESTER GROUP,	500 to 800 feet thick.
ST. LOUIS GROUP,	50 to 200 "
KEOKUK GROUP,	100 to 150 "
BURLINGTON LIMESTONE,	25 to 100 "
KINDERHOOK GROUP,	100 to 150 "

CHESTER GROUP.—The calcareous members of this group are a grey and closely-granulated limestone, well fitted for building purposes, and are characterized by the presence of an immense nautiloid shell nearly two feet in diameter (*Nautilus spectabilis*), together with some sixteen species of fishes, besides Crinoids and Brachipods.

THE ST. LOUIS LIMESTONE is a regularly-bedded, light-grey, or bluish-grey limestone, and in composition is a nearly pure carbonate of lime. The *Melonites multipora*, resembling the fruit of the tomato, and the *Poteriocrinus missouriensis* are characteristic Crinoids. This rock is highly cavernous, and in the vicinity of St. Louis there are many sink-holes, which indicate the entrance to these caverns.

THE KEOKUK LIMESTONE is, at Nauvoo and Keokuk, a regular-bedded, grey rock, well fitted for building purposes. Above this, in position, is the Geode-bed, which has furnished so many fine specimens of quartz crystallizations. The geodes occur disseminated through shaley limestone, sometimes so aggregated as to touch one another, and again so disseminated that several feet of the shale will afford not more than a single specimen. Sometimes the cavities are filled with asphaltum, and at others with water, and there often occur splendid groups of calcite crystals, implanted on crystalline quartz.*

THE BURLINGTON LIMESTONE, in its upper part, is a light-grey, or yellowish limestone, and consists almost entirely of a mass of Crinoids. The lower portion is more magnesian, and of a brownish color, and disintegrates so readily that it is unfit for building purposes. Worthen, in speaking of the beauty and profusion of the Crinoids in this group, says:

"No spot of the same geographical extent has yet been discovered on the surface of the earth, where those beautiful "*lily stars*" flourished in such numbers, as along the northern shores of the Sub-carboniferous ocean, during the deposit of this limestone; and no where else have their remains been found in such profusion, or in such a perfect state of preservation as in this rock. * * * More than three hundred species have already been described from this region, and many new ones are still being discovered, from time to time; and yet probably not one individual in every hundred that lived during this period, has been preserved in such a condition that their specific character can now be obtained."†

* "Illinois Geol. Rep." Vol. I, p. 96.

† Ibidem, p. 104.

THE KINDERHOOK GROUP consists of sandy and argillaceous shales, with thin beds of fine-grained, oolitic limestone, the whole being from one to two hundred feet in thickness, and constituting, according to Worthen and Meek, the base of the Sub-carboniferous system, being the equivalent of the Lower limestone seen at Burlington; of the Goniatite-bed at Rockford, Indiana; of the Waverley sandstone of Ohio; and of the Choteau, the Lithographic, and Vermicular sandstones and shales of the Missouri Reports.

The entire series of the Sub-carboniferous rocks, in Southern Illinois, attain a thickness of 1,200 and 1,500 feet; but they thin out as traced northward, and at LaSalle, the Coal-Measures are seen to repose upon the upturned edges of the Lower Silurian groups. They are, however, found to encircle the Michigan coal-field; in Ohio, they are represented by a thin group of arenaceous deposits, and are recognized in Tennessee, Arkansas, and Texas. Limestones of the Carboniferous age, highly metamorphosed, exist along the eastern slope of the Rocky Mountains, probably almost continuously from Mexico to British Columbia; on the Colorado Plateau; and in the Great Basin. They are the oldest group which has been recognized on the Pacific Slope, and often occur in connection with and conforming to the Trias.

The Sub-carboniferous rocks, like the corresponding groups in England, at certain points are productive in galena. In Southern Illinois this ore is intimately associated with heavy veins of fluor spar, a substance so rare in mass, that it deserves more than a passing notice; and particularly, when it is understood that it can be obtained in an unlimited quantity, and that it may be extensively employed in the metallurgic arts.

FLUOR SPAR-VEINS CARRYING GALENA.—There is a series of flexures in Illinois, first noticed by Norwood and confirmed by the observations of Worthen, running about N. 30° W., which have brought to the surface the Silurian rocks, and have disturbed and given a quâquâversal dip to the Coal-Measures. This system is at right angles to Appalachian system, and conforms to that of the Rocky Mountains. Thus, in the valley of the Ohio River, we find the Coal-Measures of Illinois separated from those of Kentucky by an axis which has brought up both divisions of the Chester group, the St. Louis limestone, and the Upper Devonian shales. The crown of this axis is well displayed in the vicinity of Rosiclare, Hardin County, where, in a bluff, two hundred feet or more in height, overlooking the Ohio River, are exhibited the sandstones, shales, and argillaceous limestones of the Chester group, and about fifty feet of the St.

Louis limestone beneath, which is here a grey-tinted rock, often oolitic in structure, and chemically an almost pure carbonate of lime. While the fissures traverse both groups, it is only in the St. Louis limestone that they develop their true metalliferous character.

These phenomena are illustrated in the following

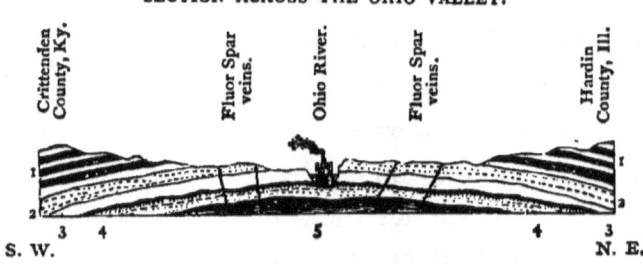

SECTION ACROSS THE OHIO VALLEY.

1. COAL-MEASURES.
2. CHESTER GROUP (Upper Division).
3. CHESTER GROUP (Lower Division).
4. ST. LOUIS LIMESTONE.
5. UPPER DEVONIAN SHALES.

The Sub-carboniferous groups are intersected at right angles to their bearing by a set of veins of fluor spar, ranging about N. 20° E., and apparently of indefinite depth. These fissures present all of the phenomena of true veins. They cut through different mineral planes, their gangue differs from the enclosing walls, there is a lining of of *flucan* on either side, and they pursue a nearly undeviating course, except where they enter the sandstone which becomes shattered and tilted up, often at an angle as high as 45°, at the point of contact. This is represented in the annexed woodcut, which exhibits the following section of one of the veins:

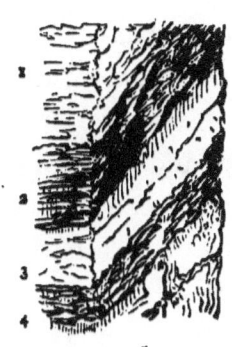

1. SANDSTONE.
2. FLUCAN, or shale, 6 feet.
3. FLUOR SPAR, 4 feet.
4. FLUCAN, 3 feet.
5. LIMESTONE of indefinite depth.

The vein at this point has a width of 13 feet, and as traced downward is observed to expand, and at the depth of 150 feet, exhibits the annexed section; but here, even, the entire vein has not been cross-cut. Throughout the gangue is distributed at intervals, galena of a steel-like fracture and color, which, on assay, is found to be both argentiferous and auriferous.

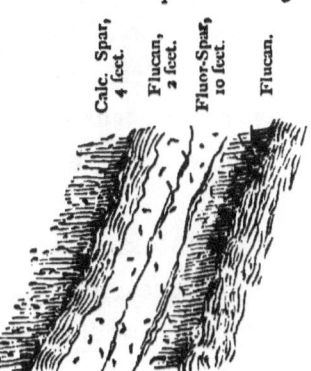

The fluor spar is ordinarily crystalline, and of a straw-color, but where cavities occur, there are found beautiful cubical crystals of an amethystine tint.

THE SOUTHWESTERN LEAD-REGION OF MISSOURI.—The famous Granby Mines are in this formation, and in productiveness are probably unsurpassed in the United States. They now give employment to about 500 miners. The amount of mineral raised annually, reaches 10,000,000 pounds, yielding 7,000,000 pounds of lead.* The ore occurs in three zones, the lowest about sixty feet beneath the surface, and each zone is capped by a layer of chert about eighteen inches in thickness. Before the war, the annual product of lead-ore was not far from four and one-half millions of pounds. Zinc, in the form of sulphuret, occurs here abundantly, as well as the carbonate; in fact, both of these ores accompany galena in its range throughout Missouri. In Taney County, however, I have observed veins of the silicious carbonate of zinc, which, in strength and purity, surpass all deposits of the kind which I have observed elsewhere.

The metalliferous deposits of Mexico are, in part, included in heavy masses of limestone which have been elevated in rugged ridges, running west of north and east of south; and the age of these

* Parker, "Missouri as it is." 1867.

rocks, according to the best observers, is referable to the Carboniferous epoch.

(*b.*) COAL-MEASURES.— In the whole range of rocks which compose the crust of the globe, there is no group which contains materials so valuable to man as this. Closely as, in the past, coal and iron have been identified with the progress of man, they are to be still more closely identified with his future triumphs over matter, and with all that pertains to his temporal prosperity. If there is any thing which distinguishes this age above all others, it is the result of their cooperation in the infinite variety of operations performed by machinery, to the superseding of human muscles. The steam-engine is, perhaps, the most marked example of this union; and in the rapidity, precision, and skill with which it performs its multifarious tasks, it seems to be endowed almost with intelligence,— to be almost "a thing of life." "Its action is so regulated, as to make it capable of being applied to the finest and most delicate manufactures, and its power so increased as to set weight and solidity at defiance. It has become a thing stupendous alike for its force and flexibility,— for the prodigious power it can exert, and the ease and precision and ductility with which that power can be varied, distributed, and applied. The trunk of an elephant, that can pick up a pin or rend an oak, is as nothing to it. It can engrave a seal, and crush masses of obdurate metal before it,— draw out, without breaking, a thread as fine as gossamer, and lift a ship of war like a bauble in the air. It can embroider muslin, and forge anchors,— cut steel into ribands, and impel loaded vessels against the fury of the winds and waves." *

The benefits which this invention has conferred upon the world can not be overestimated. In Great Britain it performs the labor of fifty millions of men, and in every civilized country it has vastly augmented the amount of its productions, and become the basis of additional wealth and population. It lies at the foundation of an improved and more expeditious commercial intercourse, and on the land it has annihilated distances. It has become a tremendous engine in war, and in peace it has armed the feeble hand of man with an instrument by which nearly every mechanical process can be performed,— and yet it is in its infancy, and each year develops new applications.

In these elements of industrial art — coal and iron, — no region is so bountifully supplied as the Great Valley. We have already traced the range and extent of the iron ores; it remains to trace the distribution of the coals. Let any one glance at the Geological Map (p. 272), and he will at once

* Jeffrey. Miscellanies :—" Character of James Watt."

see the vast area over which the Coal-Measures constitute the prevailing rocks, divided into several distinct fields, and intersected by navigable waters by which the products of these fields are made accessible to the markets of the Great Valley. Instead of lying in basin-shaped depressions as in England, where the coal-seams can be approached only by deep-penetrating shafts, they range with the enclosing strata over large areas, and can be mined by drifts and adits, driven above the ordinary drainage of the country.

THE ALLEGHANY COAL-FIELD ranges through Western Pennsylvania and Virginia, Eastern Ohio, Kentucky, and Tennessee, and terminates in Northern Alabama. Its area is estimated at 60,000 square miles. The assemblage of shales, limestones, and sandstones, is estimated at 2,500 or 3,000 feet in thickness. The workable seams of coal at Pittsburgh, have an aggregate thickness of $25\frac{1}{2}$ feet, and in Southern Ohio, of $22\frac{1}{2}$ feet.

THE ILLINOIS COAL-FIELD occupies about two-thirds of the area of that State, and parts of Indiana and Kentucky. The area is about the same as that of the Alleghany coal-field. The thickness of the associated rocks is about 800 feet, and of the workable seams, in Southern Illinois, 19 feet.

THE MISSOURI COAL-FIELD occupies the northwestern portion of that State; the eastern portion of Kansas; a large area to the north, in Iowa and Nebraska; and is protracted south into the Indian Territory. Its area is the largest in the United States, and even in the world, being not less than 100,000 square miles. According to Swallow, the coal-rocks of Kansas are 2,000 feet thick, and contain from 12 to 15 feet of workable coal. The Upper Measures, so far as we have observed, are nearly barren. Isolated patches, outliers of this great coal-field, occur on the Arkansas River.

THE MICHIGAN COAL-FIELD is extremely shallow, being about 100 feet thick, and extending over an area of 5,000 square miles. The coal, for the most part, is mined for neighborhood purposes.

The boundaries of the TEXAS COAL-FIELD, of which Fort Belknap is the centre, have been but imperfectly defined. It is known to occupy several of the northern counties of that State, but it is so covered with arenaceous deposits, that its presence can only be determined by boring, and the region has not become sufficiently populated to render such explorations necessary. Coals have been mined along the Brazos River for use at Fort Belknap, and the seam varies from two to four feet. Fossils of the coal-measure limestones have been observed by Newberry in the valley of the Rio Grande; by Stansbury in the South Pass, and at Laramie Ridge; and by Meek and Hayden in the Black Hills. Thus, while, as before remarked, the Carboniferous limestones, and even the limestones of the Coal-Measures, have been observed, at frequent intervals, along the entire eastern slope of the Rocky Mountains, there is yet to be discovered, in all that region, a true seam of coal of the Carboniferous epoch; and the reason for this is, we think, obvious. In the western portion of the Great Valley, during this epoch, conditions existed which were adverse to its formation; while to the east, the waters were shoaling, giving origin to a series of lagoons, on whose borders flourished in rank luxuriance, developed under a tropical climate, and in an atmosphere, perhaps, surcharged with carbonic acid gas, a peculiar vegetation, such as grasses, yucca-like *Lilliaceæ*, and *Palms*, and also *Coniferæ* and *Cycadeæ*. *Calamites*, somewhat like our bamboos and rushes, shot up in arborescent forms, and the *Lycopodiaceæ*, like our club-mosses, assumed tree-like dimensions. *Lepidodendra* and *Sigillariæ*, with accurately-arranged markings or with fluted trunks, reached sixty feet or more in height, while the *Stigmariæ*, which are found ordinarily in the fire-clay beneath the coal, have the markings of the Cactus. There were, too, tree-like ferns of great variety, asterophyllites with whorl-like leaves, and Araucaria-like *Coniferæ*. Such was the vegetation which flourished during that period, and which we now employ, consolidated into coal, to warm our dwellings, to light our cities, and to propel our machinery.*

As the region rose and fell, the torrents swept in their silts of sand, mud, and clay, now consolidated into sandstones, shales, and slates; and when the ocean invaded the land, limestones were formed by precipitation, enclosing forms of animal life exclusively marine. In all the Western coal-fields, the alternate dominion of land and water is clearly indicated by the character of the organic remains. While such conditions existed to the East; on the other hand, to the West, stretched out an ocean

---

* The shales which overlie our coal-seams often contain, in great perfection, the most delicate forms of these vegetable structures. Buckland (Bridgewater Treatises, Geology,) thus describes the roof of a coal-mine in Bohemia:

"The most elaborate imitations of living foliage upon the painted ceilings of Italian palaces, bear no comparison with the beauteous profusion of extinct vegetable forms with which the galleries of these instructive coal-mines are overhung. The roof is covered with a canopy of gorgeous tapestry, enriched with festoons of most graceful foliage, flung in wild, irregular profusion over every portion of its surface. The effect is heightened by the contrast of the coal-black color of these vegetables, with the light ground-work of the rock to which they are attached. The spectator feels himself transported, as if by enchantment, into the forests of another world; he beholds trees, of forms and characters now unknown upon the surface of the earth, presented to his senses almost in the beauty and vigor of their primeval life; their scaly stems and bending branches, with their delicate apparatus of foliage, all spread out before him, little impaired by the lapse of countless ages, and bearing faithful records of extinct systems of vegetation, which began and terminated in times of which these relics are infallible historians."

with no visible shores, whose waters were tenanted only by marine forms, and upon whose floor only limestone sediments were deposited. Fanciful as these speculations may seem, they become of practical utility in discussing the great routes of continental and oceanic communication. They are questions which come home, as Bacon has said, "to men's business and bosoms."

The coals derived from these different fields, and even from the different seams, and, it may be said, from different parts of the same seam, are far from being uniform in character. The anthracites are restricted to the eastern slope of the Alleghanies, where metamorphic action has been most manifest, which is supposed to have driven off the greater portion of the volatile materials. The semi-bituminous coals next succeed, where that action has been less marked; and finally, where it has been but feebly exerted, we have the fatty, bituminous coals.

The most valuable coals, perhaps, thus far developed on the western slope of the Alleghanies, are those of Northern Ohio and Northwestern Pennsylvania, derived from the lowest seam in the series, and known as Brier Hill or Ormsby. It is a splint coal, so thoroughly compacted as to bear repeated handling and distant transportation, and is capable of sustaining the burden of a furnace without crushing. It contains from 62 to 64 per cent. of fixed carbon; from 2 or 3 per cent. of hygrometric moisture; from 33 to 35 per cent. of volatile combustible matter; and less than 3 per cent. of ash, nearly white. While valuable as a domestic fuel by reason of its freedom from sulphur, its inflammability, its small amount of ash, and its disposition not to agglutinate or give off an excess of sooty matter; its preeminent merit is that, in a crude state, it is an iron-making coal; and hence in the Mahoning and Shenango Valleys, the facilities for iron-smelting are almost unsurpassed. Within a few years, a coal, having similar properties, has been developed in the vicinity of Brazil, Indiana, and has been applied to the same purposes. This is the lowest seam in the Illinois coal-field.

More recently, in the vicinity of Chester, Illinois, an iron-making coal has been discovered, which will be made available in reducing the immense deposits of specular and magnetic iron of Missouri; and a coal having similar properties, is said to have been reached by a shaft near Springfield. We discovered, some years ago, a coal having similar properties in Iowa, west of the Des Moines River, but it is too remote from the iron-ores to be made available.

The Pittsburgh coals, which include those of the Monongehala and Youghiogheny, rank deservedly high. They contain more gaseous matter, and are, therefore, unavailable for iron-making, without undergoing the preliminary process of coking. The coals of Southern Ohio are equally good; those of Central Ohio, about Zanesville, are so fatty as to agglutinate in burning, and are excellent for coking.

The coals of Northern Illinois are ordinarily highly charged with water, often containing as high as 12 per cent., and are so sulphurous as to disintegrate on exposure to the atmosphere. Still they are extensively mined for domestic fuel, and for generating steam in stationary engines and locomotives.

The Kansas coals have not been developed sufficiently to show their true character. The Burlingame coal, near the upper portion of the Measures, shows impurities such as appertain to those of Northern Illinois, but the seams in the lower portion, which come to the surface in the southeastern part of the State, are said to be of considerable thickness (7 feet), and the coal is of an excellent quality.

Apart from coal, other economic materials exist. The brine-springs of Western Pennsylvania and Virginia, and of Southern Ohio and Eastern Kansas, have their reservoirs at the base of this group. The manufacture of salt has been prosecuted for many years, and in the older States, has proved a source of great revenue to the respective regions.

The impure carbonates of iron abound in the Alleghany coal-field, but in those which lie farther west, few productive beds have been observed.

Permian System.—This series of rocks is wanting in the older States, and is by no means abundantly developed in the Mississippi Valley. The existence of these rocks was first made known by Swallow, and were observed by him near Fort Riley, on the Kaw River of Kansas. Here they consist of a series of drab and dove-colored limestones, with intercalated marls and shales, variously-colored red, green, and grey, with gypsum-beds more or less abundant. They flank the western outcrop of the Coal-Measures, which here dip northwest, and rest conformably upon them. As the lower portion is made up of transition beds, clearly indicating gradually-changing conditions in the character of the sediments and of organic forms, it becomes difficult to draw the line where the Carboniferous ceases and the Permian begins.

Near Manhattan, a limestone is quarried from this series for architectural purposes, which is so soft that it may be sawed with a hand-saw, and planed with a jack-plane, and yet is very durable. It is the cheapest material of which the pioneer can construct his house — cheaper even than it would be to resort to the forest, if such existed, for logs. Hayden notices the occurrence of a similar limestone, and belonging to the same age, in Nebraska.

In passing up the valley of the Kaw, in the vicinity of Fort Riley, these rocks are seen lining the bluffs which attain a height of 250 feet. The unequal power to resist the weathering effects of the atmosphere, causes the more enduring strata to stand out in bold relief; and, as their inclination is very slight, the bluffs for miles have the appearance of being crowned with Titanic walls which conform to all the curvatures of the ravines. Hayden has identified the extension of these rocks into Nebraska; Shumard recognizes their existence in the Gaudalupe Mountains of Texas; and Meek and Hayden in the Black Hills, and the Big-Horn Mountains.

Triassic and Jurassic Series.—These rocks have hitherto occupied a subordinate place in the the text-books of American geology, but recent explorations on the Pacific Coast show that they are widely developed, and enter largely into the orographical features of this continent. It is not improbable that they will be found coterminous with the whole Rocky Mountain system, flanking the great granitic masses, and proving the main repositories of the precious metals.

The sandstones and intercalated traps which fill the lower valley of the Connecticut, belong to this series, and from thence it is traced, in interrupted ranges, through New Jersey, Pennsylvania, Virginia, and North Carolina. It is supposed that these rocks represent both of the great divisions, Jurassic and Triassic; but it has been found impossible to draw the line of demarcation between them, and in the Mississippi Valley the same difficulty exists.

Above the Permian, in Kansas, Swallow observed a series of variegated sandstones and marls which he assigns to the Trias. In the Colorado Valley, Newberry saw a series of marls, 2,000 feet thick, but destitute of fossils, interposed between the Carboniferous and Cretaceous systems, which he regards as Triassic. Occurring at the Black Hills of Dakota and at the Red Buttes, on the North Platte, Meek and Hayden describe beds subordinate to the Jurassic, which probably belong to the Trias; and they subsequently recognized this formation along the eastern slope of the Laramie, Big-Horn, and Wind-River Mountains.

The Upper Trias, according to Le Conte, is exposed in the deepest part of Purgatoire Cañon, and also farther south, near the Sandia Mountains, and along the Rio Grande. Triassic rocks also occupy a broad belt in Nevada, extending from the meridian 117°, west to the California boundary.

But the development of this system, or rather the Triassic, in all of its importance, is the result of the California Geological Survey. The generalizations brought out are of the most striking character, and such as to afford us a clue to unravel the age of the auriferous deposits of the Rocky Mountains. The palæontological evidence would indicate that these rocks are equivalent to the Upper Trias, or the Hallstadt limestone of the Austrian Alps — a group of rocks which, up to a recent time, was thought to be barren of organic forms, but which, under the auspices of the Austrian Survey, has added 800 specimens of Radiates and Mollusks to the fauna of this epoch.

"This great Triassic belt of the Pacific Coast," according to Whitney, "has been explored by the Survey in the latitude of 40°, and over a width, east and west, of nearly four degrees of longitude (117° to 120°). * * [Triassic fossils have been collected] from the three parallel ranges in longitude 117° to 118° in Nevada Territory, known as the Humboldt Mountains, or the Humboldt mining region, and from localities in Plumas County, California. But sufficient palæontological evidence has been obtained to enable us to state, that this formation extends from Mexico to British Columbia, and that it occupies a vast area, although much broken up, interrupted by eruptive rocks, and covered in many places by heavy accumulations of volcanic materials." *

* Palæontology of California." Vol. I.

THE GOLD-BEARING ROCKS OF CALIFORNIA consist of metamorphic sandstones, with intercalated beds of quartz, in which the gold is segregated. The beds almost invariably have the same range and dip as the associated rocks, and are not, therefore, true fissure-veins. The strike of the rocks is pretty uniform, being about north 30° west, except where they have been disturbed by volcanic outbursts, subsequent to their first uplift. As you ascend to the High Sierra, the crests are found to consist of great masses of granite, often dome-shaped, whose culminating points reach 15,000 feet above the sea, constituting, as conjectured by Whitney, the highest land in the United States. While gold is not absent in these igneous rocks, it has not been found profitable to mine it.*

THE COPPER-BEARING ROCKS OF CALIFORNIA are of the same age, and occupy the western flanks

---

* The product of this series of rocks, in the precious metals, is estimated by Ross Brown for the year 1867 (Mineral Resources of the United States), at $75,000,000, apportioned as follows:

CALIFORNIA,	$25,000,000
NEVADA,	20,000,000
MONTANA,	12,000,000
IDAHO,	6,500,000
WASHINGTON,	1,000,000
OREGON,	2,000,000
COLORADO,	2,500,000
NEW MEXICO,	500,000
ARIZONA,	500,000
UNKNOWN SOURCES,	5,000,000
	$75,000,000

of the Sierra. The copper, which appears mainly as a sulphuret, is segregated in beds which are included in chlorite and talcose slates. In the vicinity of Copperopolis, they have been extensively mined, and the monthly product has been known to exceed 3,000 tons of ore. In 1864, the shipments from San Francisco reached 14,315 tons, valued at $1,094,660. The excessive cost of transportation to the coast, and the absence of a supply of proper fuel by which to reduce the ores to a matte, operate adversely to copper-mining, so that only the richer ores are selected. Besides, the fall in the price of copper the world over, has caused the export almost entirely to cease.

Rémond, before quoted, has shown that the Sierra Madre of Northern Mexico, is similar in geological structure to the Sierra Nevada. The Triassic rocks of Sonora consist of heavy beds of quartzite and conglomerate, with coal-bearing shales, and rest on greenstones, porphyries, and granites. Wherever metamorphosed, they are both auriferous and argentiferous.

These observations show that, during this epoch, both Europe and the United States were convulsed, and the dynamical forces were such as to lift up some of the most stupendous mountain chains to be found on the surface of our planet.

Cretaceous System.—The three great axial lines which determine the contour of the Mississippi Valley, had assumed their form and direction before these deposits, exceeding in places 2,000 feet in thickness, had been made in the Cretaceous sea. The boundaries of that sea may be described as follows: There were entering bays along the Atlantic Coast from New Jersey to North Carolina. The sea washed the southern flanks of the Alleghanies, and formed an estuary which penetrated inland as far as the mouth of the Ohio. It swept round the southern portion of the Northwestern coal-field, extending south into Mexico, and north beyond the limits of the United States. All that portion of the country lying between Central Kansas and the eastern slope of the Rocky Mountains was open water. On the Pacific side, the Cretaceous sea washed the base of the Sierra Nevada, extended up the valley of the Colorado, and even penetrated the Great Basin. There is no one formation in the United States, which is so widely distributed. The beds of this series in New Jersey attain a thickness of only 400 feet, while on the Upper Missouri, they reach 2,500.

To Meek and Hayden we are mainly indebted for a thorough investigation of the Cretaceous strata of the Upper Missouri, which they have grouped in the following order:

SECTION OF THE CRETACEOUS ROCKS OF THE UPPER MISSOURI.

Upper Series.—Gray, ferruginous and yellowish sandstones, and arenaceous clays, containing *Belemnitella bulbosa, Nautilus dekayi, Ammonites placenta, A. lobatus, Scaphites conradi, S. nicollet, Baculites grandis, Busycon bairdi, Fusus culbertsoni, F. newberryi, Aporrhais americana, Pseudo-buccinum nebrascencis, Mactra warrenana, Cardium subquadratum,* and a great number of other molluscous fossils, together with bones of *Mosasaurus missouriensis.*	**Fox-Hill Beds, No. 5.**—Fox-Hills, near Moreau River; near Long Lake; above Fort Pierre; along base of Big-Horn Mountains; and on North and South Platte Rivers. Thickness, 500 feet.
Dark-gray and bluish plastic clays, containing near the upper part, *Nautilus dekayi, Ammonites placenta, Baculites ovatus, B. compressus, Scaphites nodosus, Dentalium gracile, Crassatella evansi, Cucullæa nebrascencis, Inoceramus sagensis, I. nebrascensis, I. vanuxemi;* also, bones of *Mosasaurus missouriensis,* etc. Middle Zone nearly barren of fossils.	**Fort Pierre Group, No. 4.**—Sage Creek; Cheyenne River, and on White River; above the Mauvaises Terres, Fort Pierre, and out to Bad Lands; down the Missouri, on the high country, to Great Bend.
Lower fossiliferous Zone, containing *Ammonites complexus, Baculites ovatus, B. compressus, Helicoceras mortoni, H. tortum, H. umbilicatum, H. cochleatum, Ptychoceras mortoni, Fusus vinculum, Anisomyon borealis, Amauropsis paludiniformis, Inoceramus subulatus, I. tenuilineatus;* also, bones of *Mosasaurus missouriensis,* etc.	Great Bend of the Missouri, below Fort Pierre.
Dark bed of very fine unctuous clay, containing much carbonaceous matter, with veins and seams of gypsum, masses of sulphuret of iron, and numerous small scales of Fishes, local, filling depressions in the bed below.	Near Bijou Hill, on the Missouri. Thickness, 700 feet.
Lower Series.—Lead-gray calcareous marl, weathering to a yellowish or whitish chalky appearance above, containing large scales and other remains of Fishes, and numerous species of *Ostrea congesta* attached to fragments of *Inoceramus,* passing down into light-yellowish and whitish limestone, containing great numbers of *Inoceramus problematicus, I. pseudomytiloides, I. aviculoides,* and *Ostrea congesta;* Fish Scales, etc.	**Niobrara Division, No. 3.**—Bluffs along the Missouri, above the Great Bend, to the vicinity of the Big Sioux River; also below there, and on the tops of the hills. Thickness, 200 feet.
Dark-gray laminated clays, sometimes alternating, near the upper part, with seams and layers of soft gray and light-colored limestones, *Inoceramus problematicus, I. tenuirostratus, I. latus? I. fragilis, Ostrea congesta, Veulia mortoni, Pholadomya papyracea, Ammonites mullani, A. percerinatus, A. vespertinus, Scaphites warreni, S. larvæformis, S. ventricosus, S. vermiformis, Nautilus elegans,* etc.	**Fort Benton Group, No. 2.**—Extensively developed near Fort Benton, on the Upper Missouri; also along the latter, from ten miles above James River to Big Sioux River, and along the eastern slope of the Rocky Mountains, as well as at the Black Hills. Thickness, 870 feet.
Yellowish, reddish, and occasionally white sandstone, with, at places, alternations of various colored clays, and beds and seams of impure lignite; also, silicified wood, and great numbers of leaves of the higher types of dicotyledonous trees, with casts of *Pharella? dakotensis, Axinea siouxensis,* and *Caprina arenarea.*	**Dakota Group, No. 1.**—Hills back of the town of Dakota; also extensively developed in the surrounding country in Dakota County, below the mouth of the Big Sioux River, thence extending southward into Northeastern Kansas and beyond. Thickness, 400 ft.

The Cretaceous strata of this country, notwithstanding their extraordinary development, are, in position, above the Older Cretaceous beds of Europe.

The Lower series is the equivalent of the Lower, or Grey chalk and Upper green-sand of British geologists; while the Upper series is the equivalent of the Upper or White chalk and Maestricht beds.

The Cretaceous rocks, if the more recently formed Tertiary strata were removed, would probably be found every where abutting against the first-formed strata of the Rocky Mountains, but there are places where they have been disturbed by more recent volcanic eruptions. At the Raton Pass, the eruptive rocks have broken through the lower and middle series, which for a long distance form a very conspicuous terrace. Intercalated with these strata, are beds of coal of sufficient thickness and purity to prove of great economical value. In the Raton Pass, they are eight feet thick, and lie horizontally, and in Vermejo Cañon, they reach ten feet. Forts Lyon and Union are supplied with fuel from these sources. Near Tijeras and west of Los Lunas, and also east of Don Pedro, near the Rio Grande, and in San Lagaro Hill, twenty-five miles west of Santa Fé, coal has been observed, and at the latter place it forms a very pure anthracite, the metamorphism being due to a trachytic overflow. (Le Conte.) Similar deposits have been observed in the Puerco Valley, and also in those of San José and Ojo Pescado, showing an extension of the coals two hundred miles west of the Rio Grande, and in many instances the igneous protrusions have converted them into anthracite. (Parry.)

The Coast Ranges of the Pacific are made up largely of Cretaceous and Miocine-Tertiary strata. They are, at numerous points, invaded by igneous products which have not only tilted them up at high angles, but metamorphosed them into jaspery materials, obliterating every trace of organic life. Like the same formations on the eastern slope of the Rocky Mountains, there are intercalations of valuable seams of coal; and to this epoch may be referred the deposits of Mount Diablo, near San Francisco; of Bellingham Bay, in Washington Territory; of Nanaimo, on Vancouver's Island; and those along the shores of the Straits of Fuca and Puget's Sound. All of these coals are soft, are charged with a large percentage of water, and are apt to exfoliate on exposure to the air. They contain not to exceed 45 per cent. of fixed carbon, and are, therefore, unfit for use where a strong, concentrated heat is required.

The Coast Ranges are not destitute of metallic

wealth. It is claimed, even, that the rocks are sparingly impregnated with gold; but quicksilver, in the form of cinnabar, is found at several points. The most productive mines, however, are at New Almaden, where the yearly product reaches 3,000,000 pounds. The supply is far in excess of the wants of the mining community, and the surplus is shipped to China and the South American States. The ores occupy a series of irregular cavities, mostly confined within a space of one hundred and fifty feet square, and extending downwards for about four hundred feet,— dipping to the north at an angle of 30° to 35°,— and the cavities are scattered through the enclosing mass without any approach to regularity. *

All the way, according to the California Survey, between Fort Téjon and Fort Reading, along the foot-hills of the Sierra, are to be seen, except where removed by denudation, strata of Marine-Tertiary and Cretaceous, reposing in a horizontal position upon the upturned edges of the auriferous slates. In the vicinity of Shasta, however, which, as before remarked, is a volcanic cone of extremely recent origin, both of these formations have been disturbed,— the result of this uplift,— but there is little doubt that they were once continuous across the valleys of San Joaquin and Sacramento, to the

---

* Whitney. "Geological Survey of California." P. 69.

Pacific Ocean; on the one hand, exhibiting striking evidences of metamorphism, and on the other, reposing, for the most part, in an undisturbed position.

According to Gabb, the Cretaceous of California is represented but by a single member of this formation, corresponding with the Fort Pierre group, or No. 4, of Meek and Hayden. The peninsula of California may belong to the same group, although, on the authority last quoted, it is regarded as an open question.

In Northern Mexico, as we have seen, the Cretaceous strata occupy the same relation to the Sierra Madre that they do to the Sierra Nevada.

The close of the Cretaceous epoch would seem to indicate an important change in the history of the earth's progress towards the condition of affairs which we now behold. Whilst organic forms were represented by the four great divisions of the animal kingdom; still, the condition of the globe seems to have been unfitted for the introduction and sustenance of the warm-blooded animals, such as now roam over its surface, although there are a few exceptions to this general rule. The Cretaceous period was emphatically the age of reptiles. Immense saurians swarmed the seas, and winged lizards, known to us as pterodactyles, cleft the air. The vegetable remains, in this country, show a near approach to existing forms. These consist of dicotyledonous plants, among which Newberry identifies species belonging to the genera *Populus* (poplar); *Salix* (willow); *Alnus* (alder); *Platanus* (sycamore); *Liriodendron* (tulip); *Ficus* (fig-tree), and others; and European botanists, while admitting the Cretaceous age of the Nebraska flora, unequivocally assert that it is closely allied to that of the Miocine-Tertiary of the Eastern Continent.

In the following table, are given the results of the analyses of coals from the different formations in the United States, by which it will be seen, that while those of the recent epochs are more highly charged with water, and contain less fixed carbon, which is the heating power, they are yet of great economical value.

ANALYSES OF COALS.

DESIGNATION.	HYGROM. MOISTURE.	FIXED CARBON.	VOLATILE MATTER.	ASH.	CHEMIST.
CARBONIFEROUS.					
Brier Hill, Ohio	2.40	67.60	28.00	2.00	Blaney.
Marietta Run, Ohio (Upper)	3.20	54.61	36.80	5.39	"
" " " (Lower)	3.80	53.80	39.68	2.72	"
Pittsburgh, Pa.	2.34	55.82	34.31	7.16	Chilton.
Youghiogheny, Pa.	1.00	58.40	35.00	5.60	Peters.
Ormsby, Pa.	4.00	66.56	26.93	2.50	Blaney.
Greenup County, Ky. (Cannel)	2.00	56.01	37.89	4.10	Huyes.
" " " (Lower Seam)	1.13	29.14	61.29	8.42	"
Brazil, Ind.	6.17	59.17	33.16	1.50	Blaney.
Chester, Ill., Layer No. 1, 20 i.	6.31	62.75	28.68	2.25	"
" " " " 2, 14 i.	7.50	50.00	40.62	1.87	"
" " " " 3, 21 i.	9.25	46.66	29.50	5.12	"
" " " " 4, 18 i	6.22	61.57	26.50	5.30	"
" " " " 5, 16 i.	8.47	56.24	25.28	10.00	"
Du Quoin, Ill.	7.00	61.20	28.60	3.20	"
LaSalle, Ill. (Upper)	10.00	55.00	27.40	7.60	"
" " (Middle)	10.00	54.60	27.40	8.00	"
" " (Lower)	10.00	56.00	25.20	8.80	"
Ottumwa, Iowa.	11.20	59.80	22.60	6.40	"
Hillsborough, Iowa.	7.92	46.76	41.74	3.58	Whitney
Farmington, "	8.62	47.42	38.08	5.88	"
New Buffalo, "	3.13	49.08	38.77	9.02	"
Cote sans Dessein, Mo.		50.81	34.06	15.13	Chilton.
Callaway County, "		50.78	34.20	15.02	"
Johnson County, Ark.		51.16	43.50	5.34	Frazer.
TRIASSIC AND JURASSIC.					
Chesterfield, Va.		80.30	9.98	9.72	Rogers.
Richmond Coal		59.25	32.00	8.75	Andreas.
Mid Lothian		61.08	28.45	10.47	Johnson.
Stonehenge		58.70	36.50	4.80	"
Coalbrook Dale		66.48	29.00	4.52	Rogers.
CRETACEOUS.					
Mount Diablo, California.					
Clark's Mine	13.47	40.65	40.36	5.52	Whitney.
Black Diamond	14.69	46.84	33.89	4.58	"
Cumberland	13.84	44.92	40.27	0.97	"
Peacock	14.13	44.55	37.38	3.94	"
Corral Hollow	20.53	36.35	35.62	7.50	"
Bellingham Bay, W. T.	8.39	45.69	33.26	12.66	"
Nanaimo, "					
MIOCINE-TERTIARY.					
Coos Bay, Oregon	20.09	41.98	32.59	5.34	Whitney.
Bellemonte, Colorado		48.36	47.00	4.64	Kent.

CHAPTER X.

GEOLOGY (*Continued*),— SEDIMENTARY ROCKS.

TERTIARY SYSTEM — MARINE OF THE ATLANTIC SLOPE — FRESH-WATER OF THE MISSOURI BASIN — MARINE OF THE PACIFIC COAST — ECONOMIC VALUE OF THE TERTIARY COALS — IGNEOUS PRODUCTS OF THE GREAT BASIN — COMSTOCK LODE AND ITS YIELD IN SILVER — DRIFT-EPOCH — DRIFT-ACTION IN THE MISSISSIPPI VALLEY — EROSIVE ACTION ON THE PACIFIC SLOPE AND IN THE COLORADO PLATEAU — TERRACES OF MODIFIED DRIFT — LOESS — SAND-DUNES — THE GREAT LAKES — DRIFT-PHENOMENA IN THEIR BASINS — DENUDATION, AREA, DEPTH, AND ELEVATION — RESUME.

The Tertiary System.—The organic remains entombed in this series of strata, inaugurate an epoch when the forms of animal and vegetable life begin to approach nearer to existing species. In fact, many of the forms which tenanted the seas of that age are identical with those now living, and the aborescent vegetation was not unlike that of the subtropical latitudes of this day. We, too, have evidence of the existence of large fresh-water deposits, and consequently of the proximity of large areas of dry land. The Tertiary deposits are widely distributed throughout the United States, and are both of marine and fresh-water origin.

THE MARINE STRATA occur in the immediate valley of the Lower Mississippi, above its junction with the Ohio Valley, and along the Texas, Gulf, and Atlantic Coasts, as far as Richmond, Virginia; and patches are found, even, as far north as Martha's Vineyard. Lignite beds occur inland, as at Brandon, Vermont, and at other points.

What are known as the Pine Barrens, in the Southern States, is a belt of country more than 1,700 miles long, and often 170 miles broad, stretching from Richmond, along the Atlantic and Gulf Coasts, to beyond the western line of Louisiana, where the soil, derived from the decomposition of the newest member of the Tertiary series, is sandy, and where the principal arborescent form is the long-leaf pine (*Pinus palustris*). It is emphatically the "poor man's region." These forests, while affording a valuable article of lumber, also yield pitch, tar, and turpentine.

In this series, three epochs have been recognized. 1. THE CLAIBORNE beds of Alabama, and those of JACKSON and VICKSBURGH, Mississippi, which are referred to the oldest, or *Eocine*. 2. Those of YORKTOWN, Virginia, to the middle, or *Miocine*.

And 3. Those of SUMTER and DARLINGTON, to the newest, or *Pliocine*.*

According to Hilgard's general section, the combined Tertiary series, embracing the Northern Lignite, the Claiborne, Jackson, Vicksburgh, and Grand-Gulf groups, have a thickness of more than 750 feet.† The most interesting fossil, perhaps, in the whole series, is that from the Jackson group, known as the *Zeuglodon cetoides*, a marine animal of the whale tribe, which resembled the saurians in shape, and attained a length of seventy feet.

On the Atlantic Coast, the rocks which compose this series, are variable in character,—consisting at times of beds of sand and clay; at other localities, of compact sandstones; at others, of calcareous sandstones and shell-beds; and in South Carolina occurs a cellular Buhr-stone, adapted to mill-stones. The clays and sands often contain lignite and hæmatitic iron-ore in such quantities as to be of economic value; and the clays are of sufficient purity to make fire-brick, and, when washed, are

---

* These three divisions were established by Lyell: *Pliocine*, because the major part of the fossil testacea of this epoch are referable to existing species; *Miocine*, because a minor part only of the species is referable to existing forms; and *Eocine*, because in this formation, we recognize the dawn of forms allied to existing species.

† "Geology of Mississippi," p. 108.

of such whiteness as to be used in giving opacity to writing paper.

The northern limits of the Marine-Tertiary do not appear to have extended far up the Ohio Valley; but in Pulaski County, Illinois, Worthen found marine shells of the genus *Cucullæa* and *Turritella*, in a green-sand, and a shark's tooth, near Caladonia, where there is a thin bed of lignite at low-water mark in the Ohio River. The hills in Southern Illinois are capped occasionally with beds of ferruginous conglomerate, which may be referred to this age. A few miles west of St. Louis, at Webster station, Mr. Freeman has lately obtained specimens of that peculiar American shell, now inhabiting the Gulf of Mexico, known as *Gnathodon*, and Worthen has collected detached sharks' teeth at Warsaw, and near the mouth of Skunk River, Iowa.

FRESH-WATER TERTIARY STRATA.—These are largely developed in the region lying between the Missouri River and the Rocky Mountains, and even penetrate the Great Basin. They have been carefully studied by Meek and Hayden, who find that they are referable to four distinct periods, indicated by the entombed organic remains. Their classification is as follows:

GENERAL SECTION OF THE TERTIARY ROCKS OF THE UPPER MISSOURI.

NAMES.	SUBDIVISIONS.	THICKNESS.	LOCALITIES.	FOREIGN EQUIVALENTS.
Loup-River Beds.	Fine, loose sand, with some layers of limestone; contains bones of *Canis* (dog), *Felis* (cat), *Castor* (beaver), *Equus* (horse), *Mastodon* and *Elephas* (elephant), *Testudo* (tortoise), etc., some of which are scarcely distinguishable from living species; also, shells of the genera *Helix*, *Physa*, and *Succinea*, probably of recent species. All fresh-water and land types.	300 to 400 feet.	On Loup-Fork of Platte River, extending north to Niobrara River, and south to an unknown distance beyond the Platte.	Pliocene.
White-River Group.	White and light-drab clays, with some beds of sandstone, and local limestone. Mammalian fossils: *Oreodon*, *Titanotherium*, *Chæropotamus*, *Rhinoceros*, *Anchitherium*, *Hyamonodon*, *Machairodus*. Reptilian: *Trionyx*, *Testudo*. Shells (fresh water): *Helix*, *Planorbis* and *Limnea*. Petrified wood, etc. All extinct. No brackish water or marine remains.	1,000 feet or more.	Bad Lands of White River, under the Loup-River bed; on the Niobrara; and across the country to the Platte.	Miocene.
Wind-River Deposits.	Light-gray and ash-colored sandstones, with more or less argillaceous layers. Fossils: Fragments of *Trionyx*, *Testudo*, with large specimens of *Helix*, *Vivipararus*, Petrified wood, etc. No marine or brackish water types.	1,500 to 2,000 feet.	Wind-River Valley; also west of Wind-River Mountains.	?
Fort Union or Great Lignite Deposits.	Beds of clay and sand, with round ferruginous concretions, and numerous beds, seams, and local deposits of lignite. Great numbers of dicotyledonous leaves, stems, etc., of the genera *Platanus*, *Acer*, *Ulmus*, *Populus*, etc., with very large leaves of true Ean-Palms. Also, fresh or brackish water shells of the genera *Helix*, *Melania*, *Vivipararus*, *Corbicula*, *Unio*, *Ostrea*, *Potamomya*; and scales of fishes, *Lepidotus*; with reptilian bones of *Trionyx*, *Emys*, *Compsemys*, *Crocodilus*, etc.	2,000 feet or more.	Occupies the whole country round Fort Union, extending north into the British Possessions to unknown distances; also southward to Fort Clark; seen under the White-River group, on the North Platte River, above Fort Laramie; also on west side of Wind-River Mountains.	Eocene?

We shall describe this series in the descending order, in accordance with this classification.

1. THE LOUP-RIVER GROUP.—This group yields no economic materials, but the entombed mammalian remains, as determined by Leidy, are of striking interest. Among them may be enumerated three species of the camel, a rhinoceros, a mastodon smaller than the *M. ohioticus*, an elephant (*Elephas imperator*) a third larger than the *Elephas americanus*, four or five species of the horse, and a deer allied to the musk-deer of Europe,— all extinct. It is singular, that while there was no living representative of the equine or horse tribe on this Continent when first known to the European, there should be found not less than seventeen species in a fossil state, some of them having teeth not distinguishable from the living species. Prof. Marsh has lately described a fossil horse from the region of Nebraska (*Equus parvulus*), which could not have been more than two or two and one-half feet in height, although full grown, as the ossification of the various bones clearly proves.[*]

2. WHITE-RIVER GROUP.—On the White River there are fresh-water beds of drab-colored clays, and bands of sandstone and limestone, which have been denuded and left standing in a thousand fan-

---

[*] O. C. Marsh. Silliman's "American Journal," Nov., 1868.

tastic and irregular forms, so that, viewed at a distance, they resemble the ruins of a mighty city, or more appropriately, the tombstones in a vast cemetery.* And such it has proved; for in these deposits are entombed some of the most wonderful forms of extinct life that have been revealed to the gaze of the palæontologist. The orders Mammalia and Chelonia are largely represented. Not less than forty species of the former, and five species of the latter, have been discovered. The mammalian remains include Carnivores, like the hyena, dog, and panther; and Herbivores, like the rhinoceros, and animals allied to the tapir, peccary, deer, camel, and horse.

Many of these extinct forms have the most discordant characters. In the *Archaeotherium* of Leidy, are united the molar teeth of the hog, the canines of the bear, and the cheek-bones of the cat. The *Oreodon* of the same author, had the grinding teeth of the elk, and the canines of the thick-skinned, omniverous animals, and was fitted to live on both flesh and vegetables, and at the same time was ruminant like the ox. Hundreds of fossil turtles were observed by the early explorers scattered over the surface, some of which were estimated to weigh a ton, whose remains it was found impossible to remove.

* Vide Owen, D.D. "Geological Survey of Iowa and Minnesota."

Cuvier was the first who introduced us to a knowledge of the animals of this era, determined from the fragments of bones collected in the gypsum beds of Montmartre, near Paris. Here, he remarks, he found himself as if placed in a charnel-house, surrounded by mutilated fragments of many hundred skeletons, of more than twenty animals, piled confusedly around him. "At the voice of comparative anatomy, every bone and fragment of a bone resumed its place."* So conclusive and exact were his demonstrations, that we know what were the forms and habits of these extinct species, as well as if they were now animated with the breath of life, and clothed with flesh and skin. Wonderful as were these revelations, they are not only paralleled, but surpassed by those of the Fresh-water Tertiary basins of the Upper Missouri.

The basin of *Mauvaises Terres*, or Bad Lands, is estimated by Hayden to cover a region at least of 100,000 square miles; and, from isolated patches on both sides of the Missouri River, he infers that this great fresh-water lake must have spread over 150,000 square miles,— an area nearly five times greater than that of Lake Superior, the largest fresh-water lake of the present day.

3. THE WIND-RIVER GROUP.—These beds have no great geographical range, as thus far determined,

* "Ossemens Fossiles." Introduction.

although, locally, they attain a thickness of 1,500 or 2,000 feet. They furnish no materials of economic value, nor are they replete with forms of organic life.

4. THE GREAT LIGNITE GROUP.—This is the most important member of the series, both by reason of its geographical range and its economic materials. It has been traced in a series of basins along the foot-hills of the Rocky Mountains from Pike's Peak (and future explorations may make it continuous to Mexico) to the Upper Missouri and into the British Possessions; and from the testimony of Sir John Richardson, and other Arctic explorers, there is every reason to believe that it is almost continuous to the Arctic Sea.*

In a recent report, Hayden gives a description of the lignite deposits of the Laramie Plains.

"I found," he remarks, "the lignite of excellent quality, in beds of from five to eleven feet thick, and I estimated the area occupied by the basin at 5,000 square miles. Its most eastern limit is about ten miles east of Rock Creek, a branch of the Medicine-bow River. Outcroppings have been seen all along Rock Creek, Medicine-bow, on Rattlesnake Hills, on the North Platte, Muddy Creek, Ham's Fork, Echo Cañon, and all along Weber River, nearly to Great Salt-Lake, showing that one connected series of deposits covers this whole area." †

* The reader is referred to a valable paper by F. B. Meek, on the "Geology of the Mackenzie River," determined from the collections of the late Robert Kennicott. "Transactions of Chicago Academy of Sciences." Vol. I., p. 61.

† Silliman's "American Journal," March, 1868.

On South Boulder and Coal Creek, between Denver and Cheyenne, eleven distinct seams of coal have been explored, one of which is eleven feet in thickness, and the combined seams are from thirty to fifty feet. Externally these lignites present the appearance of a light, bituminous coal, and on assay, give about equal parts of volatile matter and fixed carbon, and only two or three per cent. of ash. Like most of the coals, more recent than the Carboniferous epoch, they contain a large amount of water, ranging from twelve to twenty per cent.

In the Great Basin, lignites have been observed along the eastern base of the Sierra Nevada, in the Pine-Nut Mountains; in the volcanic district of Esmeralda; in El Dorado Cañon; and at Crystal Peak, where considerable mining has been done, but with indifferent success. Towards the eastern rim of the Great Basin, the deposits are more abundant, and promise to be of greater economical value. Lignite occurs west of the Black Hills, and is traced almost continuously to Salt-Lake Valley. At Argenta, 400 miles from Sacramento, on the line of the railroad, a deposit is reported of such excellence as to fit it for locomotive use. The principal deposits of lignite, so far as known, are indicated on the Geological Map (p. 272), by the deeply-shaded, oblique lines.

MARINE STRATA OF THE PACIFIC COAST.—On the Pacific Slope, the Tertiary rocks, which are referred to the Miocine age, appear to be coterminous with the Cretaceous. They enter into the frame-work of the Coast Ranges, stretching from the Columbia to San Louis Bay, and probably to Cape St. Lucas; and, throughout the entire extent, the strata are upheaved, plicated, and metamorphosed, and, at frequent intervals, invaded by igneous products. They repose in horizontal strata upon the foot-hills of the Sierra, but are in a disturbed position where they fold around Shasta. The entombed fossils, like those of the Atlantic Coast, are of marine origin.

Like the Missouri beds, they contain valuable seams of coal, restricted for the most part to the State of Oregon. The mines in the region of Coos Bay, according to Gabb, are in this formation, and probably those of the Willamette Valley.

The ancient vegetation of the Upper Missouri, now incorporated into coals, consisted of cryptogamic land-plants, fan-palms, and coniferous trunks like our pines and firs, and of *Juglandaceæ*, like the black walnut, and of *Acerineæ*, like the maple, all allied to existing forms.

ECONOMIC VALUE OF THE TERTIARY COALS.— Thus, it would appear that, contrary to the opinion formerly entertained by geologists, nature has not restricted the useful deposits of coal to rocks of the Carboniferous epoch; and that while, perhaps, those of the true Coal-Measures are, in purity, in freedom from hygrometric moisture, in ability to produce concentrated heat, and to resist atmospheric action, superior to those of a later age; yet, in our own country, valuable coals are extracted from the Oolite, the Cretaceous, and the Tertiary formations. Tertiary coals are now successfully employed to propel the Pacific steamers, and to heat the dwellings of the Colorado miners; and Providence, as if to facilitate the intercourse between the two oceans, has so distributed these deposits throughout that vast treeless region west of the Missouri, in such accessible positions, and in such a state of purity, that they may be made available for propelling the locomotive across the western portion of the Continent.

Tertiary Igneous Rocks.—The Washoe Mountains, according to Richthofen, form an intermediate link between the Sierra Nevada and the ranges of the Great Basin. "To the Sierra Nevada they are related by the metamorphism of their sedimentary formations, which farther east appear more regularly stratified and less altered. With both, they have, in common, the considerable part which Tertiary and Post-Tertiary eruptive rocks, partly of pure volcanic origin, play in their architecture."

Mount Davidson is lithologically syenitic, and probably a continuation of the granitic axis of the Pine-Nut Mountains which are flanked by a series of rocks, as determined by Whitney, of Triassic age, forming the *ancient* series.

> "They partly preceded," remarks the Baron, "and partly were contemporaneous with the gradual emergence of the Sierra Nevada, the Great Basin, and the entire chain of the Cordilleras from the ancient sea, whose traces are left in saline incrustations and salt-pools at the bottom of the numerous basins between the Sierra Nevada and Rocky Mountains, which had formerly remained filled with the water of the retiring sea. The Washoe Mountains formed, undoubtedly, an elevated range during the long period which elapsed till the commencement of the formation of the recent series of rocks which are eruptive and volcanic, and belong to the latter part of the Tertiary and Post-Tertiary periods." *

In a volcanic rock, technically called *propylite*,— a paste of greenish or brownish color, with imbedded crystals of feldspar,— is contained the farfamed COMSTOCK LODE which, in the short space of six years, has yielded $75,000,000 of silver, and whose annual product is equal to that of all Mexico. And yet, this magnificent lode, in whose success the fate of an entire state is involved, has arrived at that pass when, at the depth of nearly a thousand feet, by reason of the accumulation of water,

---

* Richthofen, Baron. "Report on Comstock Lode."

imperfect ventilation, and increase of internal temperature (90° where, after brief exertions, the miners are required to repose), the explorations have nearly ceased to be profitable, with the certainty that they will become absolutely so, if the present system of mining is persisted in. A tunnel, (projected by Mr. Adolph Sutro, and bearing his name,) four miles long, and affording drainage into a valley, can be constructed to cut this lode at a depth of 2,000 feet; and to accomplish this object, national aid has been invoked.

The Comstock vein, while pursuing a general course of north and south, appears to partake of the flexures of the inclosing rock, which is folded round and invests the syenitic nucleus of Mount Davidson, conforming to its irregularities, passing the ravines in concave bends, and inclosing the foot of the different ridges in convex curves. It has been traced for about 19,000 feet, and, at a depth of from 400 to 600 feet, it is from 100 to even 200 feet in width, but contracting in places to a mere seam. Its dip is far from uniform, first inclining to the east, then assuming verticalness, and finally turning to the west, and expanding towards the surface in a fan-like form. It has, therefore, individual features which detach it from other systems of veins.*

* Richthofen. *Ibidem.*

Drift-Epoch.—During the Tertiary age the relative area of land and water, as we have shown, was different from what we now behold. The ocean, on the east, invested the land up to the flanks of the Appalachians, and on the west up to the flanks of the Sierra Nevada; while, in the form of an entering bay, it extended up to the mouth of the Ohio; and fresh and salt-water, as indicated by the brackish character of some of the shells, commingled far up the Missouri. The Colorado was an arm of the sea, a prolongation of the Gulf of California. A chain of great fresh-water lakes stretched along the eastern slopes of the Rocky Mountains and penetrated the Great Basin. The sun glowed with a more genial heat, and a semi-tropical vegetation, such as that which flourishes in the lower latitudes of the United States, prevailed as far north as Disco Island and the sources of Mackenzie's River. Immense saurians tenanted the sea, and numerous forms of pachyderms, allied to those of the warm climate of India, roamed over the land.

But a change was at hand,—a change for which science has thus far failed to find a satisfactory solution. The sun was shorn of a portion of his vivifying rays; the seas became cold; shells of an Arctic type tenanted the waters, and an Alpine vegetation penetrated far into the Temperate Zone. A new race of quadrupeds, represented by the mastodon and the mammoth, sprang into being, clothed with a raiment of wool to protect them from the rigors of the climate, and furnished with teeth of peculiar complexity to enable them to browse upon a sub-Arctic vegetation; and the musk-ox and the reindeer roamed south to where now grow the olive and the vine.

In order that we may realize the character of the climate which formerly prevailed over what are now the most favored portions of the earth's surface, we need but go north and plant ourselves on the shores of Greenland. Here is a continent which for three-fourths of the year is moulded in snow and ice. The coast is lined with glaciers which, descending through the fiords, jut far out into the sea, and, becoming detached by tidal action, float off in the form of bergs, while the supply is kept up by the melting of the great snow-fields lying in the interior. These bergs, freighted with masses of rock, earth, and gravel, float off into warmer waters, where they dissolve and scatter their contents over the bed of the ocean.

What can be more desolate than an Arctic landscape: — the flashing splendors of the Northern Lights; the gloomy solitude which every where reigns unbroken, except by the cracking of the ice; the coruscations of the stars in that pure, cold atmosphere; and the strangeness of a midnight sun hanging like a great fire-ball in the southern sky, lighting up the pinnacles of icebergs and causing them to glitter with opalescent hues.

The rigors of such a climate reigned over what now are the temperate regions of both hemispheres. Cold oceanic currents swept from the north, floating innumerable icebergs, and the land itself was in a state of glaciation, attested by the striation of the rocks, by long trains of boulders, by moraine-like accumulations of gravel, and by mingled sands and clays, as if deposited amid turbulent currents and shifting eddies.*

---

* If we read the narrative of Kane and other Arctic explorers, our ideas will become enlarged as to the extent of these ice-fields, and the restless energy with which they move. Take his description of the great glacier of Humboldt, presenting at the sea a perpendicular cliff of three hundred feet, and stretching inland as far as the eye can reach, in the form of a great table-land, with a relief and depression corresponding with the surface of the soil.

"Repose," says Kane, "was not the characteristic of this seemingly solid mass; every feature indicated activity, energy, movement." While the external air might have a temperature of $-30°$, the glacier indicated $+20°$, yielding an uninterrupted flow of water during the whole year.

The glacier is a viscous mass, slowly advancing to the coast, urged on by a power behind, until it is forced so far into the sea, that the water becomes capable of sustaining the projected mass, when it becomes detached from the parent glacier, not by a violent debâcle, but quietly, and is floated off in the form of a berg, to be dissolved in the milder temperature of southern seas. Thousands of these bergs are thus detached and throng the Arctic seas, freighted with tons and tons of rounded and angular blocks of stone, and other detrital matter, to be dropped in the sea-bottom of lower latitudes.

Now, if the ocean-bed along the track of these ice-rafts were elevated and made dry land, it would doubtless exhibit all the phenomena of the Drift,—detrital materials almost void of stratification, long lines of boulders, the direction in no degree conforming to the ine-

DRIFT OF THE MISSISSIPPI VALLEY.— In traversing the prairies the observer is struck by the almost entire absence of those long trains of boulders, those moraine-like accumulations of rounded and water-worn pebbles, and those heavy beds of sand and gravel discordantly stratified, which characterize the the Drift-phenomena of the Atlantic Slope, and particularly of New England. Instead of these, he finds the surface sometimes composed of comminuted materials of marly clay, and at other times of materials more silicious, with an occasional boulder standing up like a landmark. This diversity in character is owing probably to two causes.

1. That while every Drift-region shows the intrusion of materials of a northern origin, still the great mass is derived from the destruction of the rocks in the immediate neighborhood; and we should,

qualities of surface, and grooved and polished rocks, where the bergs had struck and become stranded.

The lowest temperature of sea-water recorded by Kane, amid drifting ice-bergs, is between 28° and 29°.

He describes Cape James Kent as a lofty headland, where the land-ice was covered with rocks from the cliffs above. "As I looked," says he, "over this ice-belt, loosing itself in the far distance, and covered with millions of tons of rubbish, greenstones, limestones, chlorite slates, rounded and irregular, massive and ground to powder, its importance as a geological agent in the transportation of Drift struck me with great force. Its whole substance was covered with these contributions from the shore; and farther to the south, upon the now frozen waters of Marshall Bay, I could recognize raft after raft from last year's ice-belt, which had been caught up by the winter, each one laden with its heavy freight of foreign material." ("Arctic Expedition.")

therefore, *a priori*, infer that the ruins of the Silurian and Carboniferous strata of the Mississippi Valley, would present a soil of a far different mechanical texture from that derived from the crystalline and metamorphic rocks of New England; that while the tremendous energy of the Drift-agency might grind the one class of rocks into an impalpable powder, it might leave the other of a coarser texture, together with innumerable rounded pebbles.

2. That as the force of the Drift-agency subsided, there was probably an interval sufficiently long, during which only the finer sediments were deposited upon a lacustrine floor. These sediments, for thousands of years, have borne annual crops of grass, whose ashes or decaying leaves have mingled each year with the soil, and contributed to its fertility; and hence it has the lightness and almost the mobility of an ash-heap.

The materials composing the Drift-series are loam, sand, and gravel more or less stratified, and yellow and blue clay,— the latter resting on rocks previously grooved and polished where sufficiently firm to retain the impressions. The maximum thickness of the Blue clay in the vicinity of Lake Michigan, is at least one hundred feet, and the combined thickness of these superficial materials is one hundred and fifty feet. Boulders are found embedded in the Blue clay, as well as reposing on the surface of the prairies, but more abundantly near the base of the series. The Blue clay may be regarded as a slow deposit of mud produced by the shifting action of tides, while the boulders were dropped from floating ice-bergs; for it is very evident that both classes of materials could not have been accumulated by the same set of currents.

THE DRIFT-PHENOMENA are by no means conspicuously displayed on the Plains. We have never noticed the etching of the rocks, or the distribution of boulders at points far west of Leavenworth. Dr. Hayden remarks, that on the Platte, at the mouth of the Elkhorn, there is a ledge of limestone which has been planed so smoothly by glacial action that it makes a most excellent material for caps and sills, without further working,— a phenomenon which he has not before observed in any part of the far West. Sometimes there are deep grooves and scratchings, all of which have a direction northwest and southeast. The evidences of glacial action are also to be seen at Plattsmouth, and if the detrital covering were stripped off, the limestones would appear to be planed in this way.*

* "Report to Commissioner of General Land Office," 1867, p. 129.

Erosive Action on the Pacific Slope.—The great swell, on which rise the crested ridges of the Rocky Mountains, appears to have acted as a barrier against the encroachments of the Northern Drift. All traces of its existence, also, are absent on the Pacific Slope.

"The explorations of the Geological Survey of California," says Whitney, "have demonstrated that there is no true Northern Drift within the limits of this State. Our detrital materials, which often form deposits of great extent and thickness, are invariably found to have been dependent for their origin and present condition on causes similar to those now in action, and to have been deposited on the flanks and at the bases of the nearest mountain ranges, by currents of water rushing down their slopes. While we have abundant evidence of the former existence of extensive glaciers in the Sierra Nevada, there is no reason to suppose that the ice was to any extent an effective agent in the transportation of the superficial deposits now resting on the flanks of the mountains. The glaciers were confined to the most elevated portions of the mountains, and although the moraines which they have left as evidences of their former extension, are often large and conspicuous, they are insignificant in comparison with the detrital masses formed by aqueous erosion. There is nothing, any where in California, which indicates a general Glacial epoch, during which ice covered the whole country and moved bodies of detritus over the surface, independently of its present configuration, as is seen throughout the Northeastern States." *

The same condition of things prevails throughout Oregon, British Columbia, and Alaska.

The configuration of the whole coast is such as

---

* "Proc. Cal. Acad. Nat. Sciences." Vol. III., p. 272.

to protect it from the ice-floes of the Polar Sea, and such an event could not take place without presupposing a very great change in the relative level of land and water. And yet, perhaps, there is no region of the earth which bears such unmistakable evidence that the mountains were once "moulded in ice," to a far greater extent than at this time; none which shows such wide-spread denudation and such deep accumulations of detrital materials. On the plains of Los Angeles they reach 300 feet in depth, and at Table Mountain, as before shown, 200 feet, with a denudation of 2,000 feet. In this tremendous erosive action nature has broken up, pulverized, and assorted those materials charged with gold, constituting "placer" or "gulch diggings," and thereby relieved man of an infinitude of toil in gathering the precious metal.

In the peninsula of Lower California, according to Gabb, there are extensive deposits of gravels in a horizontal position, filling or bordering on all the valleys, capped by porphyries and other volcanic rocks, one hundred or more feet in thickness, and extending over immense areas.

The great cañons of the Colorado, forming gorges from 3,000 to 6,000 feet in depth, amid whose intricacies the traveler is liable to become almost hopelessly involved, are regarded by Newberry, as belonging to this vast system of erosion, and wholly due to the action of water. On the other hand, when we see, for instance, along the rock-bound coast of Lake Superior, upon which the waves have dashed for thousands of years, the most delicate etchings on the rocks perfectly preserved, we confess that, in running water, we fail to recognize an adequate cause to account for the excavation of these profound gorges; and although the geologist, like the actor, should ever have in mind the advice of Horace,

> "nec Deus intersit
> Nisi vindice nodus,"

yet here is an instance in which, we think, the Fire-God may be properly invoked, and to his interposition, these tremendous events may be, in part, ascribed,— or in other words, that the form and outline of these chasms were first determined by plutonic agency. Every explorer describes the heavy accumulations of volcanic matter which cover the most superficial materials in the elevated region between the Rio Grande and the Colorado Desert, and in fact throughout the entire range of the Rocky Mountains.

It would thus seem that while aqueous causes were in full activity over all these regions, igneous causes exhibited an activity equally conspicuous.

Anticipating the order of succession, it may be

stated that almost everywhere in the Great Basin, and the same may be said of the Colorado Plateau, there are observed the evidences, within a recent period, of a climate much more humid, and of a soil much more fruitful than now prevail. On some of the mountain sides are seen yet standing, considerable tracts of dead forests; the borders of the lakes and streams show water-lines two and three hundred feet above their present levels; alluvial bottoms, now bare and desolate, contain the entombed remains of a luxuriant arborescent vegetation; cañons which must have been the channels of abundant streams, are either dry, or discharge an insignificant flood; springs originating in the melting snows are absorbed as soon as they reach the thirsty plain; and in certain parts are the remains of populous towns, where now it would be difficult for man to eke out a subsistence. All these phenomena attest that this wide-spread desolation is of extremely recent origin, but for which it is difficult to offer a satisfactory solution. With the relative area of land and water as at present maintained, we must suppose that the conditions of climate have remained constant; but with a depression of the country to such an extent as to admit of the flow of the ocean through the Colorado Desert to the rim of the Great Basin, and if we suppose that throughout this basin there existed a series of lakes two and three hundred feet in depth, we can conceive that the climate would be essentially modified. No currents of air would arise from a heated expanse to dissipate every forming cloud; evaporation from large surfaces of water would reduce the temperature and moisten the atmosphere; and trees, clothing the slopes of the hills, would shade the fountains and render them perennial. We are disposed to believe, therefore, that the volcanic action, of which Mount Shasta is but an example, combined, perhaps, with a gradual elevatory movement exerted within the historic period, has so far changed the relative level of land and sea as to produce this diminished moisture.

Terraces of Modified Drift.—Loess.—If we examine the shores of our Great Lakes, we find them bounded at intervals by stair-like ridges known as terraces, often three in number, the uppermost attaining, as at Mackinac, an elevation of one hundred feet above the present water-level, and a still higher elevation along the shores of Lake Superior. The same appearances are observed in the principal river-valleys. We here find ordinarily an ancient Drift-terrace indenting the hills, next a terrace of Modified Drift, and at last the Alluvial

Bottom which is often ridged with numerous steps, indicating successive levels in the river-channel.

These phenomena are represented to some extent in the subjoined

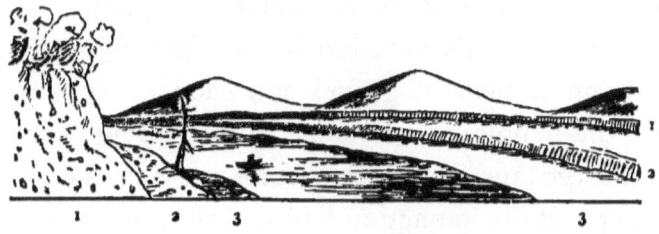

SECTION OF A RIVER VALLEY.

1. ANCIENT DRIFT.   2. MODIFIED VALLEY DRIFT.
3. ALLUVIAL BOTTOM.

These terraces would indicate a gradual emergence of the land from the ocean, with sufficient pauses in the movement to admit of their formation. When we consider the topographical features of the country, it is evident that, during this emergence, the relative area of land and water throughout the Mississippi Valley, must have varied very much, and have been far different from what we now behold. But the terraces along the Great Lakes do not represent the whole emergence. Observations on the raised beaches, both of the Atlantic and Pacific Slope, indicate that the submergence was not less than 2,000 feet, which would be sufficient to cover the great plateau in which the four great rivers, the Mississippi, the Saskatchawan, the Mackenzie, and the St. Lawrence, have a common source, though flowing in different directions, and to create an open sea between the Arctic Ocean and the Gulf of Mexico. When we examine the structure of the terraces and bluffs, we find that, in northern latitudes above the parallel 38°, and where the Drift-action is conspicuous, they are made up of beds of gravel and sand rudely stratified, the pebbles for the most part of foreign origin, with large angular blocks from the vicinage, indicating that the ice-action had not altogether ceased.

In lower latitudes, and along the Upper Missouri, remote from the Drift-influence, the bluffs of the great rivers consist of a yellowish loam, almost impalpable in its divisions, and resembling the *Loess* of the Rhine,—a term which Western Geologists are disposed to naturalize.

LOESS, OR BLUFF FORMATION,—The Loess, as observed by Hayden on the Missouri, commences at about the foot of the Great Bend (latitude 44°), and continues thence with occasional interruptions to its mouth. At Council Bluffs and Sioux City, in Iowa, it forms a conspicuous feature in the landscape, and in its thickness is from fifty to one hundred and fifty feet. This deposit is not restricted to the main valley, but lines the valleys of very many of the principal affluents. It is for the most part devoid of stratification, and the enclosed remains of shells are all of fresh-water origin, and belong to existing species. The remains of Mammalia, however, such as the mastodon, peccary, horse, lion, musk-ox, etc., belong to extinct species, thus showing that the fresh-water fauna survived changes which were fatal to many of the air-breathing animals.

Swallow, in his Survey of Missouri, was the first to recognize this deposit in all its importance, and gave it the distinctive name of the "Bluff Formation."

On the Lower Mississippi it is well developed, extending from above the junction of the Missouri to its delta. In the river counties of the State of Mississippi, according to Hilgard, it occupies a belt ten to fifteen miles in width, and in places is seventy feet thick, running parallel with the stream. In its lithological character, it resembles that of the Upper Mississippi and Missouri, being a fine, silicious loam of a buff color.

The loess is undoubtedly a lacustrine formation, and to account for its present level we must presuppose an elevation of the land to an extent of at least two hundred feet.

SAND-DUNES.—As among the phenomena of the Post-Pliocine epoch, for it was one of long continuance, may be included the Sand-dunes which often form conspicuous landmarks along the eastern shore of Lake Michigan. They consist of irregular heaps of sand which have been accumulated by the winds blowing in a certain direction, and upon specific shores. Hence, their accumulation is confined, almost exclusively, to the eastern shore of the lake.

In many countries these dunes exercise an important influence on the national industry. Holland owes its prosperity to the shelter which they afford to navigation, by forming a natural barrier against the sea; whereas, in other countries, they are dreaded on account of their encroachments on the cultivable land.

The dunes of Cape Cod rarely exceed eighty feet in height; and there, perhaps, they are as conspicuously developed as upon any portion of the Atlantic Coast. The dunes on this inland sheet of water are equally high, and even higher,— exceeding, in some places, one hundred feet. It is generally found, too, that they assume a *lee* and *strike* side,— the gentle and long slope being to the windward, and the steep acclivity towards the sheltered position. The Sleeping Bear and Pointe Aux Chênes, near the foot of Lake Michigan, are conspicuous examples of these dune-like formations,—while at the head, at New Buffalo and Michigan City, they are equally conspicuous. Sand-ridges extend from the head of the lake far into the interior, as far even as Tippecanoe, Indiana, having great uniformity in direction, and resembling what the Swedish geologists denominate *osars*.

In searching for the origin of these silicious materials, it may be asserted that the rivers which enter the lake, transport at this day only fine, argillaceous sediments, and, therefore, their accumulation is not due to existing causes. The Potsdam sandstone which skirts the southern flanks of the Azoic system of Lake Superior, is a slightly-coherent rock, which must have been powerfully acted on during the denuding agency of the Drift-epoch; and it is to this source that we may look for the origin of these materials. As to the mode of their accumulation, it may be said, that the waves, in positions where the winds have full sweep, carrying the suspended particles, strike the shore with a momentum greater than the recoil, which admits of a deposit of the materials held in suspension. Thus each wave, as it expends itself upon a shelving beach, makes a deposit of sand. After the waves have delivered their freight upon the shore, it is taken up by the winds. The particles of sand drifted inland, are subject to the same laws which control the drifting of snow. The strike-side of a dune is an inclined plane, with an inclination not to exceed 5° or 10°, up which the sand is driven, while the lee side may exhibit an angle of 30°. Wherever there occurs an obstacle like a tree or a rock, a deposit is made, and this process goes on until the general level of the obstacle is attained. As the wind shifts, particles are borne in a different direction, so that, instead of a continuous bank, the sands are generally arranged in a series of conical hills.

All dunes are found to be moist to within a few feet of the surface, as though derived from capillary attraction, and, hence, they become clothed with an appropriate vegetation, of which the pine-tribe is the most conspicuous. The slopes present the same ripple-marked surface observable on a shelving shore, which is the result of the assorting of the materials according to their specific gravity,—the lighter portions forming the crests, and the heavier the troughs.

Between the parallel ridges which, as before remarked, extend far inland, and have become clothed mainly with pines and aspens, ponds have been formed, which, from their sheltered position and slight currents, are peculiarly adapted to the growth of peat-producing plants, such as the sphagnous mosses, and of the order *Nymphæaceæ*, etc.

The ancient channel by which a portion of the waters of the Upper Lakes was formerly discharged into the Mississippi through the Illinois River, is clearly indicated.

THE GREAT LAKES.

Drift-Phenomena.—The Great Lakes, whether we consider their area, depth, or the facilities for inter-communication which they afford to the interior of the Continent, form one of the grandest features in the geography of North America. They may have existed from a remote geological epoch, as longitudinal valleys, determined by the different systems of mountain chains; but that their respective areas were greatly modified and enlarged during the Drift-epoch, admits of no doubt,— for all along their shores, the rocks where sufficiently firm to retain the markings, have been planed down, grooved, and striated, by a tremendous force which appears to have operated over the entire area of their connected basins. This planing process was not restricted to the subjacent rocks, for at Marquette, and at other points on Lake Superior, may be seen mural faces of highly-metamorphosed slates which have been polished and grooved by a force acting longitudinally, and Newberry has observed similar markings on the limestone cliffs of Lake Erie.

The grandest exhibition of the Drift-phenomena

which it has been my fortune to observe, occurs on the southern coast of Lake Superior, between Granite Point and Dead River. The rocks,— a tough feldspathic porphyry, almost indestructible,— are not only simply polished, but some of the grooves are four feet wide and two feet deep, with all the markings as sharp as though done but yesterday by some great planing-machine. Here are two sets of striæ, one running north and south, and the other north 20° east, south 20° west. Examples of this character, nearly equally conspicuous, are to be seen in the limestone surfaces at Sandusky and Buffalo.

Denudation.—That there was a wide-spread denudation of the lake-beds during the Drift-epoch, as before suggested, admits of no doubt.

Lake Superior occupies an immense depression, which has, for the most part, been excavated out of the Potsdam sandstone, and a few islands of this material, like Caribou, Maple, Parisien, and the Apostles, have escaped the general ruin. The outlines of its shores have been mainly determined by the presence of the igneous rocks which opposed an effectual barrier to the glacial action. The configuration of Keweenaw Point is due to a trappean range which juts far into the lake; and the fiord-like character of much of the Northern Shore and

Isle Royale, results from banded trap of unequal hardness and firmness, which opposed an unequal resistance to the denuding process.

The basins of the two great lakes, Michigan and Huron, and this observation will apply to Erie and Ontario, appear to have been excavated out of that series of rocks included between the Niagara limestone and the Portage and Chemung groups, consisting of the Onondaga salt-group, the Coniferous limestone, and the Hamilton and Marcellus shales, which are slaty, or slightly-coherent in structure, and, therefore, little fitted to withstand denudation. The Niagara limestone, as before shown, is a firm and comparatively indestructible rock, which stretches in an almost unbroken belt from the Great Falls to the head of Lake Michigan, giving configuration to the whole northern shore of Lake Huron, and the western shore of the former lake. Green Bay is excavated in the soft, marly shales of the Cincinnati Blue limestone.

Their Area and Elevation.—The combined area of the Great Lakes is approximately estimated to exceed 90,000 square miles, and the depression in most of them is sufficiently profound to reach below the sea-bed. The following table, though not strictly accurate, is believed to embrace their principal features.

TABLE—SHOWING THE AREA, DEPTH, AND ELEVATION OF THE GREAT LAKES.

THE GREAT LAKES.	GREATEST LENGTH. MILES.	GREATEST BREADTH. MILES.	GREATEST DEPTH. FEET.	HEIGHT ABOVE SEA. FEET.	AREA IN SQUARE MILES.
SUPERIOR, - -	355	160	900	605	32,000
MICHIGAN, - -	310	84	600	583	22,000
HURON, - - -	168	120	600 ?	578	20,400
ERIE, - - - -	246	60	300	564	9,600
ONTARIO, - -	190	50	800	233	6,300
TOTAL AREA, - - - - - - -					90,300

Col. Whittlesey, who has studied the regimen of these lakes more thoroughly, perhaps, than any other physicist, has kindly furnished me with the following notes:

"It is not practicable to fix the elevation of the surface of these lakes, until their mean fluctuation is known. The results I propose to give, are, therefore, only approximate.

"From observations made on Lake Erie since the year 1796, an extreme though transient change of level is known, amounting to seven feet, and a secular or permanent change of five feet. Of the variations on Lake Huron little is known. Observations on Lake Michigan have been made with great care, but they cover only a few years of time. An extreme fluctuation of six feet has been observed.

"On Lake Superior, the greatest known range of level is three feet, with indications of a much greater range. Lake Ontario has a variation of four feet nine inches, well determined by water-registers, since the year 1812.

"The Surveys of the Upper Lakes, by the United States

Government, now in progress, will eventually fix the mean level of all the lakes, by observations which are made twice each day.

"For present use, I give the mean results of instrumental surveys between tide-water and the lakes, and between the different lakes.

"Before doing this I must remark, that in none of them is the stage of water noted, whether above or below the mean. There is, therefore, room for a plus or minus error of two or three feet, when referred to a place which shall be fixed upon as the mean level of each lake. There is also another ground of error. The lakes are not strictly level, but have an inclination or descent towards their outlets, though this may be small and in part corrected by the action of winds.

"To fix the elevation of the lakes, I begin at those nearest the sea, to which instrumental surveys have been made. The Upper Lakes are not thus connected by direct lines, but their height above tide is determined by reference to those below.

"There is quite a discrepancy in the results which can be accounted for as I have above stated.

LAKE ONTARIO.

"By lockage in the St. Lawrence Canals, above mean tide,	234¼ feet.
By Canal Surveys of New York, above mean tide,	232 "
Mean elevation,	233¼ feet.

LAKE ERIE.

By Canal Survey of New York, 1817,	561.20 feet.
By Capt. Williams's Report of 1834, Niagara Ship-Canal,	563.00 "
By Surveys of Catskill and Portland Railway, 1828,	565.33 "
By locks of New York Canal,	567.00 "
Mean,	564.13 feet.

LAKE HURON.

S. W. Higgins, (Geological Report of Michigan, 1838),	577 feet.
A. Murray, (Geological Report of Canada, 1849),	578 "
Mean,	577½ feet.
Lake St. Clair, (Geological Report of Michigan),	570 "

LAKE MICHIGAN.

Michigan Southern Railway, J. H. Sargent, Engineer, survey of 1856, south end, - - - - - - 583 feet.

LAKE SUPERIOR.

By Capt. Bayfield's Barometical Measurements in 1824, 627 feet, evidently too great.
A. Murray's determination, (Geological Survey of Canada, 1849), 599.41 feet, say - - - - - - - 600 feet.
Survey of Bay de Noquets and Marquette Railroad, 1859, 610 "

Mean, - - - - - - - - - - 605 " "

RESUME.

It is deemed needless to enter further into the physical history of the revolutions of the earth's surface, as attested by these geological monuments, which reach back to the dawn of organic life. While to some they may indicate the reign of waste and chaos, yet, throughout all these phases, we can detect design; — in the concentration of the useful metals in veins and beds; in the storing away of vast supplies of fossil fuel; in the consolidation and upheaval of the strata, giving relief and depression to the surface; in their subsequent erosion and dispersion to form soil; and in all the changes which these material elements have undergone; — a design to fit the earth for the habitation of man, and to afford him useful materials for the exercise of his industry, and the promotion of his comforts and conveniences.

CHAPTER XI.

INFLUENCE OF CLIMATE ON MAN.

GEOGRAPHICAL RANGE OF MAN, AS COMPARED WITH THAT OF PLANTS — CONDITIONS OF HUMAN LIFE UNDER DIFFERENT ZONES — ARCTIC LIFE — TROPICAL LIFE — LIFE IN NORTHERN TEMPERATE ZONE — HUMAN ENERGY DISPLAYED WITHIN CERTAIN ISOTHERMAL LINES — IN EUROPE — IN NORTH AMERICA — CLIMATE OF THE SOUTHERN STATES AND THE CONDITION OF SOCIETY — CLIMATE OF THE NORTHERN STATES AND THE CONDITION OF SOCIETY — EFFECTS OF THESE DIFFERENCES SEEN IN THE REBELLION — PHYSICAL DEVELOPMENT.

Geographical Range of Man.— Every living organism, whether animal or vegetable, has a certain geographical range which is determined by the conditions of soil and climate. Within a particular zone, certain animal and vegetable forms attain their full development, but deteriorate when transferred to a different zone. Man is not an exception to this great law, and "the same influences which keep the smallest moss-plant to its rock, bind man to his mountain side or valley."*

* Johnson. "Physical Atlas."

These influences are less apparent when traced along a line of latitude than along a line of longitude, for the reason that the conditions of climate are less abrupt. It will be seen, however, that it is only under peculiarly favorable conditions of soil and climate, and embracing only a limited portion of the earth's surface, that man has developed, to the full extent, his physical and intellectual vigor.

Man is by nature, perhaps, the weakest and most defenceless of the Mammalia. For a long time after birth, he draws his nutrition from the mother, and it is a long time before he acquires the ability to walk. His food must be artificially prepared and his body artificially clothed. Other animals surpass him in keenness of vision, in rapidity of movement, in strength, and, in fact, in the acuteness of most of the senses. But he is endowed with reason, by the exercise of which he can make up for all these deficiencies, can repel or subdue all other animals, and make them subservient to his use. He can clothe himself to endure the rigors of an Arctic winter, and can shield himself from the burning rays of a tropical sun; he can lay up a stock of provisions in one quarter of the globe to be consumed in another; and, in fact, at this day, the intellectual man, so intimate are his commercial relations, commands the luxuries of every climate. Other animals live in the immediate vicinity of the region which affords them the means of subsistence, and hence their migrations are determined by this cause.

While, therefore, the range of man is greater than that of any other organism, whether vegetable or animal; yet, outside of certain lines of temperature, that range is at the expense of his physical and mental powers. At one extreme, he becomes effeminate and incapable of vigorous and prolonged exertion; at the other, he becomes dwarfed in stature, and so unremitting are the exertions required to procure the means of subsistence, that his animal propensities are developed at the expense of his intellectual, and his instincts become little exalted above those of the beast of prey. In the region, however, embracing the happy mean, where the climate is such as to invigorate the system, and nature is so far genial as to require the appropriation of a part of his time only to secure the means of support, leaving a portion to be devoted to the cultivation of the intellect, man attains his full physical and intellectual development; and here we meet with that system of artificial wants and refinements which is peculiarly the offspring of a high civilization. External nature, also, undoubtedly moulds the character of the individual and determines the idiosyncracies of a people. So intimate is this relation that man

> "Becomes
> Portion of that around him; and to him
> The mountains are a feeling."

The Swiss villagers, brought up beneath the shadow of the Alps, must have far loftier ideas of the grandeur of the universe than the Bushmen of the Cape, who are so degraded that they can not even build huts, — "the burning sky being their canopy, and the scorching sand their bed." In every age, the Swiss have been noted for their love of liberty, and among all the partitions of Europe, they have been able to preserve their national independence. While such traits have, with them, remained constant through many generations, it is probable that the traits of the Bushmen have been equally constant, and that it would require a system of training persevered in for generations, to lift them out of their degradation, and bring them to realize their true position in the scale of creation.

Arctic Life.—The Esquimaux, living upon the dreary ridges or boundless ice-fields which gird the Arctic shores, are compelled to maintain a constant struggle with nature for the means of subsistence. The active exercise and the out-door exposure which they undergo,— the thermometer often dropping to $-40°$,— is attended with an enormous loss of carbon in the system, which must be supplied by the most concentrated animal food.*

Burrowing in their snow-covered huts, and deriving their artificial heat from oil burned in the *kotluck*, by which the temperature within is raised to + 90° while without it may be — 40°, with an ample supply of walrus-meat, the Esquimaux recline, *in puris naturalibus*, and realize the height of human felicity.

But this dream is of short duration. Soon they are compelled to wander in quest of their precarious food, and there are long, dreary intervals, dependent upon the ice-floe, in which they experience the pangs of an all-consuming famine. In this primitive and abject state, generation succeeds generation, without producing any elevation of the race. A few hundred words comprise the vocabulary to express their wants, their desires, their hopes, their aspirations. The means of multiplying the race are limited by the austerity of the climate. Arts, laws, and society are unknown, and the individual is slightly distinguished in intel-

* Dr. Kane estimates the Esquimaux ration at eight or ten pounds of animal food a day, with soup and water to the extent of half a gallon. The walrus, the seal, and the bear, are the staples of life; and it is a matter of indifference to them whether the flesh of the animals be eaten cooked, or raw. In fact, Arctic navigators find that the raw walrus-meat is a rare tit-bit, and it is the best remedy for those scorbutic diseases which, in that region, result from intense cold and the long exclusion of the sun from the heavens. (Arctic Expedition.)

lectual endowment above his congeners of the animal kingdom.

Tropical Life.—In intertropical America, on the other hand, so prodigal is nature of her bounties, that man has but slight incentives to labor. A few posts driven into the ground, secured at the tops, and over all a roof thatched with branches of the palm, furnish his shelter. The hammock is his lounge by day, his bed by night. An acre of land, reclaimed from the forest and set out with plaintains, will, within a few months, furnish the staple of his food for life. If luxuriously disposed, he may cultivate some beans, tobacco, a few bushes of coffee or pepper, perhaps some Indian corn, and raise a few chickens. The forest furnishes him with game, the river with fish. He has no struggle with nature for the means of subsistence; his wants are simple, his surroundings primitive. Clothing for himself and family causes the slightest concern of all. Wealth has no attractions, ambition no incentives. He lives a life of inaction; he dies, is forgotten, and is succeeded by children but too well contented to pursue the same routine. So much for the dwellers in the valleys of the great rivers in the tropics.

Upon the plains, the ranging-ground of the vast herds of cattle and horses, the desire for ownership in them naturally arises; but life remains very much the same. The cattle increase with but slight care, and wealth is still comparatively valueless; for when the native has gained enough for the purchase of the long sword in its silver scabbard, the bit, stirrups, and spurs, all of silver, and the bridle and saddle, profusely ornamented with silver dollars, his ambition is gratified; and on gala days he appears well mounted, with embroidered shirt fluttering outside his other garments, his naked feet adorned with the precious spurs, and thrust into the equally precious stirrups,— content to employ his brief hour in useless display, and then lay aside shirt and ornaments, for his daily avocation of swinging in the hammock. The long, listless days of sultry heat, pass away in sleeping and smoking; his habits are irregular,— now a feast, again nothing but parched corn or beans. The family occupy but one room, shared also by the passing traveler. All the household implements are of the rudest description, and life is but existence after all.

Upon the rivers, during the rainy season, the sultriness is indescribable. Insects torment the body, and utter idleness corrodes the mind. On the return of the dry season, with the subsidence of the waters, and the decay of the accumulated vegetable matter exposed to the sun, miasma stalks up and down the valleys like an angry fiend, with wasting disease and delirious death following in his train. Thus the climate lays its embargo upon the best-devised plans of man.*

Life in the Northern Temperate Zone.—Europe.— If we examine a chart of the world and trace the isotherms 40° and 70° across the Eastern Hemisphere, we shall find that they include China, Thibet, the region of the Caucasus, Greece, Italy, that portion of Africa bordering the Mediterranean which is separated from the Desert by the High Atlas, the Germanic States, the southern peninsulas of Norway and Sweden, France, Spain, and the British Isles. Now it may be confidently asserted that, within this belt, the human form has been developed in all of its perfection, and the human intellect has put forth its most vigorous manifestations. Here has originated, almost without exception, every name associated with greatness, whether in art, literature, poetry, painting, or sculpture; in fact, in all those pursuits which dignify and adorn life. Among the warriors, we find Alexander, Cæsar, Alaric, Attila, Charlemagne, Charles XII., Frederick the Great, Napoleon, and Wellington: Among the poets, Homer, Virgil,

---

* These notes on tropical life were communicated by my old and valued friend J. B. Austin, Esq., whose pursuits have led him to pass many years in that region.

Dante, Shakspeare, Milton, and Goethe: Among the sculptors, Phydias, Praxiteles, Angelo, and Canova: Among the painters, Raphael, Reubens, Titian, Leonardo da Vinci, and Turner: Among the philosophers, Socrates, Plato, Aristotle, Pliny, Copernicus, Galileo, Bacon, Kepler, Newton, Liebnitz, Des Cartes, and Cuvier: Among the orators, Demosthenes, Cicero, Bourdaloue, Massillon, Mirabeau, Chatham, and Burke: Among the historians, Herodotus, Thucydides, Livy, Tacitus, Rollin, Gibbon, Hume, and Macaulay: Among the inventors, Faust, Watt, Hargreaves, Arkwright, Cartwright, and Stephenson: And among the navigators, Columbus, Magellan, Sebastian Cabot, and Gama. In fact, what name is there, illustrious in art or science, whose birth-place is not to be found within this zone? The art of printing, the mariners' compass, and the science of alchemy subsequently transformed into chemistry, may have been derived from the East; but their uses and applications were developed by the people of the West. They, too, may claim the invention of the telescope and microscope; the investigation of the laws of heat, light, and magnetism; of the rotation of the aerial currents; of the mathematical figure of the earth, and the movements of the heavenly bodies; and, in fact, of nearly all of the great phenomena of the universe. They invented the steam-engine, the steam-ship, the power-loom, the telegraph, and the railroad; they discovered and applied illuminating gas, the explosive properties of gunpowder, and the expansibility of air and water, as practically applied. These are they who, in the application of the arts, have done so much to mitigate human suffering, and contribute to the comforts and conveniences of man. These are they who have established such close ties of commercial intercourse with the whole habitable globe, bringing the products of every clime within this zone for consumption and re-distribution. Every steam-ship or sailing vessel, to whatever region she may go, is owned here and returns to some port within these lines. Here is accumulated capital, invested in manufactures, in mines, in railroads, and in navigation. Here are brought the crude materials to undergo additional processes and to receive an enhanced value, before they are finally consumed; — the furs of Hudson's Bay, the wools of South Africa, the cotton of Egypt and India, the copper of Chili, the gold of Australia, the sperm of Behring's Sea, and the ivory of Africa. Among these nations alone, we find stable governments for the administration of justice and the preservation of order. The rights of life and property are adjusted by judicial forms, and public faith and public credit are not obsolete virtues. How different this social economy from that which prevails outside of this zone! And to what cause, other than climate, shall we attribute this difference? Even those nations occupying its borders, have not the methodical industry, the persevering application, or the business capacity of those who occupy a central position in this zone.*

---

* This point has been well illustrated by Buckle, in his "History of Civilization." (Vol. I., Chap. 2).

"Climate influences labor not only by enervating the laborer, or invigorating him, but also by the effect which it produces on the regularity of his habits. Thus we find that no people living in a very northern latitude, have ever possessed that steady and unflinching industry for which the inhabitants of the temperate regions are remarkable. The reason for this becomes clear, when we remember that in the more northern countries, the severity of the weather and, at some seasons, the deficiency of light render it impossible for the people to continue their out-of-door employments. The result is that the working-classes, being compelled to cease from their ordinary pursuits, are rendered more prone to desultory habits; the chain of their industry is, as it were, broken, and they lose that impetus which long-continued and uninterrupted practice never fails to give. Hence, there arises a national character more fitful and capricious than that possessed by a people whose climate permits the regular exercise of their ordinary industry. Indeed, so powerful is this principle, that we may perceive its operation, even under the most opposite circumstances. It would be difficult to conceive a greater difference in governments, laws, religion, and manners, than that which distinguishes Sweden and Norway on the one hand, from Spain and Portugal on the other. But these four countries have one great point in common. In all of them, continued agricultural industry is impracticable. In the two southern countries, labor is interrupted by heat, by the dryness of the weather, and by the consequent state of the soil. In the two northern countries, the same effect is produced by the severity of the winter and the shortness of the days. The consequence is that these four countries, though so different in other respects, are all remarkable for a certain instability and fickleness of character; presenting a striking contrast to the more regular and settled habits which are established in countries where climate subjects the working-classes to fewer interruptions, and imposes on them the necessity of a more constant and unremitting employment."

North America.—The same diversity in the habits of the people and their business pursuits, is to be found as we trace the isotherms 40° and 70° across the North American Continent. The line of 40° mean temperature nearly intersects Quebec, and thence strikes north of Lake Huron and the extremity of Keweenaw Point, on Lake Superior; when, leaving that lake, it is rapidly deflected northwardly to the Rocky Mountains, and reaches the Pacific Coast at or near Sitka. The line of 70° mean temperature, starts on the Florida Coast below latitude 30°; ranges along the northern shore of the Gulf of Mexico, and is protracted west until it strikes the highlands of New Mexico; when it curves rapidly north as high as latitude 35°; then it curves south, crossing above the head of the Gulf of California, and strikes the Pacific about latitude 30°.

The region of the British Possessions, north of the isotherm 40°, is doomed to everlasting sterility. Its only available wealth is its fur-bearing animals; its only inhabitants, apart from the Indians, are roving bands of trappers,— the employés of the Hudson's Bay Fur-Company. It has no villages, except what are called Fur-Factories, which are depots for receiving and forwarding supplies. Nature is every where so inhospitable that there is no inducement to exercise that methodical industry, characteristic of a more temperate climate. At Quebec, even, the business of the year is compressed within the short summer of ninety or one hundred days, succeeded by a long winter which, to the inhabitants is a period of listless inactivity, when all the streams are bridged with ice, and the highways are obstructed by deep snows. An embargo is laid upon every thing. No rivers, no ships, no animals are to be seen, but an unbroken sheet of snow prevails, except where the forests and houses break the monotony. But this climate has its compensations. To the inhabitants, winter is the carnival season. They sally forth with horse and cariole, well protected from the frosty air by ample buffalo robes, and drive over the snowy plain, where the course is indicated by pine branches, stuck up at frequent intervals. The long winter evenings are given up to social amusements, often enlivened by the dance, and every one considers it a duty to contribute something to break the otherwise listless tedium. In April the streams are unloosed, and the St. Lawrence is filled with floating masses of ice, freighted with fragments of earth and rock gathered from its upper source. Business is at once resumed with an activity which indicates an awakening from a long hybernation.

Social Organization of the Southern States.— Directing our attention to the southern portion of this zone, embracing what are known as the Planting States, we find that, before the Rebellion, a far different social organization prevailed from that characteristic of the Northern, Middle, and Western States. The climate is, during the summer, so hot and enervating, that it is shunned by the stranger of European descent, and even the acclimated planter would fain seek the cool and invigorating breezes of the north. The whole white population were averse to out-door labor, believing it ignoble; nor did they exhibit any aptitude for those mechanical and manufacturing pursuits which form so important an item in the industry of more temperate climes. Although nature had supplied a fruitful soil, and capable of producing those raw materials which enter so largely into commerce and manufactures, yet we find that they were exclusively raised by the physical exertions of those who had little or no share in the proceeds of sale; and, at the same time, the business of conveying them to market and converting them into useful forms, was confided to strangers.

Society was separated, by an impassable gulf, into two classes,— the planter and the slave. The planter possessed a sort of suavity of manner that passed for high breeding. He was generous in his hospitalities and profuse in his expenditures. While exhibiting a certain degree of intellectual vigor, he was averse to that patient study and that continuous train of thought, by which substantial results are wrought out; and hence, his contributions to science and literature, but above all, to the practical arts of life, have been insignificant. Possessed of an abundance of leisure, politics became to him a source of excitement, and place an object of ambition. Accustomed to rule over slaves, he firmly believed in the miserable sophism of Burke, that where slavery prevails, "those who are free, are far more proud and jealous of their freedom; and that the haughtiness of dominion combines with the spirit of freedom, fortifies it, and renders it invincible." This spirit was carried into the halls of national legislation, and its display was often offensive to the representatives of other sections.

On the other side of the gulf, was the slave whom a long course of oppression had rendered docile, and wholly subservient to the will of his master. "His only business was to labor, his only duty to obey." The negro, undoubtedly, is far better fitted for a southern climate than the white man. He will toil beneath a hot, burning sun, when the white man will wilt, or in the rice-swamps of the Carolinas, whose miasms, generated in stagnant waters, are shunned even by the acclimated planter. Patient of toil, confiding, and susceptible of strong personal attachments, with a vein, too, of deep religious feeling, he has ever been the faithful ally of the white man, and has manifested no desire to strike out independent paths for self-exertion. While the former was restless under imaginary grievances, and plunged the country into war for the maintainance of a theoretical sentiment, the latter did not repine under his unmitigated lot; and, throughout the Rebellion, with the prospect of freedom within his grasp, in no instance did he turn upon his task-master. He organized no conspiracy, he committed no atrocity, but was content to cultivate the field while his master went to the war; and in those instances where he sought his freedom, it was by flight to the lines of the invader.

But this system of oppression has been swept away. The negro is now invested with citizenship. He has a voice in the making of the laws by which he is governed. He is free to appropriate the wealth which his own industry creates. The vision of the poet has been realized:

> "Their vines a shadow to their race shall yield,
> And the same hand that sowed, shall reap the field."

Let us trust that, in the new relations he assumes,

he will acquit himself as a worthy and dutiful citizen.

Social Organization at the North.—Turning now to the central portion of this belt, embracing New England, the Middle, and Western States, we find society organized on a basis of equality, with far different social and business pursuits. The people exhibit methodical industry, provident habits, and a spirit to adopt and improve upon the practical arts of life. This spirit is manifested in accumulated wealth, in inventive capacity, in labor-saving machinery, and in associated capital to carry out gigantic schemes, beyond the means of a single individual however opulent. Their practical benevolence and desire for improvement, are exemplified in the various institutions founded for intellectual culture and for the relief of the ills incident to humanity. To labor is not ignoble, and the climate is such that while the labor enriches, it does not exhaust.

Here are brought the crude materials of other zones — the products of agriculture, of the forests, of the sea, and of the mines,— to undergo mechanical and chemical processes preparatory to their distribution and application to human comforts. The dense cloud of smoke that hangs over every city, the ringing sound of the anvil, the loaded trains which constantly arrive and depart, and the thronged streets where each passenger seems intent on some business errand, all indicate that a spirit of restless activity pervades and permeates the mass of inhabitants. Between the prosperous merchant and the day-laborer there exists a great disproportion of wealth, but the lapse of a single generation ordinarily scatters the most colossal fortune. Besides, those who possess such wealth, have been, for the most part, the architects of their own fortunes, and the same avenues through which they passed, are open to all.

This belt necessarily receives the bulk of immigration from the Old World, which now exceeds three hundred thousand souls each year. The Gulf-Stream is not more accurately defined than this flow of human life. The ports of this belt are open at all seasons; those of the St. Lawrence are blocked by ice one-half the year, while those of Charleston, Norfolk, and New Orleans are, for an equal length of time, scorched with heats so oppressive that the immigrant does not care to encounter them. Besides, he who has forsaken friends and country, often with nothing to rely upon but the full possession of his physical faculties — his ability to toil, — will naturally seek a new home where the climate is agreeable, and where labor is honorable. Hence, the South has heretofore held out few inducements to this class of population.

There is no portion of the earth where man is so well clothed and fed, where the rewards of industry are so certain, and where life and property are so secure as here; and society may be said to have attained the highest degree of perfection. Artificial distinctions, arising from the accident of birth or the accumulation of wealth, are not recognized; and the unrestrained freedom of the individual, in the exercise of his physical and intellectual powers in a manner not inconsistent with the public welfare, is amply secured.

Effect of these Differences, seen in the Rebellion.—The differences in the local organization between the two sections of the Republic, were so great as to be irreconcilable; and every calm observer of events, foresaw that whatever temporary expedients were resorted to, there must ultimately come a rupture. The South, though outnumbered in population, through their unity of action and compact organization, had been able to possess the Government and to dictate its policy, almost uninterruptedly, from its origin; but when they saw that the sceptre of their power was about to depart, they took the initiative, fully believing that they could found a government based on human slavery. They overestimated the value of their products, because they went abroad to adjust national balances. They also believed that commercial necessity would sanction a system of compulsory labor, which was condemned by the enlightened sentiment of every Christian community. They underestimated the force of that great moral sentiment underlying all legislation, before which human statutes, conceived in a spirit of temporary expediency, and however solemnly enacted, must sooner or later give way. They underrated, too, the strength of the people of the North, who, though less impulsive and mercurial, had an indomitable will, a tenacity of purpose backed by numbers, and a fertility of resources in skilled labor, machinery, and in reserved capital brought out and tendered to the Government in the hour of need, which gave assurance that, however protracted the contest, the issue could not be doubtful. Great as was the expenditure of treasure and of blood, it was incurred without repining. There was one all-prevailing sentiment, originating in convictions of temporal prosperity, and, also, in the higher convictions of religious duty and of national grandeur, that the Republic must be preserved,—and preserved, too, stripped of those elements which, from its origin, had been the source of its weakness.

RESUME.

From this survey it will be seen that, only under certain favored latitudes, has man attained to his full physical development, and exhibited that "sanctity of reason"— that divinity of mind,— which distinguishes him so preëminently above the brute.

The region of the Black Sea is supposed to have been the original seat of the Caucasian race,— a race in which the moral feelings and the intellectual powers, as well as the beauty and perfection of the physical structure, have been in the highest degree displayed. Between this region and the prairie region of the West, the conditions of soil and climate are, in a marked degree, similar. If, to climatic causes, we are to attribute the diversities of character in the great family of man, it may be said, that here exist those conditions best fitted for the development of his physical and intellectual nature. *

---

* In a region which has been populated so rapidly as the Western States, and where immigrants form so large an element of that population, it would be unsafe to draw conclusions as to the effects of the climate on physical development; but it may be stated, that the average height of nearly 26,000 recruits to the volunteer regiments of the United States, during the late Rebellion, (three-fifths of whom were gathered in the States of Michigan, Iowa, Indiana, and Minnesota, and two-fifths from the New England States), was $68\frac{20}{100}$ inches.

The average height of nearly 28,000 soldiers recruited for the British Army, for 1860, was $66\frac{20}{100}$ inches.

The average height of French conscripts for thirty years,—1831-62— was $65\frac{17}{100}$ inches.

Unfortunately, we have not measurements of the circumference of the chest, weight, tests of muscular lifting-strength, and capacity of chest, as determined by the spirometer, so far as relates to the Western recruits, for the purposes of comparison with the recruits and conscripts of other nations; but the facts already quoted, show that in height, at least, they are superior. (See an elaborate paper by E. B. Elliot, submitted to the International Congress, at Berlin, 1863, on "The Military Statistics of the United States.")

CHAPTER XII.

ORIGIN OF CIVILIZATION.

VALLEY OF THE MISSISSIPPI, ITS PROSPECTIVE POPULATION — GREECE, THE CRADLE OF CIVILIZATION — ROME, THE INHERITOR OF THAT CIVILIZATION — ORIGIN OF TEUTONS AND CELTS — CHARACTERISTICS OF EACH RACE — COLONIZATION OF NORTH AMERICA — TEUTONIC AND CELTIC COLONIZATION CONTRASTED — NATIONAL UNITY — CAUSES WHICH PROMOTE IT — ENGLISH CHARACTER — ITS HOMOGENEITY AS COMPARED WITH THAT OF THE PEOPLE OF THE UNITED STATES — THE CIVILIZING EFFECTS OF THE CHRISTIAN RELIGION.

THE valley of the Mississippi and the region of the Great Lakes, are destined, before the close of the century, to become the abode of fifty millions of the Teutonic race, speaking the English language, and developing a peculiar civilization. Since first known to history, they have exhibited certain idiosyncracies, both as individuals and as members of the body politic, which have widely separated them from the Celtic or Latin race. It, therefore, becomes a matter of interest to inquire into the origin of that civilization, of which they are the peculiar exponents. In tracing up the stream of history, it will be found that they have always displayed a sturdy independence, a freedom of will, and a self-governing capacity which belong to no other race. They are the only people who, in modern times, have founded stable governments, either of representative monarchy or representative democracy.

Greece, the Cradle of our Civilization.—Our civilization, appropriating the term to the advancement which modern nations have made in art, science, and literature, is directly traceable to Greece. In her we recognize the source from which we derive our knowledge of all those arts which embellish civilized life. She communicated the first impulse, by which the human mind was lead to enter upon those trains of thought, which have resulted in our social and intellectual elevation. She has been, in fact, the mother of nations, teaching her offspring those great principles of public faith and public honor which, though often violated, have yet influenced the conduct of the world's affairs. And when we consider the topographical features of that wonderful country, its soil and climate, we shall see that they were such as to make her the most favored of nations; and that she occupied a position to collect and absorb whatever of art or science there was in the barbaric world.

It is true that she recognized human slavery, but this blot upon her career is compensated by the nobler gifts of virtue and genius. "Each of her citizens was a freeman, who dared to assert the liberty of his thoughts, words, and actions; whose person and property were guarded by equal laws; and who exercised his independent vote in the government of the Republic." *

The inhabitants of Greece possessed a soil of great natural fertility which was rendered more fruitful by cultivation. They dwelt beneath a sky of great serenity, and in a climate which was favorable to the full development of the physical and intellectual man. The relief and depression of the surface was such as to give origin to a diversified landscape; — rugged peaks, thickly-wooded slopes, luxuriant meadows, precipitous water-falls, running brooks, and an ocean sublime in the play of its constantly-changing tints; and thus they were brought in intimate communion with the noblest aspects of nature, which left an indelible impress upon their imaginations, reflected in their poetic works, their oratory, and even their architecture.

Her deeply-indented shores, washed on the one hand by the Adriatic, and on the other by the Ægæan, with its archipelago of islands,— serving both as landmarks to guide the adventurous navi-

* Gibbon. "Decline and Fall." Chap. 48.

gator in his course, and as places of refuge in a storm,— tended to develop a maritime spirit among her people, which led them gradually to extend their voyages to the entire coasts of the Mediterranean and Black Seas. Commerce, thus inaugurated, was the great civilizer. In this intercourse, they became acquainted with the discoveries and inventions of surrounding nations, which they adopted and improved upon; and even the elements of their philosophy were derived from foreign sources. So humanizing has this spirit proved, that it may be said that no nation, isolated from the sea, has ever attained to a high state of civilization.

Under such conditions of soil and climate, the Greeks developed a degree of culture whose influence has attended the intellectual man in all of his migrations. Whatever there is of heroic action in human conduct; whatever there is of intensity of expression in the passions; whatever there is of sublimity in poetic diction or oral discourse; whatever there is that relates to the beauty of the human form, or the just proportions of human structures, as manifested in sculpture and architecture; was displayed in all of its perfection by these Hellenic tribes.

Rome, the Inheritor of this Civilization.—From this source, the Romans derived their civilization and their knowledge of the arts; and even after they had subdued, by the power of numbers, that magnificent territory, their statesmen and poets did not hesitate to resort to the vanquished for instruction, and adopt their illustrious names as exemplars for their own guidance. At the dawn of the Christian Era, the Roman Empire is computed to have extended over 400,000 square miles. It reached from the western extremity of Europe to the Euphrates, and from Gætulia south to the confines of the Libyan Desert, comprehending the greater portion of the known world. In their career of conquest, the Romans had annexed not only Greece, with all her art and refinement, but also that region which is supposed to have been the cradle of the race, and where God had condescended to hold intercourse with man, and proclaim His will. Every known tribe and kindred rendered tribute to the Cæsars, and even our Saviour recognized the civil obligation.

Origin of Teutons and Celts.—To the north of Italy and beyond the Alps, lay a country divided into several principalities, known as Celto-Galatia, Germania, Cimbrica, and Scandiæ Insulæ, comprehending northern France, Germany, and Sweden, whose people, born beneath a cooler sky, and in a less enervating climate, and nurtured in a manner which required, from necessity, the practice of the hardier virtues of temperance, both in eating and drinking, were destined to subvert the Roman Empire and establish dynasties of their own upon its ruins, and to become even, the dominant race of the world. Little is known of these people prior to the invasion of their country by Cæsar. He found the valley of the Rhine mainly occupied by tribes of the Celtic family, while the frontiers were possessed by the Teutonic or German tribes. Thus, the population was partly Celtic and partly German, but both were branches probably of the great Indo-European family of the Caucasian type. Motley thus describes the characteristics of each:

"Physically the two races resembled each other. Both were of vast stature. The gigantic Gaul derided the Roman soldiers as a band of pigmies. The German excited astonishment by his huge body and muscular limbs. Both were fair, with fierce blue eyes, but the Celt had yellow hair floating over his shoulders, and the German long locks of fiery red, which he even dyed with *woad* [a plant growing in the temperate zone from which indigo is extracted] to heighten the favorite color, and wore twisted into a war-knot upon the top of his head." *

The Roman Empire contained the elements of its own dissolution; and it is well, perhaps, for the

---

* "Dutch Republic." Vol. I.

progress of the race, that this vast fabric, reared with so much toil and cemented by so much blood, was leveled to the ground by the pressure of its own weight. When the Roman soldier was so far enervated by luxury that he could not sustain the heavy armor, or wield the heavy weapons of his ancestors, he became an easy victim to the missile weapons of the Goth and Hun. The short sword and the pilum, with which the ancient Romans had subdued the world, dropped from the nerveless arms of their effeminate descendants. They were fain to recruit their armies from the ranks of the Barbarians, and confide to them the public defence. The foreign soldiers who had thus been incorporated into the Roman army, and subjected to its discipline, were they who subverted the Empire and founded dynasties on its ruins. The victorious Goths, fortunately for the cause of humanity, renounced their ancient superstitions, and adopted the Christian faith; and, at the same time, they received the use of letters so essential to the understanding of the Sacred Book, nor did they reject the inestimable treasures of ancient learning, preserved in the Greek and Latin languages. Thus the vanquished Romans communicated to the victors their religion, their language, their laws, and whatever of constitutional liberty they possessed.*

* Vide Gibbon's "Decline and Fall." *Passim*, Chap. XXVIII., XXX., XXXVI.

At the middle of the seventh century, we find the scale of their dominion contracted to the narrow limits of a small tract in Southeastern Europe,— to the lonely suburbs, as the great historian expresses it, of Constantinople; and in the meanwhile were laid the foundations of those governments, carved out of Roman territory, which, in modern times, have monopolized the arts, the sciences, and the civilization of the world.

Theodoric, Clovis, and Alboin, who thus founded dynasties out of the conquered provinces of the Roman Empire, were of Teutonic origin.

At this day, the Celtic division of the Indo-European family occupies Spain, Portugal, France, and parts of Belgium, Switzerland, and Britain; while the Teutonic division occupies Norway, Sweden, Denmark, Germany, Holland, and parts of Belgium, Switzerland, and Britain. Each, too, has distinct national characteristics which have clung to him in all of his subsequent migrations.

The Teuton.—The Teuton is fond of independence, and is little disposed to surrender his will to the control of another. He is restless under even venial grievances, and claims to be heard in the making of the laws by which he is to be governed. Hence, the governments founded by him, are either a representative monarchy, or a representative democracy. He makes a good colonist, adapts himself readily to altered conditions, and evinces a power for self-government. Wherever settled, his love of free thought, and his disregard of ceremonies, have made him a Protestant in religion, with a strong tendency to divide into a multiplicity of sects, and upon points of doctrine which, we would fain believe, are not essential to salvation. While the invigorating climate of the temperate zone is best adapted to his full development, he has pushed his conquests to the remotest parts of the earth; and wherever he has come in conflict with other races, he has proved himself the victor.

The Celt.—The Celt has never exhibited the same desire for personal freedom and civil liberty. He has been content to live under an absolute or slightly limited monarchy; and in those instances where he has thrown off the yoke of oppression and founded republics, as in South America, they have proved but another name for anarchy and misrule. With a disposition to superstition and a blind observance of forms, he is every where found the zealous and devoted adherent of the Catholic Church, whose imposing ceremonies awe his imagination, and captivate his judgment. Without protest, he surrenders his individual will to that of his superior, and submits to his teachings with an unquestioning faith. Hence, the uniformity of belief,— hence, the universality of the Catholic Church. Its doctrines are the same, whether expounded beneath the vaulted dome of St. Peter's, beneath the palm-thatched hut upon the banks of the Amazon, or in the log-cabin beneath the hyperborean sky of Lake Superior.

It is a striking historical fact, that the principles of the Reformation have never taken root in the purely Celtic regions, while they were at once accepted in those of the Teuton, and have accompanied him throughout all of his migrations. In the Old World, the boundaries between Catholicism and Protestantism remain about the same as at the death of the Great Reformer; and in the New World, the currents, springing from two distinct fountains, have flowed side by side, without any tendency to commingle.

The Celt loves the soft and balmy air of the tropics; and hence, in the New World, he relapsed into a life of luxurious ease, which the equable climate and the profusion of nature greatly encouraged; and to attain this end, he did not hesitate to press into his service the unrequited toil of an inferior race. But, beneath the glare of a Northern sky, where, to sustain life, were required unremitting exertions, all of his attempts at colonization have proved signal failures. In his contact with the aboriginal tribes, he has evinced a disposition to descend to their level, rather than to exalt them to his own standard of excellence.

Colonization of North America.—On the 7th of October, 1492, in mid-ocean, Pinzon, the companion of Columbus, observed a flight of parrots winging their way to the southwest, in consequence of which the course of the exploring expedition was changed to that direction; and ere long, instead of the "solid continent," the West-Indian Isles greeted the longing gaze of the adventurers. This apparently insignificant event, as remarked by the historian, had an all-controlling influence upon the destinies of the people of this Continent. It diverted the Celtic or Latin colonization, represented by the Spanish and Portuguese nations, to the tropical and southern portion of the hemisphere, while it left open to the Teuton, represented by the English and the German, the northern portion.

Thus, then, to these two great branches of the human family, was confided the task of subduing a hemisphere. Although the French and Spanish acquired a foothold upon the northern portion, and invested the narrow belt of Teutonic settlement on the Atlantic border, yet they were ultimately expelled, and the whole Continent was surrendered to the dominion of the Teutonic race; and now, after the lapse of less than four centuries, how different have been the results!

The Celt had the advantage in the race, for the United States were not colonized until a century later than Spanish America. Nature, too, had apparently dealt more kindly with the one region than with the other. In the one, there were luxuriant forests of extraordinary beauty, and bearing fruits most grateful to the appetite; and its fertile valleys and slopes were capable of rearing the coffee-plant and sugar-cane, whose products are so highly prized by all civilized nations. The temperature of the one was so mild and unvarying that little protection was required beyond a tent, or a thatch of palm-leaves; but, above all, and this was the most attractive feature to the adventurers, nearly all the streams rolled down their golden sands. Thus, in this serene and equable climate, surrounded by a profusion of vegetable forms which yielded their spontaneous fruits, and with a soil whose quickening powers produced those luxuries most highly esteemed by man, nature offered to the colonist an easy and indolent life.

The other region furnished a soil of indifferent fertility, covered with a forest which must be subdued before it was fitted for cultivation; and its wealth was extracted only after long and assiduous labor, going through the routine of seed-time and harvest, and garnering up, with economic care, and storing away the crops for future use. The climate was so inhospitable that elaborate houses were to be constructed, and every precaution taken to keep out the wintry blasts.

Thus, the differences of soil and climate were calculated to generate differences in the character of the two races. In the one case, with habits of order and intelligent industry, and with an aptitude for self-government, the people have built up a social system the best ever devised for the happiness of man, and developed a strength and unity which have made them the most powerful nation of the earth; while, in the other, whatever development of material resources has been made, is the result, in the main, of compulsory labor, extorted from an inoffensive race; and whatever governments have been instituted, by whatever name called, they have afforded little security to life or property.

Thus it will be seen, that our modern civilization has been a plant of slow growth, originating under peculiar conditions of soil and climate, and propagated only over such portions of the earth's surface as afforded similar conditions. Personal servitude was a part of the civilization of Greece and Rome; and the Barbaric tribes, in their primitive settlements, were accustomed to reduce not only their captives, but their criminals, and even those who had incurred the obligation of debt which they could not discharge, to this condition. Hence, then, among every nation, from the earliest times, and continued until times comparatively recent, slavery has been the lot of the greater portion of mankind. Its abolition, by the most enlightened nations of Christendom, certainly affords substantial evidence of the progress of humanity.

National Unity.— European philosophers, speculating on the origin of our people, derived from so many sources and composed of elements so discordant, have predicted for the American Republic a short-lived career. The only disturbing cause — human slavery — which, from the outset, has proved the source of deep-seated discord and internecine strife, and which, in its culmination, threatened the disruption of the Republic, has happily been removed; and, great as has been the expenditure of treasure and blood, no true patriot can regret the sacrifice, in view of the permanent benefit which has resulted to the cause of free institutions.

There are several causes which have contributed to the fusion of our people into a nearly homogeneous union. Among these may be enumerated the democratic tendencies of our institutions, where each elector is required to pass upon the measures, not only of the National and State legislatures, but even those relating to the details of township organizations; and if he fail to arrive at independent conclusions by reading and reflection, he has at least the advantage of hearing such measures discussed by those who have informed themselves.

Next may be mentioned the system of common schools, where all of the youth are brought under such a system of instruction as to qualify them for the ordinary pursuits of life. This tends to fix the principles of the language and produce a uniformity of pronunciation. Webster's Spelling Book was issued as far back as 1783, and since that time probably more than fifty millions of copies have been published, and it is yet retained as a text-book in the schools.

Next may be mentioned the press, whose freedom is expressly guarded by constitutional enactments. The conductors of the press not only inform the people of current events, but they express the public sentiment and often create that sentiment. Every projected measure, at the present day, is fully discussed outside the halls of legislation, before it becomes incorporated into the statute-book. The power thus wielded over the morals, the intelligence, the habits, and pursuits of the people, is a tremendous one; and the experience of nearly a century, since all restrictions were thrown off, has proved that little is to be feared from its licentiousness. The electric telegraph, too, has become its ally in the diffusion of intelligence, and there is hardly a well-to-do farmer on the verge of settlement, who is not, at the end of the week, fully advised as to what has transpired in the busy world. A free press, having the ear of the whole community, and acting as a public instructor, is essentially an American institution. Wherever a colony is planted, and the people aggregated into a village, there, too, is to be found the newspaper.

Last, but not least, may be mentioned the close commercial relations which exist between widely-separated parts, and the ease and expedition, through navigable rivers and innumerable railroads, by which those relations are maintained. There are few Americans who do not visit some one of the commercial centres at least once a year, while the mercantile class penetrates to the remotest hamlets. This direct intercourse tends to break down provincial antipathies, to produce a homogeneity of character, and to bind together all classes and conditions of men. The infusion, too, each year, of large bodies of immigrants into the New States from regions widely-separated, destroys all tendency to a clannish spirit, and leads to the formation of new associations, independent of birth and nationality. Thus, it may be said, that the Western people exhibit a far more cosmopolitan spirit than those of the Older States. In such a mixed community, provincialisms of speech are at once observed and criticised; and, without criticism, the provincial man is insensible to his errors. Language is the strongest bond of union, and it is spoken with the greatest purity, where the intercourse between the different parts of the country is most intimate. The attrition, so to speak, which is constantly going on between the individual members of a society thus constituted, tends to rub off the angularities of character and produce a homogeneous union.

In the higher walks of science and literature, while we have accomplished much, yet it must be confessed, that we have not attained to that commanding rank which is to be desired; but in a country where there are few hereditary fortunes which permit the inheritors to indulge in a course of travel or learned ease, and where the investment of capital is so remunerative, it is idle to expect that a large body of men, corresponding to what are known as "German students," should be abstracted from the active pursuits of life. "The state of a nation," as long ago remarked by Dr. Johnson, "is the state of common life;"— and if we go to our farm-houses, our work-shops, and factories, and inquire into the condition of those who hold the plough, or forge the iron, or weave the warp, we shall find a degree of thrifty industry, of sturdy independence, and general information, such as are possessed by no other people. Combining the land-grants of Congress for agricultural colleges, and the school-funds of the several States, as well as the voluntary endowments of individuals, it may be boldly asserted that no nation has made such liberal appropriations for the cause of education as the United States.

Under these influences the American character has already acquired a distinctive national type, whose elements are not a conglomerated mass, but a crystallization into definite forms and angles. Take such an assemblage as the Congress of the United States. Trace back the ancestry of each individual member for a few generations, and see the different stocks from which they draw their origin. He may be the descendant of one of the Puritans who came over in the Mayflower; of a substantial burgher of Bruges, who loaned his credit to the Prince of Orange; of a God-fearing Huguenot, driven out of France by the treachery of Henry of Navarre; of an Irish Catholic who fought the "bloody Oliver" at Drogheda, or William III. at the Boyne; or of the peace-loving courtier, William

Penn; or of the gentle-minded Roger Williams, who founded Rhode Island; — yet, among these men there is as strong a spirit of national pride as among the peers of England, who can trace their lineage to William the Norman.

In the settlement of the United States, there have been no barriers sufficiently formidable to check, except temporarily, the flow of population. Those barriers are, or soon will be, effectually overcome, and intimate commercial relations will be established with every part of the Republic, producing homogeneity of character. Go into the Highlands of Scotland, and you will see at this day some descendant of the Græme, or the Campbell, clothed in his kilt; go to the miner's cabin in Colorado, and you will see the mistress of that rude abode wearing a bonnet of a fashion received in New York a month previously. Discordant, then, as the elements of our population may seem, there is an all-pervading spirit whose influence is to blend and harmonize the materials into a homogeneous union.

Our population, then, may be compared not inaptly to the Great River, whose regimen we have attempted to describe. Its waters, springing from fountains far remote, and under different conditions of sky, are first gathered into trickling rills which, increased by fresh affluents, expand into brooklets, and then into broad streams. As the river advances in its course, it absorbs tributary after tributary, each nearly as large as itself, until its rolls on a uniform volume, broad and deep,— the emblem of restless power,— floating upon its surface richly-laden barges, supporting on its banks populous cities, and diffusing blessings over a continent.

Other nations have attained to greatness, or maintained it, through the power of their aristocracy, or the far-seeing sagacity of a single controlling mind, like that of Alexander, or Cæsar, or Charlemagne, or Napoleon. While we have produced great men, it may be said that we have produced no one man, (not excepting Washington), who has impressed his policy on the nation. While we have developed such marvelous resources, such a commercial spirit, such a productive industry, and such a power to subjugate a continent,— these results have been achieved by the recognition of the doctrine of the sovereignty of the people, and their will as supreme in the legislation of the country.

English Character.—The English are regarded as a homogeneous people; and the Englishman has peculiarities, both mental and corporeal, by which he can be recognized the world over; yet in his veins flows the mingled blood of Celt, Goth, Saxon,

Dane, and Norman; and out of this amalgamation of races, has sprung a nation with a distinctive character, which is perpetuated from one generation to another.

While a fusion so thorough and effectual, had taken place centuries ago among the people of the Lowlands, beyond the Cheviot Hills, amid the Highlands of Scotland,— about the same distance from London that the Adirondacks are from New York,— there dwelt, and yet dwells, a race of men, under different conditions of soil and climate, who have persistently clung to the traditions of their ancestors, and resisted all attempts to intermingle. It is only as far back as 1773, that Dr. Johnson published his "Tour to the Hebrides," in which he describes the manners and customs of a people as different from the English, as though they belonged to the antipodes.

In another portion of the empire, embracing seven millions of people, there has been, for centuries, a war of races and religions, at times so fierce as to lead to the distraction of the country and the depopulation of its cities; and, at this day, the feeling of discontent towards the throne is as deep-seated and intense as at any time in the previous history of the union. A native historian has had the boldness to expose the national crimes and follies which have been practiced upon this member of the empire,—"but a withered and distorted member, adding no strength to the body politic, and reproachfully pointed at by all who feared or envied the greatness of England." *

The diffusion of language is, perhaps, the most conclusive evidence of the homogeneity of a people; and we venture the assertion, that the tongue of Shakspeare and of Milton, is spoken with greater precision and purity by the mass of the people of the United States, than by the inhabitants of the British Isles. In estimating their intelligence, we are apt to form our own conclusions from our knowledge of those who have graduated in the universities, and have had the benefits of foreign travel and observation. But this view is erroneous. When we descend to the sub-stratum of society to determine the degree of intelligence, we shall find that it is to be rated by a much lower standard. In Ireland, throughout pretty extensive districts, a dialect of Gaelic is spoken almost to the exclusion of the English; in the Highlands of Scotland, the Erse; and in Wales, a dialect different from both. But coming to England itself, the provincialisms of the districts of Northumberland, Yorkshire, and Cornwall, are broader and more uncouth than prevail in any portion of the United States.

* Macaulay. "History of England."

"Language, more than any other attribute, forms a binding link among a people;—by its idiomatic properties it severs them."

Civilizing Effects of the Christian Religion.— In tracing the career of a people — their progress in moral and intellectual development, in these modern times, no candid observer, even in a purely philosophical treatise, can justly ignore the influence of the Christian religion. And while it is to be deplored that the full force of those doctrines,— first promulgated by Him who, in a human light, was the son of a carpenter of Nazareth, and which were propagated by the humble fishermen of Galilee,— has been greatly impaired by the dissensions of the Christian church and its division into a multiplicity of sects; yet, as a *political* element, Christianity has tended to make better citizens, more orderly, more sedate, and less given to turbulent passions; it has tended to awaken a spirit of national unity by making even the humblest feel that they were co-heirs in a common inheritance, and had a common object to accomplish; and, at the same time, it has tended to establish a bond of unity between nations geographically separated, by inculcating the doctrine that the rights of a people are not to be ruthlessly stricken down by mere brute force. And while this sentiment has not, in the conduct of the world's affairs, found its full expression, it has so far acquired a foothold that no ruler at this day, however powerful, dare venture upon a step which shall shock the enlightened sentiment of mankind.

Christianity, in the general diffusion of its doctrines among the people, has awakened thoughts of a nobler origin; has brought man within the sphere of higher impulses; has given him clearer ideas of his duties here and of his destiny hereafter; has laid the foundation of every scheme of practical and all-comprehensive benevolence; and has combined and crystallized a public sentiment, that governments are not instituted for the benefit of a particular class, but for the prosperity and well-being of the people; and finally and preëminently, it recognizes the common humanity of the whole family of man, and inculcates the necessity of breaking down those barriers which pride, and prejudice, and power, have been able to erect, throughout the world's history, to hamper the human race and to prevent them from assuming that position in the scale of creation, for which they were, of a aforetime, designed.

CHAPTER XIII.

PROGRESS OF DEVELOPMENT.

ORDINANCE OF 1787 FOR THE GOVERNMENT OF THE NORTH-WESTERN TERRITORY — ITS EFFECT UPON THE CHARACTER OF THE COLONIZATION — FIRST SETTLEMENT OF THE REGION — RELATIVE GROWTH IN POPULATION — AREA OF WESTERN STATES — AGRICULTURAL PRODUCTS — THEIR RAPID INCREASE — THE ASSESSED VALUE OF REAL AND PERSONAL PROPERTY — INDIANS — THEIR HABITS — GOVERNMENT POLICY TOWARDS THEM — THE MOUND-BUILDERS — THEIR CIVILIZATION — ANTIQUITY OF THEIR WORKS — CONCLUSION.

Ordinance for the Government of the Northwestern Territory, and its Effects on the Character of Colonization.—On the 11th day of July, 1787, the Congress of the United States, sitting at New York, passed "An Ordinance for the Government of the Territory of the United States, northwest of the Ohio." This region, at that time, was an unreclaimed wilderness—unvisited by the white man, if we except a few Moravian missionaries, who had penetrated to near the sources of the Muskingum, and established a mission on its banks, at a point above the present town of Coshocton, in the State of Ohio. The passage of this Ordinance, as justly remarked by Hildreth,* was a a measure second in importance only to the Constitution itself; for, by the sixth clause, the whole of this territory, out of which have been carved the five great States of Ohio, Indiana, Illinois, Michigan, and Wisconsin, was irrevocably dedicated to free labor. It was the turning point in the controversy which even then had enlisted the action of the statesmen of the two divisions of the Union, and which subsequently found its solution in the sword,—whether the States should exist all free or all slave. The South consented to its passage with the understanding, afterwards acted upon, of securing, under future cessions, the extension of slavery into the territory south of the Ohio River.

This Ordinance was a measure of profound political sagacity, and one which, in the lapse of years, proved the salvation of the Republic. But for that, the people of the Border States of Virginia and Kentucky, would have crossed over the boundary thus established, with their slaves, and the institution of slavery would have taken root and flourished in a fertile soil, and amid a genial climate. As it was, when, in 1861, this question culminated, there were found, within this territory, seven millions of people, educated in the belief that labor

---

* "History of the United States." Vol. III.

was honorable, who rallied almost unanimously to uphold the Government, and evinced their patriotism by contributing to the army a relative numerical strength far in excess of that of the New England or Middle States; and with no vaunting spirit, it may be said, that the men thus contributed, and the services which they performed, broke the power of the Rebellion.

At the time of the adoption of the Ordinance, the Government, by treaties with the Six Nations, the Wyandots, the Delawares, and the Shawanese, had extinguished the Indian title along the northern bank of the Ohio, and for a considerable distance inland, as far west as the Wabash; and the territory thus secured, embraced seventeen millions of acres. Thus, this region became open to American colonization only through the channel of the Ohio River. The French, however, as far back as 1720, built several forts within the present limits of the State of Illinois, of which Fort Chartres was the principal. This was one of a chain which stretched from Canada to the mouth of the Mississippi.

First Settlement.—There is not, in the whole history of the colonization of man, so striking an instance of the increase of population and of material wealth, as is exhibited in those States which occupy the Upper Valley of the Mississippi and the region adjacent to the Great Lakes, comprehending Ohio, Michigan, Indiana, Illinois, Wisconsin, Minnesota, Iowa, Missouri, and Kansas. In 1778, within the memory of men yet living, the first colonists of English extraction,— gathered in Massachusetts, under the leadership of Rufus Putnam,— entered this region and established themselves at Marietta, where the Muskingum unites with the Ohio. This was the origin of that colonization which, in ninety years, has peopled this region with more than twelve millions of souls; has subdued and brought under cultivation an area nearly twice as great as the cultivated land of England; has connected together the principal commercial points by a net-work of railroads more that 12,000 miles in extent, at a cost exceeding $413,500,000, and whose annual earnings reach nearly $50,000,000; and has built up a domestic industry whose annual value is in excess of $300,000,000, giving origin to an internal trade far greater than the external trade of the whole country.

In order to show the relative growth of the different sections of the United States, the following table is submitted, compiled from the Census Returns of 1860, in which the several States are grouped in reference to geographical position, climate, productions, and the business pursuits of the inhabitants:

TABLE—SHOWING THE GROWTH OF POPULATION AND THE RATIO OF INCREASE.

STATES.	POPULATION, 1850.	POPULATION, 1860.	RATE OF INCREASE.
NEW ENGLAND STATES—Maine, New Hampshire, Vermont, Massachusetts, Connecticut, & Rhode Island,	2,728,116	3,135,283	$14\tfrac{9}{10}$
MIDDLE STATES—New York, New Jersey, Pennsylvania, Delaware, and Maryland,	6,573,301	8,258,150	$25\tfrac{6}{10}$
CENTRAL STATES (Slave)—Virginia, North Carolina, Tennessee, Kentucky, and Arkansas,	4,485,719	5,289,875	$17\tfrac{9}{10}$
PLANTING STATES—South Carolina, Georgia, Alabama, Florida, Mississippi, Louisiana, and Texas,	3,770,640	4,969,142	$31\tfrac{7}{10}$
PACIFIC STATES—California, and Oregon,	105,891	432,439	
TERRITORIES,	124,618	295,275	$1.37\tfrac{8}{10}$
WESTERN STATES—Ohio, Michigan, Indiana, Illinois, Wisconsin, Minnesota, Iowa, Missouri, and Kansas,	5,403,595	9,064,896	$67\tfrac{7}{10}$
Total population,	23,191,876	31,445,080	

It will be seen that the ratio of increase in the Western States, between 1850-60, was more than two-fold greater than in any other section, except in the Pacific States and Territories, where the population was too insignificant to form a basis of comparison.

That increase was 3,661,301, which is three-fold greater than the whole population of the Colonies in 1750, and more than 1,500,000 greater than the whole population of the United States, when, in 1776, they declared their independence.

With regard to the relative progress of settlement in the northern and southern belt of the Western States, it may be said, that population of Anglo-Saxon origin* began to flow into the latter region as early 1778, and continued without interruption. The region adjacent to Lake Erie was not sought by the immigrant, to any considerable extent, until after the completion, in 1825, of the New York and Erie Canal, opening the lake-region to the seaboard, — a work which will stand as an imperishable monument to the genius of Clinton. The

---

* The Romanic or Latin race was the first to discover and establish posts in the Great Valley.

In 1541, De Soto, then Governor of Cuba, made an overland expedition from Florida to the Mississippi River, which he reached about latitude 35°, and was the first white man to gaze upon its turbulent flood. Crossing the river, he explored the country as far west as the Boston Mountains of Arkansas, and south to the Washita. Seeking to retrace his steps, he was stricken down by death, and his followers consigned his body to the middle current of the Great River which he had discovered.

The discovery of the Upper Mississippi is to be ascribed to Marquette, a Jesuit missionary, and to Joliet, an envoy of France, of whom little is known except in connection with this event. On the tenth of June, 1673, with five French voyageurs and two canoes, they crossed the portage between the Fox and Wisconsin, and descended the latter stream to the Mississippi. Thence continuing the voyage, they reached Arkansas (about latitude 33°), when, finding the Indians hostile, they retraced their course. Arriving at the mouth of the Illinois, they passed, by that stream and the Des Plaines, to Chicago. Thus, then, they were the first white men to survey the site of what is now a

region west of Lake Michigan, was not open to settlement until after the close of the Black-Hawk War, in 1832. Thus, the southern belt had nearly a half century the start in the career of colonization; and, taking the National Road as the dividing line through the States of Ohio, Indiana, and Illinois, the population south of that line, in 1830, largely preponderated, and maintained its ascendency up to 1840; but, in 1850, the conditions were

magnificent city. Before the close of September they reached Green Bay. Joliet hastened to Quebec and there embarked for France.

La Salle, residing at Fort Frontenac, inspired by the report of these discoveries, matured a plan to follow in their wake, and open the region to European commerce. Having received the sanction of the French minister, in 1679, he built the Griffin on the Upper Niagara, the first vessel of any considerable size that spread her canvas on the Lakes. In this bark, he proceeded with a colony of fur-traders and attendants to Green Bay. The Griffin was despatched back, freighted with furs, but was never heard of afterwards. La Salle then voyaged to St. Joseph's, near the head of Lake Michigan, where Allouez had planted the cross and gathered around him the Miamis. Penetrating the Illinois valley, he established Fort Crevecœur, below Peoria, and thence despatched Hennepin to explore the Upper Mississippi. In 1682, he descended the Great River to its mouth. In 1685, with a fleet sent out from France, he attempted the colonization of the Lower Valley, but the colonists were carried beyond the mouth of the river, and landed on the Texas coast. Two years after, he was assassinated in attempting to return to Quebec.

The French kept up their military occupation in Illinois. Kaskaskia is the oldest permanent settlement in the Great Valley. Fort Chartres was a principal rendezvous; Cahokia was founded below St. Louis, and Vincennes on the Wabash.

By the peace of 1762, France ceded the territory east of the Mississippi to Great Britain, but formal possession was not had until 1765.

During the colonial period, the British government endeavored to restrict settlements to the east of the Alleghanies, but while emigration found its way through the passes to Tennessee, Kentucky, and Western Pennsylvania, the North West remained sealed to Anglo-Saxon settlement.

reversed; and, in 1860, the preponderance was largely in favor of the north.

The southern region has a climate less rigorous, and a soil more fruitful and better adapted to stock-raising and the growth of Indian corn; but to the mass of immigrants the pure waters and the invigorating air of the lake-region have proved more congenial and attractive.

Area.—The area of the eight Western States is 525,301 square miles, which is equivalent to 326,192,640 acres, of which 52,199,050 acres are "improved," but far from being cultivated in a manner to bring out the full capabilities of the soil. This would make the improved land equal to 18 per cent. of the whole area. Portions of Michigan, Wisconsin, and Minnesota, adjacent to Lake Superior, are not attractive to settlement by reason of the inhospitable climate, and the western half of Kansas by reason of the deficiency of rain; but, with suitable cultivation, it may be safely asserted that this area is capable of supporting 50,000,000 of the human family.

Agricultural Products.—The principal products of these States, in animal and vegetable food, are embraced in the table, page 241. They comprise more than 550,000,000 bushels of cereals, more than 11,000,000 head of swine, and more than 7,200,000 head of horned cattle. Relatively this group furnished 59 per cent. of all the wheat, 39 per cent. of all the oats, 56 per cent. of all the corn, 40 per cent. of all the tobacco, 28 per cent. of all the cattle, and 33 per cent. of all the swine, raised in the United States. The total value of the agricultural products in 1860, was $1,159,605,660.

The amount of cereals which annually flows out of this region to the Eastern markets, is not less than 100,000,000 bushels, and the product of pork is not less than 100,000,000 pounds. To move this large surplus of vegetable and animal food, gives employment, during the season of navigation, to more than 1,200 vessels, and to five lines of trunk railways, to say nothing of that portion which finds an outlet through the Mississippi River, or is sent to the Plains to supply the Military posts. The commerce of the Mississippi itself gives employment to about 1,200 steam-vessels, besides a large number of barges.

Assessed Value of Property.—The assessed value of real estate and personal property in these States,—1860,—was nearly $4,000,000,000,—an increase during the decade of more than 250 per cent. The cash value of farms was nearly $2,500,000,000; of farming implements and machinery, $80,275,000; and of live stock, $382,400,000.

These facts render it obvious that the centre of population and productive industry, has already crossed the Alleghanies, and has become seated for all time in the Great Valley. Under a new apportionment of representation, the political power of this region will be dominant in shaping the legislation of the country. The physical combinations, which we have endeavored to elucidate, are such as to make it the seat of the most powerful organization of men that has ever been formed. This people will impress their peculiar civilization upon the whole country, and their influence will be felt and acknowledged by the nations of the earth.

Having thus given a sketch of the progress of development in population and material resources under the colonization of the white man, it will not be deemed out of place to refer to the characteristics of that people who formerly asserted their dominion over the whole of this region, but are now contracted, within narrow limits, on the Western Plains; and, also, to refer to that mysterious race, of whom little is known, apart from the tumuli and embankments which are scattered along many of the river-valleys. A century hence, perhaps, the memorials of the Indian will be less conspicuous than those of the Mound-Builders.

THE INDIANS.

During the whole history of the colonization of the white race on this Continent, a serious impediment has existed in the Indian, whom it has been found necessary to subdue and even to exterminate; — and a great deal of misplaced sympathy has been expressed for his apparently irrevocable fate. There is not a State whose sod has not been drenched with the blood of the white man, shed in some border strife. Even now, not a year passes by without the perpetration of atrocities shocking to humanity. The sums which have been spent in Indian wars, and paid out under treaties, would cancel the national debt. The whole breadth of this Continent must now be appropriated to commercial intercourse, sure, safe, and expeditious. That intercourse must necessarily destroy the hunting-grounds of the Indian, and it becomes a question of a very serious character whether the policy heretofore pursued by the Government, is to be persisted in. Thus far, while we have prohibited other powers from trading or holding intercourse with the red man, we have so far recognized his nationality as to consent to enter into treaty stipulations with him.

At the time of the occupancy by the European, of that portion of the Continent out of which have been carved the United States, the aboriginal inhabitants did not exceed 300,000, and that is the estimated number at this time, the greater portion of whom dwell on the western slope of the Great Valley. If they were all aggregated in one place and furnished with houses, they would form a city a little more populous than Chicago. They are, and always have been, separated into numerous tribes, between whose members there was no permanent bond of union, but oftener open feuds. Having no knowledge of the arts beyond fashioning a canoe, or chipping from flint or obsidian an arrow-head, no agriculture apart from cultivating patches of corn, no constructive faculty other than setting up poles and covering them with hides of buffalo or sheets of bark, they live a listless and degraded life, roaming in small bands from place to place in search of food, and regulating their migrations by those of the animals on which they subsist. Often subject to the gnawings of long-continued famine, when the means of appeasing it are presented, they gorge themselves like beasts of prey, and then relapse into inaction, utterly improvident of the future. With such habits, and with means of subsistence so precarious, the Indian can not live in large communities and occupy fixed habitations.

His contact with civilization has not elevated his condition. He has readily imbibed its vices, while he has shown no disposition to practice its virtues. Drafts have been made upon his moral and intellectual faculties, which, in mercantile phrase, he has invariably allowed to go to protest, with the indorsement, no assets.

The Indian was never a formidable antagonist, until he became possessed of the weapons of the white man; and even then, he did not exhibit the steady valor and efficient discipline of the American soldier; and to day, on the Plains, Sheridan's troopers would not hesitate to attack the bravest band, though outnumbered three to one. The Indian has never risen to the higher arts of strategy, such as handling large bodies of men, the carrying or maintaining of a position, or conducting those evolutions which appertain to a pitched battle. The ambush and surprise are his modes of warfare,— to strike and retreat before his foe can rally. The knife, the gun, and the horse, obtained from the white man, are the only gifts of civilization that he esteems, and the effect of conferring them upon him, has been simply to make him more powerful for evil.

Commercial necessity requires the appropriation of these lands to other purposes than hunting-grounds. We may talk of their rights to the soil, acquired by immemorial use and enjoyment; but to make that right valid, there must be some act of conversion or appropriation, beyond the mere pitching of a lodge, the cultivating a patch of corn, or roaming over the surface in pursuit of game. Population presses too closely on the heels of production, to admit of the setting apart ten miles square for the support of a single life, which is required in the hunter-state, when, with proper cultivation, half an acre would yield a less precarious support. It would have been better, perhaps, at the outset, but certainly now, for the Government to assume the full relation of guardian and ward, and to treat the Indian as the States treat the feeble-minded and incompetent,— by providing asylums where they shall be cared for, or rather place them on reservations, under close surveillance, where the experiment may be tried of instructing them in the arts of agriculture. If they die out under the experiment, we may console ourselves with the reflection, that their case is but an illustration of a law of nature, where the weaker and more sickly organisms, whether animal or vegetable, are compelled to give way before the hardier and more vigorous.

The Cherokees afford about the only example where a whole tribe has emerged from barbarism, and successfully adopted the arts of civilized life. One of their number clomb to the conception of an alphabet and reduced it to form. Situated in one of the most favored regions of the United States, where the extremes of temperature are not excessive, where the relief and depression of the surface is such as to give origin to running streams, and where the vegetable covering is about equally divided between prairie and forest,— the Cherokees have developed a capacity for farming of the highest order, and their surplus herds, in part, find their way, even, to the New York market. Their government is republican in form, and the will of the tribe finds full expression in their legislation. This example encourages the belief that the Indian can be redeemed from barbarism, and the policy of placing him on a reservation and subjecting him to a system of training in the arts of civilized life, is the only one which can rescue him from swift and certain annihilation.

THE MOUND-BUILDERS.*

At frequent intervals throughout the region of the Great Lakes and the valley of the Mississippi,

---

* Abstract of a paper, by the author, on the "Antiquity of Man in North America." Trans. Chicago Acad. Nat. Sci. Vol. I.

occasionally upon some crowning eminence, but for the most part in the rich alluvial valleys, there are found tumuli of earth—the highest of which reach from seventy to ninety feet,—long lines of embankments, often circular and often square, enclosing many acres, and pierced at intervals with entrances, and parallel roads connecting together the several parts,—the whole occupying leagues in extent, and bearing evidence of having been constructed according to well-devised plans.

When the white man first penetrated the Ohio Valley, he found growing upon them, a forest which, in the size of the trees and in their characteristic forms, differed in no degree from those of the surrounding region. Upon the origin of those structures, by what people built, and the causes that led to their extinction, the Indian occupants of the country could throw no light; except, perhaps, the obscure tradition communicated to Heckewelder, a Moravian missionary, that the Algonquins and Wyandots had expelled from the valley of the Ohio its former inhabitants, who had descended the Mississippi.

It is to be regretted that the accomplished historian* of the United States, basing his information on a hasty generalization of the late Professor Hitchcock, who, at the time, had never personally

---

* Bancroft. "History of the United States." Vol. III., Chap. 22.

EXTENT OF THEIR WORKS. 417

inspected these structures, should have indorsed and perpetuated, in a work to which every one refers as the standard of authority, the grave error, that the Mississippi Valley has no monuments;—and that where the antiquarian of a vivid imagination sees the vestiges of artificial walls, the geologist sees but crumbs of decaying sandstone; that where the one sees parallel entrenchments, the other sees but a trough that subsiding waters have ploughed through the centre of a ridge; and that where the one sees a tessellated pavement, the other sees but a layer of pebbles aptly joined by the water. It is hardly necessary to select from an ample storehouse, the facts to refute these assertions. Suffice it to say, that the geologist and the antiquary, side by side, and with pains-taking care, have explored very many of these structures, and both accord in the verdict, that these are the works of human hands.

This region, then, has its monuments, whose origin goes back to a remote antiquity,—reared, too, by a people who had at least emerged from barbarism. These works are first met with in Western New York, and are continued through Northern Ohio to Wisconsin and Minnesota. While on the southern shore of Lake Superior no traces of earth-works have been observed, there are abundant evidences of ancient mining, extending over the whole Copper-region, and there is a chain of proof which connects these exploitations with the Mound-Builders.

The valleys of the Ohio and Mississippi, however, afford a climate more equable, and a soil more genial for the cultivation of maize, which was undoubtedly the great staple of food and the basis of their civilization; and hence, in these regions, we find these earth-works vastly multiplied. In the vicinity of Grave Creek, below Wheeling; at Marietta, and up the valley of the Muskingum, and its tributary, the Licking; at Gallipolis; at Portsmouth, Piketon, Chillicothe, and Circleville, in the rich valley of the Scioto; at Cincinnati, and through the equally rich valley of the Miami;—the number and magnitude of these works indicate that here were the sites of populous settlements, whose inhabitants must have been maintained by other pursuits than those of hunting and fishing. Earthworks occur at Vincennes, Indiana, and at other points in the Wabash Valley; in Kentucky, Tennessee, and Northern Mississippi, and vestiges have been observed in the Gulf States — Alabama, Georgia, and Florida,— as far east as South Carolina.

The original site of St. Louis was dotted over with numerous mounds, and the Illinois shore opposite, in what is known as the American Bottom, contains some of the largest thus far observed.* The Rock-River region of Northern Illinois, embracing Sterling, contains many of these earth-works, some of which, like those of Wisconsin and Minnesota, represent the form of animals.

We are not aware that the Missouri Valley, above the mouth of that river, contains any vestiges of the Mound-Builders.

I do not propose to describe these works, as that task has been executed by Atwater, Squier and Davis, Whittlesey, Lapham, and others; but suffice it to say, that they appear to have been constructed to subserve a variety of purposes,— such as military defence, in which case they were undoubtedly crowned with palisades; for places of sepulture; for sacrificial altars; and, perhaps, the more conspicuous were erected as monuments to commemorate some signal event in their history.

The Mound-Builders, in the selection of the sites for their habitations, appear to have been influenced by the same motives that governed the white man, for we find that many of the most flourishing towns and cities in the West, occupy these identical sites; for example, Marietta, Portsmouth, Circleville,

* That of Cahokia is 90 feet high, and has a base of 666 feet; while the famous mound at Grave Creek, Virginia, is 70 feet, with a base of 333 feet; and the next in rank is that at Miamisburgh, Ohio, which is 68 feet, with a base of 284 feet.

Piketon, Chillicothe, Cincinnati, Vincennes, Chattanooga, St. Louis, Sterling, Beloit, etc.

When we consider the magnitude and extent of these works,— those, for instance, near Newark, Ohio, with its circles and squares, and its parallel roads and tumuli, extending over leagues of ground (and whose cubic contents exceed those of the great pyramid of Cheops); or the great mound of Cahokia, and the subordinate mounds in the American Bottom, and on the site of St. Louis,— the whole series extending over a breadth of ten miles,—we draw the inference, that these structures could never have been erected by a people who depended on the chase or the fisheries for the means of subsistence. Mere roving bands, like the Indians on the Plains, can not aggregate in communities, nor can they accumulate a stock of provisions so as to admit of the expenditure of vast labor upon unproductive works; and besides, the history of all nomadic tribes, whether in Scythia or North America, shows, that they are averse to that patient and long-continued labor which is implied in such structures. They are the memorials of the persevering industry of a people who occupied fixed habitations, and whose agriculture was so far successful, as to admit of the appropriation of a portion of their labor to other objects than procuring the necessaries of life. They imply, too, a consolidated and, perhaps, a despotic government, under which a single mind directed that labor to the accomplishment of a well-devised plan. There is a unity of purpose, carried out in all of its details, which could only be successful under such a political organization.

The civilization of Egypt resulted from the cheap food furnished by the date, which grows spontaneously in the valley of the Nile; and to bring up a child to manhood, according to Diodorus Siculus, who wrote more than two thousand years ago, cost not more than twenty drachmas, or less that three dollars. Hence, then, under a despotic government, nearly the whole labor of the country could be employed in constructing such works as the Pyramids, and such cities as Thebes, Karnac, and Luxor.

In South America, the cheap food furnished by the cultivation of corn or maize, enabled the Incas of Peru, to build up a great empire, and construct those works whose ruins, at this day, excite the admiration of every beholder.

Maize probably constituted the staple of the Mound-Builders' crop, and a single acre of ground well cultivated, would have supported from thirty to fifty people, with such animal food as they may have derived from the forests and the streams. Vestiges of their garden-plots may be seen in the valley of the St. Joseph's, Michigan, and carbonized corn has been revealed in the mounds at Grave Creek and Cincinnati. And yet they must have tilled their fields at a disadvantage, for there is no evidence of their having availed themselves of the patient labor of the ox or the horse, which, on the European Continent, have proved the faithful servants of man, — for neither of these quadrupeds existed on the American Continent at the time of its discovery by Europeans. There were, it true, two representatives of the bovine tribe, — the musk-ox, which never wandered as far south as their habitations, and the buffalo, which has hitherto resisted all attempts at domestication. In the absence, then, of the horse and ox, which mainly constitute the herds of a pastoral people, the Mound-Builders must, in the progress of their history, have passed directly from a hunter-life to one of agriculture.

Their stone-implements consisted of spear and arrow-heads chipped, with much skill, out of hornstone or chert; of hammers, generally of porphyry, grooved near the head for the attachment of a withe; of fleshing instruments of the same material brought down to a blunt edge; of pestles for cracking and grinding corn; of tabular plates of steatite or chlorite slate, pierced with holes to gauge the size of the thread in spinning; of circular discs, like weights, and concave on both surfaces, ordinarily of porphyry, and ground; ornaments like plumb-bobs, double-coned or egg-shaped, and pierced or grooved at one end for the attachment of a string,—the material being specular iron, like that derived from Lake Superior or the Iron Mountain, but sometimes limestone; and lastly, there are occasionally found elaborately-wrought pipes, which show that they indulged in the luxury of tobacco.

In the fabrication of these implements they exhibited a skill far superior to that belonging to the Stone Age of Europe, rivaling those elaborately-wrought and polished stone-works which are designated as "celts," and which are referred, by European ethnologists, to a more advanced state of civilization.

They mined extensively native copper on the shores of Lake Superior, and wrought it into knives, spear-heads, chisels, bracelets, and other personal ornaments; but, having no tin, they could not, like the ancient dwellers on the Swiss lakes, or like the inhabitants of Nineveh, of the valley of the Nile, or of Peru, impart to the alloy almost the hardness of steel. It is doubtful, even, whether their metallurgic art extended to the smelting of copper; for it often happens that the native copper of Lake Superior encloses native silver,—both metals existing side by side chemically pure,—

which, if smelted, in whatever proportions, would form a homogeneous compound. Bracelets have been found in the mounds, in which this peculiarity is preserved, thus showing that the material had not been smelted but simply hammered; and the ends are brought together by bending, without any evidence of having been soldered.

Their mining operations were on a scale of magnitude, of which no one can form a just conception, except from personal observation. There are few productive copper-veins now wrought upon the shores of Lake Superior, which were not known and explored by the Mound-Builders. Continuous lines of ancient, but now nearly filled pits, are observed, not only on Keweenaw Point, in the Ontonagon region, but even on Isle Royale; and to reach the latter point involved a passage of forty-five miles, across a lake by no means placid in its disposition. Their method of mining was, probably, to build fires on the rock and, when thoroughly heated, to dash on water, and thus fissure it in parts, when it was broken up with hammers of porphyry weighing from five and even up to forty pounds, which were derived from the rounded masses on the Lake-shore. Cart-loads of hammers were taken out of some of these excavations by the modern explorers.

Heaps of rubbish line the course of the veins;

and in the bottom of some of the pits, have been found the remains of ladders by which they ascended and descended, the bowls with which they bailed the water, and the copper-gads by which they forced the rocks apart. At the Minnesota mine, the workmen in re-excavating one of these ancient pits, at the depth of eighteen feet, came upon a mass of copper ten feet long, three feet wide, and nearly two feet thick, and weighing not far from two tons, which the ancient miners, after having raised about five feet, and propped with billets of wood, had abandoned, having first, however, removed all of the projecting points which were accessible.

They clothed themselves, in part at least, not in skins like the Indian; not like the Sandwich Islander in the macerated bark of certain trees; not like the dwellers on the Swiss lakes, in matted sheets of vegetable fibre; but in cloth of a texture approaching hemp, spun with a uniform thread, and woven with a warp and woof. The texture, while coarse, is uniform, and the border is often ornamented with tassels. It is not such a fabric as a European manufacturer would make to traffic with a barbarous nation, for cotton would be cheaper, and wool would afford more warmth; and, besides, this cloth was found under such circumstances as to preclude the idea of its being a modern substitution.

In the plastic arts, they attained to considerable proficiency. While the Indian, before his contact with the white man, was in the habit of bending up birch-bark so as to hold water, and then casting in hot stones, and thus bringing it to a boiling point; the Mound-Builder moulded his pots in clay, tempered with sand or shells, and baked them so far as to make useful utensils in most of the processes of cooking. Not content with the useful, he aspired to the ornamental. From a mound in Missouri, I have seen a water-cooler in the form of a compressed globe, the neck surmounted with the similitude of a human head. The features are symmetrically moulded, and the facial angle indicates intelligence. The features are not those of the red man, but such as distinguish the enlightened races. There is a statuette taken from the same mound, representing a captive bound ; and while portions of the figure are well moulded, taken as a whole, it is grossly incongruous.

They must have maintained a commercial intercourse with the most distant parts of North America, for the same mounds have often afforded plates of mica from a region as remote as New England; copper from the shores of Lake Superior; marine shells (*Busycon perversum*) from the Gulf or Atlantic Coast; and steatitic and porphyritic implements, the materials of which must have been derived from a region equally remote.

The crania which have been exhumed from the mounds, as determined by Morton,* differ in many respects from those of the North American Indian; — in the wider expansion of the forehead, the larger facial angle, the less obliquity of the orbit of the eye, the narrower nose, the less prominent projection of the jaws, the smaller dimensions of the palatine fossa, and the flattened occiput. Many of these peculiarities are displayed in the head from the Missouri mound, before spoken of, moulded by the unknown artist who had the skill to impress upon the plastic clay, the features of his race.

Although the Mound-Builders, from the absence of tin, made no use of bronze implements, yet, when we regard the vast number and magnitude of their structures, their perfection in weaving, in pottery, in the fabrication of stone-implements, the extent to which they employed copper in the place of bronze, and the communication which they maintained between widely-separated portions of the country, we can not but ascribe to them a place in the scale of civilization, as high as the

* "Crania Americana." p. 208.

people of the Bronze Age on the Eastern Hemisphere. Their exclusion from the beautiful valley of the Mississippi, which contains so many memorials of their industry and greatness, is not the only example which history affords of the extermination of a people considerably advanced in civilization, by a people more vigorous, and less inclined to the arts of peace.

We have no chronometer by which to measure the lapse of time since these excavations were made, and these structures were reared, except the character of the arborescent vegetation with which they are now covered. This is in every respect like that of the adjacent forest. When, therefore, we see growing upon these mounds, trees four centuries old, and the prostrate and moldering trunks of others, which once flourished on the same sites, we are justified in assuming that these works are at least a thousand years old; but in attempting to determine their absolute age we are lost in the mazes of conjecture.

CONCLUSION.

We here bring to a conclusion our sketch of the physical geography of the GREAT VALLEY. We have endeavored to portray its configuration,— the mountain chains by which it is bounded, the different epochs of their elevation, the heights to which they attain, the diversity of climate to which they give origin, and the influence which they exert on the distribution of moisture. The boundaries of forests, prairies, and arid wastes have been traced, and the causes to which they owe their origin, have been investigated. The conditions of soil and climate essential to the growth and perfection of those plants adapted to human food and human raiment, have been pointed out, and, at the same time, the materials which make up the great frame-work of the region,— the rocks from whose abrasion the soil has been derived, and whose recesses are the repositories of the useful metals, and the store-houses of fossil fuel,— all have passed under review. And, finally, we have recounted how this Great Valley, within the memory of living men, has been reclaimed from the wilderness, and been made the abode of twelve millions of human beings, who have developed an internal industry, and attained to a degree of prosperity, of which the annals of the past afford no parallel; and, indulging in visions of coming greatness, we have predicted the time, and at no remote date, when this people would impress their laws and civilization upon the Continent, and make their influence felt in the conduct of the world's affairs.

We close with the consciousness that our task has been but imperfectly executed. While we have endeavored to avoid those specialities which are required to satisfy the demands of pure science, we have endeavored to introduce those generalizations which may be comprehended and appreciated by the intelligent reader.

No one can rise from the study of the physical geography of our country, without its awakening in his mind a nobler sphere of thought, and creating a profounder impression, as to the ultimate destiny of the human race in those arts which dignify life and mitigate its sufferings.

If Burke, during the last century, in surveying the magnitude of the French empire,— the public works, the charitable foundations, and other institutions,— confessed that, in all this, he beheld "something which awed and commanded the imagination;" how much more profoundly would he have been impressed, if he could have witnessed the growth and present position of the feeble colonists whose conduct he so ably defended. He would have seen those colonists, numbering at the time they asserted their independence, less than three millions, expanded to forty millions; occupying a country stretching from ocean to ocean, and so far diversified by soil and climate, as to produce most of those plants which enter into human food and raiment; intersected by great navigable rivers, spanned by bridges of iron, and dotted with populous cities upon their banks; with an area greater than that of France, subdued and brought under cultivation, and yet with a capacity for expansion almost unlimited; with artificial communications, undreamed of in his day, between every principal commercial point; and with one iron-road, stretching like a girdle across the "solid continent." He would have seen this people living under a form of government the best ever devised for the security of personal freedom and the display of human energy, and with an inherent strength to withstand shocks, as evinced in the late Rebellion, under which any other government would have crumbled. He would have seen, in each State, ample provision for the education of every child; and hospitals and asylums, erected by public or private contributions, for the alleviation of all the ills incident to humanity.

With such elements of national power and future greatness, let us hope that the virtue and intelligence of the people will advance with equal pace.

INDEX.

A.

Abbot, cited, see HUMPHREYS AND ABBOT.
Adirondack Mountains, age of, 266.
Africa, desert of, 131.
   sources of the Nile, 132.
   rain-fall of Sierra Leone, 134.
   region of the Mediterranean, 135.
   atmospheric currents of, *ib.*
Agassiz, Louis, cited, on Primeval Continent, 255.
Age of rocks, see SYSTEMS OF UPHEAVAL.
Age of metals, 269.
Alaska, climate of, 199.
Alleghany, or Appalachian Mountains, 27.
   height of, *ib.*
   age of, 255.
   range and structure of, 28.
   coal-field of, 297.
Alluvium of the Mississippi, 16.
Alps, different lines of upheaval recognized in, 32.
Altai Mountains, 129.
Alternate wood and prairie, region of, 81.
Amazon, basin of, 113.
   vegetation of, 114.
America, see NORTH AMERICA.
Amygdaloid of Lake Superior, 275.
Andes, range of, 111.
   effects in modifying climate, 112.
   highest peaks of, *ib.*
Anthracite of Pennsylvania, 301.
   of New Mexico, 313.
Antisell, T., cited, 36.
   on the rains of California, 168.
Appalachian system, 225.
Arabia, desert of, 130.
Arctic climate, 333.
Arctic life, 358.
Argentiferous veins of New Mexico, 294.
   of Nevada, 330.
Artemisia, characteristic of a dry climate, 86.
Asia, central plateau of, 129.
   mountains of, 130.
   rainless and profusely-watered belts of, *ib.*
Atacama, desert of, 119.
Atlas Mountains, 135.
Atmosphere, currents of, 173; 186.
   height of, 183.
Auriferous slates of California, 308.
Auriferous veins, Azoic, 268.
Auroras, 201.
Austin, J. B., cited, 362.
Australia, its flora and fauna, 135.
   its deserts, mountains, and winds, 136.
Axis of elevation, 250.
   of the Alleghanies, 255.
   of Lake Superior, 254.
   of Rocky Mountains, 257.
   of the Sierra Nevada, 258.
   of the Coast Range, 260.
Azoic system, defined, 264.
   its range, 265.

B.

Bancroft, George, cited, on the ancient monuments of the Mississippi Valley, 416.
"Barren Grounds" described, 78.
Basalt, of Table Mountain, 261.
   of Lower California, 262.
   of New Mexico, 262.
   of Oregon, 36.
Basins, river, of the Mississippi, 3; 43.
   of the Missouri, 39.
   of the Ohio, 42.
Beaumont, Elie de, cited, 251.

B E C

Becquerel, on forest-barriers, 160.
Bigelow, J. M., cited. 88; 89.
Big trees of California, 94.
Bituminous coal, of Carboniferous age, 301.
    of Cretaceous age, 312.
    of Tertiary age, 326.
Blake, W. P., cited, 46.
Blodget, Lorin, Climatology of United States, 96.
    his tables of temperature, 207.
    of rain fall, 96; 208.
    on the winds of the Gulf, 104.
Blue (Cincinnati) limestone, range of, 283.
Borlander, H. N., cited, 154.
Botanical Geography, region of mosses, 78.
    of conifers, 80.
    of deciduous trees, 81.
    of the grasses, 84; 89.
    of the cacti and artemisiæ, 87.
    arborescent forms of Pacific Slope, 92
    of Mississippi Valley, 5.
Boulders, see DRIFT.
Brande's Dictionary, cited, 219.
Brazil. forests of, 113.
    atmospheric currents of, 121.
British America, lignites of, 326.
    climate of, 366.
    of the Saskatchawan region, 62.
Bross, Gov. Wm., cited, 233.
Brown, J. Ross, cited, 91; 308.
Buckle, H. T., cited, 365.
Buckland, Wm., cited, 300.
Burlington limestone, range of, 289.
Buenos Ayres, pampas of, 117.

C.

Cactus, distribution of, 87.
Calciferous sandstone, range of, 280.
California, Carboniferous rocks of, 259.
    basaltic rocks of, 261.
    Cretaceous of, 313.
    gold-bearing rocks of, 308.
    copper-bearing rocks of, 308.
    coal deposits of, 313.
    quicksilver deposits of, 314.

C L I

Triassic rocks of, 258; 307.
Tertiary rocks of, 328.
erosive action in, 338.
its mountain chains, Sierra Nevada, 34.
Coast Ranges, 36; 260.
height of principal summits, 35; 37.
vegetable productions of, 92.
Yosemite Valley in, 95.
wheat-culture of, 168.
climate of. 101.
periodic rains of, 106; 168.
Canada, climate of, 366.
Cañons of the Colorado plateau, 339.
Caraccas, llanos of, 114.
Carbonic acid gas in air, 142.
    how generated, 145.
Carboniferous series, range of, 287.
Caribbean Sea, winds of the, 103.
Carolina, pine barrens of, 319.
Cascade Range of Pacific, 36.
Caspian Sea, region of the, 125.
Catholicism, universality of, 386.
Caucasian type, characteristics of, 375.
Caucasus, region of the, 128.
Celts, their origin, 381.
    their characteristics, 385.
    their colonization, 386.
Cerealia, range and cultivation of, see CLIMATIC RANGE.
Chaco Gran, described, 116.
Chester group, range of, 288.
Christianity, effects of the spread of, 399.
Cinnabar of California, 314.
Civilization, origin of, 377.
    Grecian, 378.
    Roman, 381.
    Teutonic, *ib.*
    Celtic, *ib.*
    contrasted with that of the ancients, 69.
Classification of rock-formations, 246.
Climate, definition of, 172.
    atmospheric currents, 173.
    oceanic currents, Gulf Stream, 188.
    rains and winds, 178.
    isothermal lines, 186.
    of the United States, 192.
    of the Pacific Coast and Great

Basin, 180; 197.
of the Plains, 204.
table of temperatures in United States. 207.
table of rain-fall in United States, 208.
its influence on man, 355.
in the Arctic regions, 358.
in the temperate regions, 362.
in the torrid regions, 360.
phenomena of the seasons in North America, 200.
Climatic range of cultivated plants, 209.
of maize, 213.
of wheat, 215.
of oats, rye, and barley, 218.
of rice, 222.
of sugar-cane and sorghum, 224.
of the potato, 226.
of cotton, 227.
of tobacco, 230.
of the grasses, 231.
tables of annual production, 240.
Climatology, of the United States, 182.
of the Mississippi Valley, 180.
of the Gulf Coast, 195.
of the Pacific Coast, 198.
of the Saskatchawan Valley, 194.
of the United States compared with Europe, 187; 190.
Cloud-bursts, phenomena of, 182.
Coal, its uses, 295.
mode of formation, 299.
of the Carboniferous age, 296.
of the Cretaceous age, 312.
of the Tertiary age, 326; 330.
anthracite of Pennsylvania, 362.
of New Mexico, 313.
analyses of, 317.
Coast Ranges of the Pacific, 36; 260.
Colonization of United States, 387.
of Western States, 403.
Colorado, desert of, 46.
cañons of, 339.
Comstock lode described, 330.
Columbia, basin of, 46.
Columbus, diversion in his course, effects of, 387.
Coniferous limestone, range of, 80.

Constant precipitation, zone of, 177.
Continents, formation of, 245.
Continent, Primeval of North America, 254.
Cooper, J. G., cited, 82.
Copper, annual product of, 280.
Copper-region of Lake Superior, 279.
of California, 308.
Cordilleras of South America, 112; 117.
Corn, a generic term, 219.
Corn, Indian, range of, 213.
Cotton, range of, 227.
Cretaceous system, range of, 310.
groups of Missouri Basin, 311.
of the Atlantic Slope, 310.
of the Mississippi Valley, 14; 310.
of the Pacific Coast, 310; 313.
of the Colorado Plateau, *ib*.
flora of, 316.
coals of, 313.
Crofts, Capt., cited, 233.
Crystalline rocks, range of, 249.
Cultivated plants, see CLIMATIC RANGE.
Currents, air and oceanic, see CLIMATE.
Cuvier, cited, 325.
Cypress-swamps of the Mississippi, 6.

D.

Dakota group, 311.
Dall, W. H., on the northern extension of the Rocky Mountains, 62.
Dana, J. D., cited, on the structure of continents, 253.
on the origin of the prairies, 109.
on the Australian Alps, 136.
Davidson, on the range of fossils, 247.
Delta of the Mississippi, 16.
Denudation, in the region of the Great Lakes, 350.
in California, 338.
in the Colorado Plateau, 340.
Densely-wooded belt, in United States, 78.
Deserts, origin of, 71.
of Arabia, 130.

DES

of Atacama, 119.
of Australia, 136.
of Colorado, 46.
of Gobi 129.
of Patagonia, 118.
of Sahara, 131,
of Salinas, 116.
of the Great Basin, 37; 90.
Development, physical, in Western States, 375.
Devonian system, range of, 285.
 economic materials in, 285.
Drift series, 332.
 in Mississippi Valley, 335.
 absence, of on the Plains, 337.
 in California, 338.
 in Lower California, 262.
Dunes of Lake Michigan, 345.

E.

Earth, effects of the obliquity of its axis, 177.
Earth's crust, effects of the contraction of, 177.
Earthquakes at New Madrid, 18.
Egypt, effects of the Nile's inundation on, 133.
 ancient irrigation practiced in, 166.
Elevation, systems of, 250.
 of Lake Superior, 254.
 of the Appalachian, 255.
 of the Rocky Mountains, 257.
 of the Sierra Nevada, 258.
 of the Coast Ranges, 260.
England, climate of, 124.
English character, 397.
Eocine-Tertiary, range of, 319.
 on the Atlantic and Gulf Coasts, 319.
 in the Missouri Basin, 322.
Erosion, see DENUDATION.
Erratic blocks, see DRIFT.
Eruptions, see VOLCANIC ACTION.
Esquimaux, habits of, 358.
Europe, climate of, as influenced by the Gulf Stream, 123.
 compared with that of North America, 187.
 races of men in, 382.
Evaporation, amount of, in United States, 190.

GRA

F.

Flint, Timothy, cited, on the forests of the Mississippi Valley, 8.
 on the earthquakes of New Madrid, 22.
Fluor spar veins of Southern Illinois, 293.
Forests, distribution of, in North America, 78.
 in South America, 113.
 in Europe, 124.
 their range dependent on moisture, 81.
 their effects on health, 141.
  on animal life, 149.
 rapid destruction of, in United States, 155.
 they modify climate, 160.
 their lessons, 159.
 they retain moisture, 148; 161.
 tree-planting, effects of, 146; 152.
 effects of disrobing a country of, 152.
 they absorb noxious gases, 145.
Fresh-water Tertiaries of Missouri Basin, 322.
Fractures of earth's crust, see ELEVATION.
Frémont, J. C., cited, 87; 233.
Gabb, W. M., cited, on the Post-Pliocine of California, 262.
 on Cretaceous of California, 315.
 on the gravels of Lower California, 339.
Galena, occurrence of, in the Northwestern States, 283.
 in Southern Illinois, 293.
 in Missouri, 280; 294.
Galena limestone, range of, 282.
Geological Sketch (Map) of the United States, 272.
Geology, objects of, 245.
 subdivisions of strata, 246.
Gibbon, cited, 130; 283.
Glaciers of Greenland, 333.
Glacial action in Mississippi Valley, 335.
Gobi, desert of, 129.
Gold product in the United States, 308.
Golden Age, 270.
Grama-grass, described, 89; 233.
Granite, origin of, 253.

G R A

Grasses for pasturage, 231.
Gravel-washes, 39; 183.
Great Basin, character of, 39; 90.
Great Lakes, 349.
    their influence in modifying climate, 203.
    how formed, 350.
    altitude above ocean, 352.
    area of, *ib.*
Great lignite group, 326.
Greece, early intellectual development in, 379.
Guinea, climate of, 134.
Gulf-coast, climate of, 195.
Gulf-stream, action of, 124; 188.
    effects of diversion, 190.
Guyot, A., cited, 27.

H.

Hall, James, cited, 285; 286.
Hayden, F. V., cited, 278; 305; 326; 337; 344.
Heat, internal, of earth, 252.
Heights of mountain peaks:
    in the Andes, 112.
    in the Cascade Range, 36.
    in the Coast Range, 37.
    in the Rocky Mountains, 31.
    in the Sierra Nevada, 35.
    in the Alleghanies, 27.
    of the Alps, 36.
    of the Caucasus, 128.
Heights of water-sheds, 3.
    of the Mississippi, *ib.*
    of the Missouri, *ib.*
    of the Ohio, 26.
    of the Great Plateau, 33.
    of the Great Basin, 37; 45.
    of Lake-terraces, 343.
Henry, Joseph, on atmospheric currents, 173.
Herodotus, cited, 125.
    on the ancient corn-trade, 218.
Herschel, Sir John, on solar influence, 198.
    on tree-planting, 154.
Hewit, A. S., cited, 271.
Hilgard, cited, 320.
Himalaya Mountains, 129.
Hood, Mount, height of, 36.
Humphreys and Abbot, cited, 40; 169.
    on the physics of the Mississippi River, 3; 5; 16; 17.

J O H

    on the winds of the Gulf-Coast, 105.
Humboldt, Alexander Von, cited,
    on the structure of the Rocky Mountains, 33.
    on the llanos of Caraccas, 114.
    on solar influence, 139.
    on Central Plateau of Asia, 129.
    on nocturnal life of animals, 151.
    his system of isothermal lines, 187.

I.

Icebergs, drifting of, 334.
Ice-action, see DRIFT.
Igneous action, 249.
    in Azoic epoch, 264.
    in Silurian epoch, 275.
    in Triassic epoch, 308.
    in Cretaceous epoch, 313.
    in Tertiary epoch, 330.
    in Quatenary epoch, 339.
Illinois, galena deposits in, 283; 293.
    coal-field, 297.
Indiana coal-field, 302.
India, rains of, 130.
Indians, North American, 411.
    their character, 412.
    policy pursued towards, 413.
Indian summer, described, 205.
Indo-European race, 382.
Insect-life in northern latitudes, 203.
Ireland, climate of, 124.
    language of, 398.
Iowa, coal of, 302.
Iron, its uses, 270.
Iron Region of Lake Superior, 266.
    of Missouri, 267.
    characteristic of the Azoic, 265.
    annual product of, 261.
Irrigation, practiced by the Orientals, 165.
    by the Peruvians, 166.
    feasibility of, on the Plains, 169.
Isothermal lines of United States, see METEOROLOGY.

J.

Johnson, Edwin F., cited, 61.
Johnson, Dr. Samuel, cited, 393.

JUR

Jurassic and Triassic systems, 305.
  range of, on Atlantic Slope, 306.
  in Rocky Mountains, 307.
  in California, *ib.*

K.

Kane, E. K., on Arctic night, 148.
  on glaciers and drift, 334.
  on Esquimaux rations, 359.
Kansas, physical features of, 75.
  coal-field of, 298.
  Permian system in, 305.
Keokuk limestone, range of, 288.
Keweenaw Point, trap range of, 279.
Kinderhook group, 290.

L.

Labrador, currents of, 189.
Lakes, Great American, 349.
  effects in modifying climate, 203.
  fresh-water of Tertiary age, 325.
  Great Salt Lake, 90.
  Slave, Bear, and Athabasca, 263.
Lake Superior system, 254.
Lake Michigan, dunes of, 345.
Language, a bond of national unity, 398.
Lapham, I. A., cited, 204.
Lead ores, vide GALENA.
Le Conte, J. L., cited, 56; 312.
Leidy, J., cited, on mammals of the Loess, 15.
  of the Missouri Basin, 323.
Lesquereux, Leo, on the origin of prairies, 73.
Lignites, of Mississippi Valley, 320.
  of the Missouri Basin, 326.
  of the Columbia Valley, 328.
  of the Great Basin, 327.
Llano Estacado described, 44.
Llanos of Caraccas, 114.
Loess of Mississippi and Missouri Valleys, 15; 342.
Loup-river beds, 323.
Lyell, Sir Charles, division of Tertiary, 320.
  on the Loess of Natchez, 15.

MIS

M.

Magnesian limestone, range of, 280.
Maize, botanical range of, 213.
Malaria, origin of, 147.
  arrested or modified by tree-planting, 147.
  generated by the first breaking of the soil, 148.
Mammalian remains in Missouri Basin, 323.
  in Loess at Natchez, 15.
Marine formations of Tertiary Age, 228.
Man, effects of climate on, 355.
  geographical range of, 356.
  effects of external circumstances on, 357.
  Arctic life of, 358.
  life of, in Temperate Zone, 362.
  in North America, 366.
Map of geology of United States, 272.
  of isothermal lines, 208.
  of distribution of forests, prairies, and deserts, 140.
Marsh, George P., cited, man and nature, 152.
Marsh, O. C., cited, 323.
Mauvaises Terres, described, 325.
Mediterranean, basin of, 135.
Meek, F. B., cited, 326.
Meek and Hayden, cited, 265; 298; 305; 310; 321.
Metamorphic rocks, 254.
Meteorology, system of air-currents, 173.
  of isothermal lines, 187; 208.
  of winds and rains, 120.
Mexican Gulf, winds of, 103.
Mexico, formations of, 259.
Michigan, coal-field of, 298.
Michigan, Lake, sand-dunes of, 345.
Miocine, see TERTIARY.
Mississippi River, regimen of, 3.
  approaches to, 12.
  magnitude of, 2.
  origin of name, *ib.*
  area of valley, 3.
  length, height of sources, volume, etc., *ib.*
  sources of, 43.
  internal navigation of, 4.
  character of Lower Valley, 5.
  typical vegetation of, *ib.*

M I S

bluffs, levees, overflows, of, 10.
phenomena of waters, 13.
outlets of, 11.
geology of bed, 14.
geological structure of, 242.
alluvium of, 16.
depth and slope of, 17.
earthquake-action in, *ib.*
drift-action in, 335.
Missouri, iron-region of, 267.
Azoic series in, 265.
occurrence of tin in, 268.
lead-region of, 280; 294.
coal-field of, 297.
Missouri River, description of, 39.
water-shed of, 26.
Missouri, basin of the, 39.
Triassic series in, 306.
Cretaceous series in, 311.
Tertiary series in, 322.
Moisture, sources of, in United States, 92.
Morton, S. G., cited, 427.
Mosses and saxifrages, region of, 78.
Motley, J. L., cited, 382.
Mound-Builders, 415.
extent of their works, 418.
their agriculture, 421.
their implements, 422.
their mining, 424.
their commerce, 426.
their crania, 427.
antiquity of their works, 428.
Mountain ranges, Altai, 129.
Andes. 112.
Appalachian, 27.
Atlas, 135.
Cascade Range, 36.
Coast Ranges, *ib.*
Caucasus, 128.
Himalaya, 129.
Kuen-lun, *ib.*
Parimé. La, 114.
Rocky Mountains, 30.
Sierra Nevada, 34.
Mountain Heights:
Mount Baker, 36.
Blanc, *ib.*
Brewer, 35.
Clingman's, 27.
Diablo, 37.
Elbrouz, 128.
Gray, 31.
Frémont, *ib.*
Hamilton, 37.

O C E

Hood, 36.
Illampu, 112.
Lassan's Peak, 35.
Olympus, 36.
Long's 31.
Pike's, 31.
Ranier, 36.
San Francisco, 31.
Shasta. 35.
Silliman, *ib.*
Spanish Peak, 31.
Taylor, *ib.*
Tyndal, 35.
Washington, 27.
Whitney, 35.
Mullan, Capt., cited, 40.
on the warm air-currents of the Upper Missouri, 192.

N.

National unity, causes which produce, 390.
Negro, characteristics of, 369.
Newberry, Dr. J. S., cited, 170.
on the Cañons of the Colorado, 340.
on the alluvial of the Rocky Mountain Slope, 89.
on the origin of prairies, 109.
on the Cretaceous flora, 316.
New Madrid, earthquakes at, 18.
erosive action of river at, 9.
New Orleans, approaches to, 12.
New York, sources of her greatness, 48.
Niagara limestone, range of, 284.
Nile, valley of, 132.
ancient canals of, 166.
Niobrara group, 311.
North America, physical features of, 1.
mountain ranges of, 27.
climate of, 182.
vegetation of, 81.
river-systems of, 263.
colonization of, 387.
progress of development in, 307.
geology of, 242.

O.

Oak-openings described, 83.
Ocean, the great source of moisture, 178.

Ohio, basin of, 42.
    coal-field of, 302.
Ohio River, 3.
Oil springs, origin of, 286.
Onondaga salt-group, 285.
Ordinance of 1787, 401.
Oregon, climate of, 199.
    coals of, 328.
Organic remains, range of, 243; 247.
    absence of in Azoic, 264.
    first appearance in Silurian, 273.
    in the Loess of the Mississippi, 15.
    flora of the Carboniferous, 299.
    of the Cretaceous, 316.
    of the Tertiary, 322.
Oronoco, basin of, 113.
Oscillations of the earth's surface, 251.

P.

Pacific Coast, climate of, 197.
    elevation of, 252; 257.
Pacific Ocean, source of moisture, 101.
    periodic winds of, 106.
Pacific railroads, 51.
Pampas of La Plata, 116.
Pahranagat, described, 38.
Parry, C. C., cited, 60; 107; 313.
Passes, mountain:
    Cadotte, Snoqualmie, 61.
    South Pass, 26.
    St. Bernard, 51.
    Evans's. 61.
Passes of the Mississippi. 12.
Patagonia, climate of, 118.
Peat, origin of, 74.
Pembina, region of, 217.
Pennsylvania, coal-field of, 297.
Permian system, range of, 304.
Peru, mountains of. 112.
    rainless district of, 118.
    ancient works of, 116.
Petroleum springs, origin of, 285.
Pictured Rocks, Lake Superior, 276.
Pierre, Fort, group, 311.
Pineries, Western, their rapid destruction, 155.
Pine-Barrens of the South, 319.
Pines, botanical region of, 80; 92; 379.

character of soil essential to their growth, 80.
Plants, how they grow, 141.
    chemical constituents of, 142.
    cultivation of those useful to man, 209.
    soil in reference to their growth, 210.
    maize, range of, 213.
    wheat, oats, rye, barley, range of, 215.
    their origin, 218.
    rice, sugar, sorghum, 222.
    potato, range of, 226.
    cotton, range of. 226
    tables of production, 240.
    extension of plant-culture by irrigation, 84.
    plants peculiar to the prairies, 86.
    moisture as connected with their distribution, 84.
    cactus, 81.
    artemisia, 86.
    bunch-grass, 89.
Plata, La, pampas of, 116.
Pliny, cited, 1.
Pliocine, see TERTIARY.
Pope, Gen., quoted, 43.
Post-Pliocine, see DRIFT.
Potsdam sandstone. 275.
Potato, range of, 226.
Prairies, origin of, 71.
    their distribution, *ib.*
    not due to peat-growth, 73.
    not due to texture of soil, 76.
    not due to annual burnings, *ib.*
    due to conditions of moisture, 109.
    vegetation of, 84.
    characteristic plants of, 86.
    facilities for cultivation. 235.
Prairies in North America, 71.
    in Caraccas (llanos), 114.
    in La Plata (pampas), 116.
    in the Black-Sea region (steppes), 125.
    in Central Asia, 129.
    how far modified by tree-planting, 161.
    by irrigation, 169; 181.
Primeval Continent, 254.
Progress of development in Western States, 401.
    effects of Ordinance of 1787, *ib.*
    first settlement of, 405.

INDEX. 441

population in, 240; 408.
agriculture of, 241; 408.
Protestantism, where prevalent, 386.

Q.

Quicksilver of California, 314.

R.

Railroads:
Union Pacific, 51.
Central Pacific, 54.
Union Pacific, E. D., 57.
Northern Pacific, 61.
their effects on the progress of development, 65.
Rain-phenomena in the United States, 181.
Rains, whence derived, 178.
mode of formation, 179.
as connected with the distribution of plants, 77.
tables of the mean annual precipitation at various stations in the United States, 97; 208.
sources of moisture, 103.
periodical rains of California, 101.
Raised beaches, 349.
Rawlinson, on the ancient corn-trade of the Black Sea, 220.
Redfield, W. C., cited, 104.
Rebellion, the Great, causes of, 373.
Religion, civilizing effects of, 388.
Rémond, A., cited, on the geology of Mexico, 259; 309.
Rice-culture, 222.
Richardson, Sir John, cited, 78; 151; 203; 326.
Richthofen, Baron, cited, on the Washoe Mountains, 38.
on Comstock lode, 330.
River-systems of United States, 263.
Rocks, their physiognomy, 210.
Rocky Mountains, their range and extent, 30.
their elevation, 257.
Rocky Mountain Valleys, 45.
Rogers, W. B. and H. D., cited, on the structure of the Appalachians, 27.
Roman Empire, extent of, 381.

Russel, Robert, cited, 104.
Russia, forests of, 124.
steppes of, 125.

S.

Sahara, desert of, 131.
Salt, of Michigan, 286.
of Nevada, 91.
efflorescences of the Plains, 86.
of the Great Basin, 91.
of the Black Sea region, 128.
of South America, 116; 119.
of Central Asia, 129.
Salt Lake described, 90.
Salt Lake, desert of, 45.
Saskatchawan, basin of the, 62; 194.
Schacht, on the effects of forests in attracting moisture, 162.
Scotland, Highland races of, 398.
Scratches, or striation, of rocks, 337; 350.
Sand-dunes, 345.
Seasons, phenomena of, 200.
Section, of the Ohio Valley, 292.
of the Mississippi Valley, 15.
Sedimentary rocks, described, 272.
their distribution, 246.
See, also, SILURIAN, DEVONIAN, CARBONIFEROUS, etc.
Shasta, height of, 35.
Shumard, B. F., cited, 305.
Sierra Nevada, height of, 35.
vegetation of, 92.
Sierra Leone, climate of, 134.
Silurian system, explained, 273.
first traces of organic life, 274.
distribution of the strata, *ib*.
embraces the copper-region of Lake Superior, 279.
and the lead-bearing region of Missouri and Wisconsin, 280.
recognized in the Black Hills and on the Colorado Plateau, 278.
Silver-mines of Mexico, 259.
of Nevada, 330.
Sitka, climate of, 199.
Sky, serenity of, in Peru, 118.
of the United States as compared with England, 191.
Slates, auriferous, of California, 308.

Smith, Dr. Angus, on Sanitary Economy, 146.
Soil, whence derived, 210.
— exhaustion of, 334.
Solar influence, 139.
Somerville, Mrs., cited, 66.
Sorghum, culture of, 225.
South America, features of, 111.
South Pass, height of, 26.
Squier, E. G., cited, on the Andes, 112.
Stansbury, Capt. H., his exploration of Salt Lake, 90.
Staring, on peat-growth, 74.
Steppes, of Black-Sea region, 125.
Stephenson, George, value of his invention, 236.
St. Lawrence, basin of, 47.
St. Louis limestone, range of, 288.
St. Peter's sandstone, range of, 281.
Sugar-cane, cultivation of, 224.
Sun, universal influence of, on matter, 139.
— on organic matter, 143; 147; 150.
Systems of rocks, 246.
    Azoic, 264.
    Silurian, 273.
    Devonian, 286.
    Carboniferous, 287.
    Triassic, 305.
    Permian, 304.
    Cretaceous, 310.
    Tertiary, 318.
    Post-Pliocine, 332.
    Recent, 340.
Swallow, S. G., on geology of Missouri, 280; 284; 298; 345; 306.
Systems of elevation, 254.
    Appalachian, 255.
    Rocky Mountain, 257.
    Lake Superior, 254.
    Coast Ranges, 259.
System, river, 263.

T.

Table-lands of the United States, 33.
— of South America, 113.
— of Central Asia, 129.
Table Mountain, described, 261.
Tables of temperature, 207.
— of precipitation, 208.
— of rock formations, 246.
— of agricultural products, 240.
— of population, 241.
Temperature, lines of, 208.
— causes which modify, 177.
— agency of oceanic currents, 199.
— that of the Pacific, 198.
— of the Gulf Stream, 188.
— effects of, on forest range, 79.
Temperate Zone, life in, 362.
Terraces of Modified Drift, 342.
— along the Great Lakes, *ib.*
Tertiary deposits, 318.
— change in animal life indicated, *ib.*
— marine of Atlantic Coast, 320.
— divisions of Eocine, Miocine, and Pliocine, 320.
— fresh-water series of Missouri Basin, 321.
— Loup-River group, 323.
— White-River group, 324.
— Wind-River group, 325.
— Fort Union or Great Lignite group, 326.
— Lignites of the Great Basin, 327.
— Miocine beds of Pacific Slope, 328.
— coal-deposits of, *ib.*
— igneous products of, 329.
— silver-ores of Washoe, 330.
Teutonic race, origin of, 381.
— characteristics of, 384.
Texas coal-field, 298.
Tin, occurrence of, in Missouri, 268.
Titicaca, lake of, 112.
Tobacco, culture of, 230.
Trappean rocks of Lake Superior, 275; 277.
— of the California Coast, 261; 339.
— of the Great Basin, 329.
— of the Colorado, 261.
Trees, range of in United States, 71.
— character of Northern forests, 80.
— of the Appalachian Slope, 79.
— of the Pacific Slope, 92.
— their effects on health, 144.
— on climate, 159.
— how they grow, 141.
— effects of destroying the forest, 152.

TRE

Tree-planting, effects of, 162.
Trenton limestone, range of, 282.
Triassic system, range of, 258; 305.
    on Atlantic Coast, 306.
    on Pacific Coast, 307.
Tropical climate, on life, 360.
Turchin, J. B., cited, on the steppes of the Black Sea, 128.

U.

United States:
    geological map of, 272.
    isothermal lines of, 208.
    winds of, 103.
    rain-fall in, 96.
    vegetation of, 71.
    climatology of, 182.
    geology of, 209.
Upheaval, see SYSTEMS OF.
Upper Silurian, range of, 284.

V.

Vegetation, zones of, 78.
Volcanic products, 261.
Volcanoes of United States:
    in the Rocky Mountains, 31.
    in the Great Basin, 330.
    in the Colorado Plateau, 31.
    in the Cascade Range, 36.
Volney, cited, 104.

W.

Warren, G. K., cited, 30.
Washington, Mount, height of, 27.
Washoe Mountains, 27; 330.
    silver-ores of, *ib.*
Water-sheds, of the Mississippi, 26.
    of the Missouri, 39.
    of the Ohio, 26.
    of the St. Lawrence, 47.
    of the Canadian, 26.

ZON

Wheat, culture of, 215.
White-River group, 323.
Whitney, J. D., cited:
    on the Trias of California, 258; 307.
    on the Coast Ranges, 260.
    on structure of Table Mountain, 261.
    on the measurement of Shasta, 35.
    on quicksilver of California, 314.
    on Drift of California, 338.
Whittlesey, Charles, cited:
    on wheat-culture in Pembina, 217.
    on height of the Great Lakes, 352.
Winchell, cited, 285.
Wind-River group, 325.
Winds, region of, 120.
    of Caribbean Sea, 103.
    systems of, 173.
    map of, 140.
    of North America, 103; 195.
    of South America, 120.
    as disinfectants, 146.
    their evaporative power, 190.
Wisconsin, Lead-region of, 282.
Worthen, A. H., cited, on the Geology of Illinois, 284; 285; 288; 321.

Y.

Yosemite Valley, 95.
Youkon River, 62.

Z.

Zinc-ores, distribution of, 294.
Zones of vegetation in United States, 78.

www.ingramcontent.com/pod-product-compliance
Lightning Source LLC
Chambersburg PA
CBHW031955300426
44117CB00008B/771